W9-BPQ-434

NINE MINUTES
PAST MIDNIGHT

"A timely and moving book by a man of genuine eminence in the medical profession. Ern Crocker is living proof that a passionate Christian faith can co-exist with life-long belief in the scientific method. Many of the experiences which Crocker recounts—his own, his colleagues' and his patients'—are truly amazing. They are a testament to the awesome powers of God and to the peace of mind which comes to those who place their trust in him. Crocker writes with humility, but his words carry authority. St. Luke himself would be proud of his fellow physician."

Roy Williams, lawyer, journalist, and author of God Actually

"I love stories about doctors. All my life I wanted to be a doctor, and even when that dream was accomplished, I knew that the adventure had just begun. And adventure is what this wonderful book by Dr. Ern Crocker is all about. But the adventure is not just medicine. It is the challenge of a medical life given over to following Jesus. Every story of the doctors that Ern tells about in this book is a story of the adventure that happens when anyone chooses to follow Jesus. My father (Donald in this book) lived that adventure. Ern is living that adventure. Enjoy this book and join in the passion of this journey."

Dr. Tony Dale, Chairman and Founder of The Karis Group, Inc.
physician and author

"In a world that questions the very existence of God, a reminder that God is both sovereign and savior is vitally important. Ernest Crocker in *Nine Minutes Past Midnight* shares his wealth of experience as a highly esteemed doctor and Christian. His hope in this book is that all people see that Jesus alone is both Savior and Healer of the world."

Rev. Canon Christopher Allan,
St. Andrew's Cathedral Healing Ministry, Sydney

"The book *Nine Minutes Past Midnight* is a narrative of Dr. Ern Crocker's walk as a physician asking God to reveal himself to him in his medical practice and everyday life. Dr. Crocker's charge to you, the reader, in his preface, is to consider the role of God, 'the silent partner,' in your life.

Through the pages of this book, identify with the skeptical physician and open your heart to let God reveal himself to you and you will not be disappointed. You will find that he is not only a God of history and Dr. Crocker but one who wants to have a personal relationship with you through Jesus Christ today and forever. As you share with Ern the experiences of God through the people that cross his path as a physician, I pray that you will find God to be more than a 'silent partner' in your life. Is it nine minutes past midnight in your life? As this servant of God, you will find purpose and fulfillment of life."

Donald R. Tredway MD, PhD, Professor emeritus and former Chairman,
Department of Obstetrics and Gynecology,
Oral Roberts University and University of Oklahoma

"Ern Crocker has written from his experience as a doctor of seeing God's miracles in people's lives. He has been able to expand on this personal experience by capturing many other doctors who share their own life experiences. Ern is passionate and meticulous about the details in the experiences he shares. He lives and breathes what he writes. I encourage you to read and be inspired so you can lift your experience up to what God's Word says."

Peter Irvine, co-founder of Gloria Jean's Coffees,
author of Win in Business

"It is my hope that this book will encourage a large number of people to recognize that their hope lies with God, rather than with themselves."

Benjamin S. Carson, Sr, MD, Director of Pediatric Neurosurgery, Professor
of Neurological Surgery, Oncology, Plastic Surgery, and Pediatrics, Johns
Hopkins University, Baltimore, and author of Gifted Hands

"This book is a detailed record of God's miraculous intervention that is quite marvellous. It is made more marvellous for me, the son of a potato and pig farmer, because it is written by a highly trained medical professional, heavily practised in the scientific process of searching for empirical evidence. Dr. Crocker is as honest about the absence of the miraculous as he is about the miracle. He describes the comfort as a rational human being of learning to trust Jesus in every area of his life, family and professional career. You too will find the heart of this eminent scientist echoing the cry of the Spirit of God...'Come now, let us reason together and join me in the relationship of the Father with the Son as a real participant'."

Tom Hallas, Asia Pacific Field Director, member of International Eldership, Youth With A Mission International

"This is an inspiring and considered reflection that tells the story of one doctor and his many friends. Hear how God leads one man from work in an old pie factory, to work in central China to providing international leadership in his area of medical specialization. This is an essential read for young doctors, and many others, struggling with the considerable challenge of integrating a passion for the science of medicine, the art of compassionate holistic care and a love of the God who has created them."

Dr. Michael Burke MBBS, PhD, FRACGP, FAICD, Executive Officer, Christian Medical and Dental Fellowship of Australia

"What a read! From the time I started reading the experiences of Dr. Ern Crocker I was taken into the world of intense, high-level medicine and life-and-death decisions. Whether or not the reader has a faith they will be attracted to the story, the skills—and the unexplainable. I am full of admiration for this wonderful and dedicated doctor who is an innovator and a delightful personality."

The Hon. Alan Cadman OAM

"This is an inspirational book. I recommend it to all but especially to students and young professionals in health care. Over and over again it shows that God is faithful to those who seek him and intervenes in the lives of his followers. He is the healer whether it be through medical or miraculous means. May it encourage those in the medical world to go after God more and more and see his kingdom come in health care in the nations."

Dr. Ken Curry, Health Care in Christ, Australia

"Dr. Ern Crocker speaks from the heart with passion, empathy and experience about God's presence and influence in his life, with other doctors and patients. In *Nine Minutes Past Midnight* he writes 'One of the richest rewards in medicine is to be able to reassure a patient and allay his or her fears. The expression on the patient's face is its own reward. But it's better still if we are in that place of privilege where we can sensitively share our own faith and hope, and speak into their own situation of need'. An inspirational, must-read book which I couldn't put down."

Professor John Boyages, author of Breast Cancer: Taking Control *and Director, Westmead Breast Cancer Institute*

"Dr. Ern Crocker's book, *Nine Minutes Past Midnight*, was an amazingly interesting read to me. I found it interesting to see God working through people in the medical field; interesting to read of the miraculous interventions bringing about healings and miracles; interesting to read of providence sometimes leading to a new lease on life and sometimes grace to die early. I have been very interested in the relationship between the spiritual and the medical in relation to healing, and have conducted symposiums in the United States on Healing: Spiritual and Medical Perspectives. This book will be recommended in my symposiums, especially to those in the medical field. *Nine Minutes Past Midnight* didn't offer easy answers to difficult questions, but it did offer powerful examples of men and women of faith who were also highly trained professionals in the medical field living out their faith through their professions. I wish this book would be required reading by every medical school in the world. It would go far to reduce the effect of 'reductionistic' tendencies in medicine, to reduce us to only the physical aspect of our lives while ignoring our spirits. The living souls God created in his image consists of more than the chemicals that make up our bodies, but also his breath of life giving us our spirit, the spirit of life. You will find this book to be a book that will touch your heart, encourage your faith, and challenge your mind. Ultimately, it brings glory to God through his servants in the medical field."

Randy Clark, author of There Is More, *and founder of Global Awakening*

"I have always been intrigued by matters related to health and medicine. My childhood heroes were the medical pioneers like Edward Jenner, Alexander Fleming, Ignaz Semmelweis, Florence Nightingale and others who created breakthrough oftentimes despite trenchant traditionalism. I am no less intrigued by the Christian medical profession who on one hand exercise acute academic discipline while at the same time express great faith. To some, a Christian doctor of faith is an oxymoron in our day and age. Dr. Ern Crocker in his book *Nine Minutes Past Midnight*, demonstrates keen intellectual precision while at the same time positioning himself in a very real faith. I love the reality of the book. I enjoy the stories of incredible medical and technological breakthrough. I am in awe when healing comes when doctors know that it was not their efforts alone that won the day. Both types are stories of divine intervention. I am comforted that others struggle with the reality that healing is not effected in every case, either by divine or by natural means. The reality of our limitations as shared in this book, serves to remind us that there is still much to learn, and much to keep us humble, even while celebrating great success. This book and its heroes are worth celebrating."

David Crabtree, Senior Pastor, DaySpring Church, Australia

"*Nine Minutes Past Midnight* is a compelling book, demonstrating perfectly what it looks like when the kingdom of heaven is expressed through the hands of those in the medical field. With interviews and testimonies from professionals all over the world, Dr. Ernest Crocker has courageously painted a clear picture of what it looks like when the hand of God is upon and working through doctors surrendered to Him. This book will encourage your faith as you read about the many who have encountered God and have successfully carried Him into the world of medicine."

Bill Johnson, Senior Pastor, Bethel Church in Redding, California
author of When Heaven Invades Earth *and* Secrets to Imitating God

NINE MINUTES PAST MIDNIGHT

Medical Encounters with a Miraculous God

Ernest F. Crocker, MD

Authentic

Nine Minutes Past Midnight
© 2013 Ernest Crocker

Cover design by Kevin Keller

All Scripture references, unless otherwise indicated, are taken from the New King James Version. Copyright © 1982 by Thomas Nelson, Inc. Used by permission. All rights reserved.

The Bible text designated THE MESSAGE is from the The Message: The New Testament, Psalms and Proverbs. Copyright © 1993, 1994, 1995, 1996, 2000, 2001, 2002 by Eugene H. Peterson. All rights reserved. Used by permission of NavPress Publishing Group.

The Bible text designated AMP is from the Amplified® Bible, Copyright © 1987 by The Lockman Foundation. Used by permission. (www.Lockman.org)

The Bible text designated NIV is from the Holy Bible, New International Version®. Copyright © 1973, 1978, 1984, 2011 by Biblica, Inc.™ Used by permission of Zondervan. All rights reserved worldwide. www.zondervan.com

Excerpt from *Solzhenitsyn: A Pictorial Autobiography*, by Alexander Solzhenitsyn. English translation copyright © 1974 by Farrar, Straus and Giroux, LLC. Reprinted by permission of Farrar, Straus and Giroux, LLC.

Ernest Frank Crocker holds the following degrees: Bachelor of Medicine and Bachelor of Surgery (MBBS), Bachelor of Medical Science (BSc Med), Fellow of the Royal Australasian College of Physicians (FRACP), Diploma of Diagnostic Ultrasound (DDU).

Dr. Crocker's Australian MBBS degree is the equivalent of the Doctor of Medicine (MD) degree in the United States of America. The title "MD" is shown on the cover to indicate to the reader that the author is a qualified medical practitioner.

Published by Authentic Publishers,
188 Front Street, Suite 116-44,
Franklin, TN 37064
Authentic Publishers is a division of Authentic Media, Inc.

Printed in the United States of America
Library of Congress Cataloguing-in-Publishing Data

Crocker, Ernest
    Nine Minutes Past Midnight: Medical encounters with a miraculous god / Ernest Crocker p. cm.
ISBN 978-1-78078-104-4   978-1-78078-204-1 (e-book)

All rights reserved. No part of this book may be reproduced or transmitted in any form or by any means, electronic or mechanical, including photocopying and recording, or by any information storage and retrieval system, without permission in writing from the publisher.

To my darling Lynne, without whose encouragement and unerring support this book would never have been written, and to the glory of God.

Table of Contents

Contents

Preface

"I will stand my watch...

to see what He will say to me...

Then the LORD answered me and said:

"Write the vision and make it plain...

That he may run who reads it."

Habakkuk 2:1,2

We live in a world of increasing personal challenge and accelerating danger. The uncertainty of tomorrow and the demands of today render us vulnerable to every new onslaught. But there is One who longs to walk beside us, to comfort, advise, protect, and guide us through this jungle of life. The extent to which we entrust ourselves to Him will determine the nature and direction of our journey.

I have no doubt that God will speak to you as you read these pages. From the very outset, there grew within me a sense of urgency to faithfully record the words of the Christian doctors and patients I interviewed. As the book grew it developed a life of its own. I have come to realize again that when God is doing something all that is required is that we be receptive, obedient, and hold on tight!

I endeavored to put aside all my preconceived ideas, and remain open and receptive to what was said, prayerfully considering and weighing each experience and revelation. By so doing, I have seen the hand of the Master Weaver create an intricate cloth far beyond the creative and professional ability of mere mortals.

Please read with an open mind and an unencumbered spirit, trusting that God will reveal to you truth that has the potential to set you free from the trappings and entrapments of this life. I trust also that you will not be bound by religious orthodoxy, by convention, or by the transient, myopic values of this contemporary secular world.

Finally, it is my earnest prayer that the Spirit of God will be stirred within you, to reach out again or perhaps for the first time to the One who longs to walk by your side. I believe that you will be compelled to consider the role of God, the Silent Partner in your life.

Ernest Frank Crocker MBBS BSc (Med) FRACP DDU
Castle Hill
Australia Day, January 26, 2011

Acknowledgments

I am indebted to the many that have made this book possible: to Paul Bootes, Kyle Duncan, and the crew at Authentic Media. They caught the vision and ran with it.

To Ben Carson, Ian McCormack, Jackie Pullinger, and Donald and Penny Dale for their encouragement and support and whose lives proclaim the reality of the risen Christ.

My sincere appreciation also goes to Belinda Pollard for her advice and editorial assistance, and to Sheila Jacobs, Cristine Bolley, Mamie Long, and Rosemary Bradford for their support and editorial suggestions.

My sincere thanks also to Elizabeth West and Richard Attieh for their media support.

I shall be ever grateful to Noel and Phyl Gibson, for their incisive comments and their continuing prayer ministry and to Pete Irvine and the many others who stood by me in prayer.

To my parents who allowed me to observe, passively and without coercion, the practical outworking of their faith when I was a young man searching for truth and direction. And to my family who have faithfully stood by me through this venture giving their support, encouragement, and time.

I especially thank my wife, Lynne, for her counsel, her wisdom, her insight, and her love. She is my finest critic who never once doubted God's purpose in this book.

My sincere thanks to my medical colleagues, who testified boldly of the miracles they witnessed, and to the many others who willingly shared their lives, their hopes, their passions, and sometimes their agonies to reveal the wondrous divine intervention Above all, my thanks to a God who is there and who never fails!

> You are My witnesses, says the Lord, and My servant whom I have chosen, that you may know Me, believe Me and remain steadfast to Me, and understand that I am He. Before Me there was no God formed, neither shall there be after Me.
>
> Isaiah 43:10, AMP

Introduction

D r. William Barclay tells of a famous British surgeon. When he operated, the gallery was filled with students and other doctors, watching closely, hoping to learn from the master surgeon. Even under scrutiny, his technique was faultless.

"How do you avoid self-consciousness and errors?" he was asked.

"When I operate," he said, "as far as I am concerned there are only three people in the theater. There is myself and the patient I am seeking to help..."

"Yes, and the third, who is the third—the anesthesiologist?"

"The third person," replied the surgeon, "is God Himself."[1]

This is a book about doctors and patients who took God at His word and were astonished at what followed. It might have been written about people in any profession or calling. As it happens, my experience as a doctor over thirty-five years has allowed me to use medicine as a model to investigate the ways in which God intervenes in the lives of men and women.

I have spoken with many doctors professing to be Christians from all branches of medicine and at all levels of experience and expertise. They report times when God's agenda has taken them well "outside the square" to untested ground. They have faced challenges ranging from terrorist attacks to suicidal depression. They have been delivered from drowning and incurable diseases.

I have discovered that these men and women have an awareness of a third person involved in patient care and in the healing process—as teacher, healer, provider, protector, or even surgical assistant. That unseen person, or "Silent Partner," is perceived as the presence of Almighty God, sometimes as Father, sometimes as Son, sometimes as the Holy Spirit.

This is not a book of miracles. Even so, events are recorded that may be regarded as such. It is a record of the manner in which a personal God interacts and intervenes in the lives of doctors, their patients, families and friends, to produce radical life change.

I have taken the stance of Luke the physician to record an orderly account of those things which I have observed in my own life and witnessed in the lives of others. I have not added fictional detail to make for better narrative, but have included only factual evidence entrusted to me by reliable witnesses and which, where possible, I have been able to verify personally.

To those who may not be in a personal relationship with God I emphasize that the events recorded are not fictional, they are faithfully recorded experiences of prominent medical practitioners of sound mind and undisputed word. If reading this book causes you to search more deeply for spiritual meaning in your life, I remind you that God's Word says, "you will find Him if you seek Him with all your heart and with all your soul" (Deuteronomy 4:29).

Even among Christians, some will dismiss this book out of hand. The accounts given may not be compatible with their brand of theology. I am completely sympathetic, having argued vigorously for years with those who maintained that God intervenes today in the lives of men and women. As you read you will see that He revealed to me, the greatest skeptic, how wrong I was...

1

Now is the Time

For we cannot but speak the things
which we have seen and heard.

Acts 4:20

T he scene from the bedroom door filled me with dismay. The
patient, a woman in her forties, lay motionless save for agonal
heaving of her chest. This was medicine in its most confronting
form, real white-knuckle stuff. I was just a hospital resident moonlight-
ing to earn enough money for the deposit on a house. What could I do
to save this woman's life?

Examining her I could feel no pulse, and there were no audible heart
sounds. Pulling her from the sagging bed, I began CPR by the light of a
naked bulb dangling from the ceiling.[2]

Ribs cracked under my hands. The patient's stomach filled with air
and its contents were regurgitated, making mouth-to-mouth resuscitation impossible. I resorted to ventilating through cupped hands.

About twenty-four hours earlier, I had faced a different kind of crisis. It
was late, very late on a Sunday evening in July 1973. My wife, Lynne,
and I sat deep in thought in the living room of our Strathfield home.
Few words were exchanged. I needed an answer. I needed it now!

I had been a doctor for three years. I had long struggled to reconcile
my understanding of modern medicine with the concept that God may
supernaturally intervene in the healing process today. I needed to find a

1

position that sat comfortably with my medical training, experience, and with my Christian faith. I had witnessed healing beyond my comprehension, but these observations were often not compatible with my physician training and my prior medical research. I regarded myself as a rationalist.

Yes, I had seen migraines, backaches and "arthritis" healed. I had seen people's asthma symptoms eased and heard how infertile women had become pregnant after prayer. But there always seemed to be some psychosomatic aspect to the illness. I was aware of the powerful impact of the placebo effect and, for the believer, prayer seemed to be the ultimate placebo. Yet, to me, as a young man, keen to move on in my career, there was a real sense of urgency to resolve the question of prayer and its role in medicine.

I challenged God. "If You heal today, we need You to show us in the next seven days. If we don't have an answer within the week, we will put the issue to rest and move on."

The next morning I drove to Sydney's Royal Prince Alfred Hospital where I served as a nuclear medicine registrar. There was the usual busy schedule: patients to see, rounds to attend, a research paper to complete. I had not planned to work that evening and was looking forward to a quiet night at home. Mid-afternoon, my friend Bill called. Together we had been managing an after-hours radio-doctor service in the inner western suburbs of Sydney. This was not a job for the faint-hearted. We provided an after-hours service for approximately fifty general practitioners over an area of about sixty two square miles, extending west to Burwood, east to Balmain, north to Drummoyne and south to Mascot. The pay was about $4.00 per patient! It was a tough business, often requiring us to visit doubtful areas of Sydney alone in the early hours. Any scenario might be expected, from a child with asthma to suicide. (Only once was I assaulted.)

Bill was scheduled to cover the service that evening, but for personal reasons was unable to do so. "Could you cover me?" he asked.

By 6 p.m. there was a long list of patients all requiring home visits. It seemed that everyone in the inner west had a fever or a sore throat. But by midnight all of the calls had been attended. I made my way home and crashed in front of the TV with a cup of coffee, before turning in.

It was just after midnight when Mrs. Mac called.

"Can you come quickly, doctor? I have pains in my chest."

She sounded unwell—very unwell. I took her address, told her not to panic, to lie down, and that I would be there as soon as possible. Saying goodbye to Lynne, I grabbed my bag and was off. It was a twenty-minute drive to Hurlstone Park.

The door was ajar, and I let myself in to find a woman in her mid-forties sprawled across her bed in a dimly lit room. Though previously well, tonight she had experienced the sudden onset of severe chest pain which radiated into her left arm. She was nauseated and began to vomit. I examined her as best I could in the dim light. She was pale and sweaty, but her heart rate was regular—sinus rhythm I suspected—and her blood pressure was maintained.

I called the admitting officer at Royal Prince Alfred Hospital and asked him to accept this lady with a provisional diagnosis of acute myocardial infarction (heart attack) and then called the ambulance service, imploring them, "Please hurry!" It was 1 a.m. I sat in the kitchen to write a note to the admitting officer.

Mrs. Mac lived alone. As I wrote, there came a knock at the door. It was her son with his wife and young family. I asked them to sit quietly with her until the ambulance arrived. But within minutes the son appeared at the kitchen door, ashen-faced. "Doctor, come quickly, Mom's gone all funny!"

And so there I was resuscitating a patient that I had never met before in my life, and who had called me at home just thirty minutes earlier. Despite CPR, her pupils became fixed and dilated. I searched for a vein to administer adrenaline. But there was no vein to be found. Finally in desperation I drew up an ampule of adrenaline and injected it straight into her heart with a large spinal needle. Again, no response. By this stage I had been attempting to resuscitate the lady for about twenty minutes and was just about exhausted.

The son watched in despair. "What can we do?"

"You can pray if you like," I said, "and call the ambulance again." I don't know whether he prayed, but he did call the ambulance service. He discovered that the details of my call had been misplaced, but that they would now send an ambulance immediately! In my experience, this type of error was unprecedented.

I knelt beside the woman, exhausted and with no idea what to try next. But as I did so, a quiet voice within said, "*Now's the time, now's the time.*" My hands were already on the patient's chest and as they rested there I prayed for her under my breath. There was nothing to lose. She shuddered, as someone does when they are counter-shocked by the "crash" team in hospital, but then...nothing. I suspected her sudden movement was from some kind of hypoxic seizure caused by lack of oxygen, and continued CPR.

Ten minutes later, the ambulance arrived with only a driver. He walked into the room, hands in pockets, summarily assessed the situation and told me in no uncertain terms that I was wasting my time.

"The patient's dead."

But I was the doctor and I was adamant. We would continue resuscitation until we reached the hospital. Together we heaved the patient onto a stretcher and into the back of the ambulance.

With lights flashing and sirens screaming, the driver made record time to Royal Prince Alfred Hospital, "bells and whistles" all the way! The ambulance was one of the older style low-profile vehicles, and there was very little space for me to access the patient. I straddled Mrs. Mac and held on to a window rail with one hand to prevent being thrown around. Occasionally I managed to compress the patient's chest, but any kind of meaningful ventilation was out of the question.

We pulled into the old emergency room ambulance bay opposite the residents' quarters, to be met by a team of residents and interns who had been alerted. They quietly made their clinical assessment in the back of the ambulance to emerge and pronounce the patient DOA (dead on arrival). She would not be accepted into the ER but would be "certified" and could then be taken to the mortuary behind the hospital. But I was a medical registrar at that hospital and was able to bring some pressure to bear. Soon we had Mrs. Mac transported into the emergency room and onto the arrest bed.

I gladly stood back as the team went to work: CPR, intubation, IV adrenaline, fluids, oxygen, bicarbonate. To my absolute astonishment after about five minutes, the electrocardiogram (ECG) demonstrated a regular heartbeat. And then the patient began to breathe spontaneously. Several minutes later she regained consciousness and began to speak, complaining about her painful chest. And with good reason—I had broken several of her ribs and likely her sternum.

I had great difficulty in accepting what I had just witnessed. After scribbling a few words in the patient's notes, I walked out into the darkness of Missenden Road, bewildered. The patient had been clinically dead for over an hour and had been verified as such by the ambulance man and the emergency team. Resuscitation had been attempted alone under the most difficult circumstances, in a home with poor lighting and with no assistance. Even the ambulance had been delayed.

I had previously been involved in numerous attempts at cardiac resuscitation in the hospital, and was only too aware of the miserable salvage rate even when the cardiac arrest team has been able to attend within minutes.

Lynne listened to my story, somewhat incredulous, but accepted what I had to say. We would talk about it in the morning.

A phone call woke me at 6 a.m. It was the head of cardiology. "I don't know what you did, son," were his words, "but well done." I didn't tell him what I had done.

That morning, I went straight to see the patient, now transferred to Ward BP2 under the care of the professor. At best, I expected to find her semi-conscious and possibly intubated. She was sitting up in bed eating bacon and eggs for breakfast, and reading a women's magazine. I called for her notes and checked her ECG. It was normal. There was no evidence of myocardial infarction or indeed of any cardiac problem. She was physically well, and there was no sign of brain damage.

After two days of observation and further tests, the patient was discharged home with no firm diagnosis. I spoke to her later. She had no memory of the events of that evening and recalled no near-death experience, but admitted that she had been surprised to find herself in hospital.

Just twenty-four hours prior to that incident, Lynne and I had been on our knees in our Strathfield home asking God to prove Himself. The very next day, He showed us in a most dramatic and irrefutable way that He can, and that He does, heal today. No asthma, no back pain, no migraine this time; nothing that I could rationalize away. And there were witnesses: the ambulance man and the resident staff at Royal Prince Alfred Hospital.

I had no rational explanation for those events which occurred on a cold July evening in 1973. My Christian medical colleagues were skeptical. Others were fascinated, but could of course provide no logical explanation. At that point I opted for discretion as the better part of valor, and kept the matter to myself for some time.

It was just a few years later that I received another call, again late at night. The wife of a close friend living just a few streets away had collapsed and could not be roused. I was there within minutes to find the young mother void of life on the bathroom floor. We called for an ambulance, and I attempted resuscitation while my friend and his young children pleaded with God for the life of their mother from the next room. But no amount of CPR administered with prayer and petition could save the life of that young woman. Faces fell and tears flowed as we considered the brutal reality that Cassy was gone.

Here was a dilemma; a real dilemma. Why did God heal one woman and not the other? Were the events of that cold July evening in Hurlstone Park a one-off, or could I expect God to intervene again when I called upon Him?

On Christmas Day 1939 in one of the coldest winters in recorded English history, King George VI addressed the British people. Hitler was poised to unleash his Luftwaffe and the people needed a strong leader, a steady hand and the best possible advice.

With faltering voice but iron resolve he gave the following counsel: to place their hand in God's hand and allow Him to lead them through the dark days ahead. There was no better and no safer way.

2

Where Can a Young Man Put His Trust?

I have more understanding than all my teachers,

for Your testimonies are my meditation.

Psalm 119:99

I don't know whether it was rain or tears streaming down my face as I stood there in the semi-darkness, but I knew that life was changing. It would never be the same again. A distant figure on the other side of the Sydney showground said, "You come!" And I did.

I was one of 149,000 people to make a "decision for Christ" during that first Australian Billy Graham Crusade in May 1959. (This represented 2 percent of Australia's entire population at the time.) As a brash 14-year-old I was uncertain about most things, but from that night on I knew this: God had a plan for my life and it had to be better than the one I had been nurturing for myself.

Through high school I continued in faith. It wasn't difficult with parents who were themselves committed Christians. But despite my decision at that rain-swept showground, I coat-tailed it on their faith with little understanding of a personal relationship with God. At that time in my life, Christianity was defined as Sunday mornings in the local Baptist church, super-cool in pegged trousers and winkle-pickers,[3] counting away the minutes by the large clock on the back wall. It was a way of life, an ethic, a means to salvation, a place to hide.

God was always there in my house. One morning, hearing hushed voices, I peered from my bedroom door to hear my grandfather being told that his wife had died during the night. He bowed his head and wept as he was comforted with prayer, an embrace, and a glass of Scotch.

I recognized God's voice only once in those early years. It was dusk on a Saturday evening and I had taken off for a jog, pounding the pavement and managing to outpace the local dogs. As I ran, there came the conviction that one day I would become a medical doctor. I pondered this as I lay in bed that night, but it was not until some years later as a resident medical officer at Royal Prince Alfred Hospital that I recalled that memory.

Medical school was guaranteed to test a person's faith from the outset. From day one in the dissection room, I was confronted by the transience of life. The study of anatomy and bodily function left me in awe and wonder, but that first confrontation with a lifeless body was nothing less than surreal. Witnessing the demise of a child in pediatrics, a miscarriage in emergency, or the disfiguration of an adolescent in a motor vehicle accident raised profound questions about the meaning and significance of life.

As a novice student at St. George Hospital I was asked to take a medical history from a new patient who had been admitted with acute chest pain. With fear and trepidation I approached, notebook and shiny new Littman stethoscope in hand. The patient was a pleasant and engaging, silver-haired man in his mid-sixties. I assessed his history, examined him, and we had a good chat. Later that evening, preparing the history for presentation next day, I took some comfort in a job well done.

The next morning after lectures, my friends and I were paged to attend an autopsy. To my dismay, there was my new friend, lying naked and motionless on the post-mortem table! I lifted his hand. It was a big hand, still soft but now cold and lifeless. How different it felt from the day before, when I had examined his pulse. Where had life gone? Where was the interesting, jovial man that I had spoken to just one day earlier? How could such a small thrombus in a tiny artery terminate a life spanning sixty-five years? These questions I would ponder through student days and into the years to come.

My student undergrad rotation in psychiatry posed unique problems. Initially I was hooked. The subject appealed to my mind. Here was a well-structured and proven means of classifying patients according to their mental disorder. Most could be classified as psychotic, neurotic, or suffering from a personality disorder, and at a simplistic level this all seemed fairly straightforward. "Neurotics," they said, "build castles in the sky, psychotics live in them, and psychiatrists collect the rent."

However, it was disconcerting to learn of the vast differences between schools of psychiatric thought, even in Sydney. The professor at my university held to the belief that most psychiatric illnesses were organically based. Other staffers were behaviorists and used conditioning to treat people with phobias, compulsive disorders and sexual deviations. Elsewhere in Sydney there was a strong Freudian school. They couldn't all be right. Were any of them correct?

Our classes often took the form of roundtable discussions. It soon became clear that some of the psychiatrists were at best agnostic and not at all sympathetic to Christian beliefs, or in fact to any religious faith. Christians were often deliberately provoked. "What is this trick called life that's been played upon us?" was an opening question I clearly recall.

One of the key questions in a psychiatric interview was, "Do you believe in God?" A positive response invoked the further question, "Do you speak to Him?" To answer in the positive was damning enough, but led to the further question, "Does He answer?" This was the clincher. To say "Yes" to that question raised serious questions regarding the patient's sanity.

In one outpatient clinic an elderly lady was interviewed. She had collapsed in the rose garden of a nursing home.

"Do you believe in God?" asked the psychiatrist.

"Yes."

"Are you fearful of dying?"

10

"Not at all," she replied. "When I die, I'll go to heaven."

After the patient had been escorted from the room the psychiatrist turned to me and said, "That woman is in deep denial. She clearly has a morbid fear of death." He could not have been wider off the mark. (Despite the psychiatrist's self-confidence, he called for assistance when a patient later collapsed on the floor during an interview. One of my fellow students sarcastically quipped, "Get a real doctor.")

As the semester progressed, deep concerns grew within me. Many events recorded in the Bible could be explained as psychiatric phenomena. Delusion and hallucination seemed to provide a rational explanation for many biblical accounts. Surely the appearance of angels could be explained as hallucination. Perhaps delusional states were responsible for accounts of divine guidance. I had also learned a new term, folie en masse (group madness), which may have accounted for such miracles as the feeding of the 5,000.[4]

The tenets of my faith were shaken, and daily I became more impressed by the potential for mental illness to control the mind. One day a schizophrenic patient told me that his shoes were talking to him. There were others who talked to people who were not there, or imagined themselves pursued by non-existent predators—even Adolf Hitler, apparently, was one of our inpatients at the time!

I began seriously to doubt my beliefs and remembered how someone had said, "Ern, unless you are a Christian when you begin psychiatry, you sure won't be when you finish."

One group session was so distressing that I decided not to attend clinics that day but to go home and find a quiet place to reflect on all that had been said in class. As a student I was in awe of my teachers. They were highly qualified men, respected in their field. What they said could not be lightly dismissed. If they were correct, then the beliefs on which I had based my life for the last ten years would have to be radically revised, if not abandoned.

Nobody was home. Good, the solitude gave me a chance to think. I sat at the kitchen table deep in thought, and turned to my Bible looking for consolation. It fell open to a verse in the Psalms, one that I had never before seen in my life: "I have more understanding than all my teachers, for Your testimonies are my meditation" (Psalm 119:99).

More understanding than all my teachers! The words blazed from the page. I do not normally look for guidance in this way. But I have no doubt that God spoke to me that day, when He clearly showed me to put my faith in Him and not in the "wisdom of men."

I have since come to realize the fallibility of human wisdom and the folly of its often flawed understanding. Recorded history is often based on doubtful provenance and dubious interpretation. And where facts are unpalatable they are often massaged by political spin doctors.

Even in medicine, beliefs are constantly changing. A drug in favor ten years ago may now be abandoned as positively dangerous. Aspirin, first highly regarded as an analgesic, fell into disfavor with the discovery of its effect on the stomach lining, and on kidney function when used in combination with other drugs. Now it is widely used in patients with ischemic heart disease to prevent acute events, and is regarded as helpful in the prevention of bowel cancer.

Young people embarking on a career path in medicine are confronted by a plethora of programs, pathways, spin, and algorithms—the possibilities are legion. Where can students put their trust? What does God require of them?

There have been milestones in my life, unforgettable experiences that anchor my beliefs and point the way ahead. The events of that day in psychiatry constitute one such milestone. I have never had cause to doubt God since. I have questioned His ways many times, but always with the awareness that I am a mortal and fallible man. I am conscious that His ways are not my ways. They are far more profound and far-reaching.

What then should our response be? Mercifully, there is a simple answer, found in the Bible: "He has shown you, O man, what is good; and what does the LORD require of you but to do justly, to love mercy, and to walk humbly with your God" (Micah 6:8).

But as my medical studies progressed, Christianity—or rather, my Christianity—was not stacking up as I had hoped it might. I was assured of salvation, and I believed in a God who loved me and answered prayers. But where was the excitement and anticipation? Where was the "victorious Christian living" that I had read about? Life as a young Christian was hard work every step of the way.

My Anglican pastor directed me to John Stott's *Basic Christianity*, a fine book which I had read years before. But this was not the whole answer. Beyond this he was unable to help and, I think, a little uncomfortable.

I would have to wait a few years yet to find the key that would unlock the spiritual freedom that I so desperately sought.

If medical school was tough, residency was tougher. We worked 120-hour weeks, which included every second night and weekend. On my first night as an intern at Royal Prince Alfred Hospital, I was scheduled to cover a surgical ward somewhere high up in "the gods" of the ancient Vic block. Strolling through the ward around 9 p.m., I was alarmed to see a patient arrest before my very eyes. Never having witnessed a cardiac arrest before and as yet unfamiliar with protocol, I called for help and then proceeded to administer mouth-to-mouth resuscitation. It was soon brought to my attention by an informed young nurse in starched uniform that the patient was terminal and expected to die that evening. I spent the rest of the night in the residents' quarters trying to wash away the taste of the Vaseline that had been used to lubricate the patient's lips.

I was later recalled to the ward to replace a nasogastric tube pulled out by an uncooperative patient. I had not yet actually learned how to do this procedure, but was eager to regain my standing. I managed to replace the tube—to the chagrin of the patient and the approval of the same young nurse. I was not yet familiar with the "watch one, do one, teach one" mantra.

Old Bill was a familiar figure in Ward D2 where I spent my first surgical term. He had laryngeal cancer resulting from a lifetime of smoking. His treatment had included radical surgery and radiotherapy. Doctors were guarded about his prognosis, but he was soon to be discharged home.

Late one morning after rounds, a nurse noticed a spot of bright blood on the side of Bill's neck. The intern was summoned urgently and identified what he thought to be a small superficial bleeder, perhaps related to the effect of radiation on the skin. He called for a suture tray.

As the needle pierced the skin, a torrent of arterial blood surged from the patient's neck. The common carotid artery, one of the main blood vessels to the head and brain, had been eroded by the cancer. Compression of the neck with a large wad of gauze swabs stemmed the flow of blood while the registrar was called. He placed a large mattress suture in the neck, incorporating the wad of dressing and compressing the artery. An emergency consultation with the surgeon was sought, but it seemed that little more could be done. The patient was distressed and fearful. Morphine was administered.

That evening, I was on the night duty roster. Between tending to other patients' needs, I observed Bill carefully. Later, when the lights went out, I sat with him. He was unable to speak but understood my words, and was able to nod or shake his head. That night Bill was assured of his salvation in Christ and, in the early hours of the morning, he passed away.

Other patients taught me the importance of flexibility. In the same ward I cared for Molly, a retired barmaid of Irish descent. Her bowel cancer surgery had been successful, but postoperatively she failed to thrive and eventually refused to eat. But she was partial to the odd bottle of Guinness stout smuggled in by one of her friends. My father, not a medical man, had been a great supporter of stout for people in convalescence, so who was I to deny her the one source of nourishment that she would accept? The word of her "special" diet spread amongst her friends. Soon the cases of Guinness stored beneath her bed began to encroach on the general ward space, bringing a sharp retort from the nursing sister in charge. Molly thrived and was eventually discharged on a balanced diet. She became a lasting friend and attended my wedding two years later.

The confronting nature of the work placed far greater demands on us than the challenge of the hours alone. In my second year, I was sole doctor on duty at Bathurst District Hospital when multiple patients were brought in from a motor vehicle accident. Later that evening I stood and watched a nurse arrange flowers on the chest of a 4-year-old girl, a victim of that accident. That vision remains with me still.

As a senior resident I was seconded for a short time to the clinical research ward. This older style of open ward, painted hospital cream, occupied the lower ground floor of one of the original blond brick buildings. Rows of beds housed patients with such conditions as lupus erythematosus, the leukemias, and obscure endocrinopathies. Late one afternoon I admitted an attractive young lady in her late teens with a fever. She had acute leukemia. I assessed her history, arranged investigations, and commenced her management regime. The next morning her bed was empty. She had perished during the night.

The months spent in that ward were sobering. But it was during that time that I came to develop a friendship with my senior colleague Dr. Bob Batey, a friendship that has remained very dear to me to the present day. I observed God's intervention in Bob's life in a remarkable way. He was rescued from almost certain death by circumstances nothing short of miraculous when several of his friends were drowned while at a conference on the Gold Coast. Bob's relationship with God was not a passive, feel-good, Sunday acquaintance but a personal experience of knowing God with His sleeves rolled up, a hero in every sense. (Bob's story is recorded in Chapter 10.)

After residency came specialty training in nuclear medicine. The old pie factory at Royal Prince Alfred Hospital was an extraordinary bunker of a building. Acquired by the hospital to house the new technologies of radiation therapy and nuclear medicine, it had long ceased to produce meat pies. Located between the Page chest pavilion and King George V obstetric block, it was just sufficiently removed from the main hospital complex to calm the growing paranoia about radiation risk experienced by the powers that be. Little money had been spent on its conversion. Painted hospital cream inside and out, it housed nuclear medicine at one end and radiotherapy at the other, along with the enormous pie ovens which were a highlight of every visitor tour.

It was in the corridor of the old pie factory that an extraordinary event transpired. One midmorning in 1974, just as the day was getting into gear, I was distracted by raised voices from one of the partitioned offices. A door burst open and out bolted our Burmese exchange student, closely followed by a senior doctor who pointed bluntly at me and said, "Ask him!"

The student had been a bit of a mystery to us all, keeping to himself with little to say. But today the dam burst. Fixing me with a gaze that would have halted a charging rhinoceros, he exclaimed for all to hear: "How can I become a Christian?"

It appeared that this young man, whose family lived in Rangoon under the oppressive influence of the military junta, had acquired a Bible soon after arriving in Sydney. He had spent each evening cloistered in his tiny room, reading it cover to cover. I had the unparalleled privilege later that day of introducing Thien Tun to Jesus.

It was in that same year during College of Physician exams that I experienced the empowering presence of God in the prayers of a Christian colleague. To be successful in the oral exams, candidates must be informed, maintain their cool, and know how to play the game. And it was a game. "Show no fear and stay on the front foot," was the order of the day. "Don't let them grind you down!" they would say—using slightly more colorful language!

I entered the examination room terrified, to be met by an old friend from medical school, Dr. George Kostalas. He was a nominated "bulldog" for the day and would be my guide through the gauntlet of clinical challenges, escorting me from one examiner to the next.

"Don't worry, buddy," he said. "I'm right behind you—praying."

That evening, I saw men and women respond in tears as they tore open the envelopes holding their results. There was no need to read the letter enclosed. One paragraph meant failure, two meant a pass. The second paragraph invited successful candidates to a cocktail party with their examiners.

My letter had two paragraphs.

With college qualification came a new problem. As a doctor—now a specialist physician—and a Christian, I would have to reconcile my medical knowledge with my understanding of the role of God in the healing process. It was the 70s. The charismatic movement was sweeping Australia and people were making outrageous claims about supernatural healing. I found this alarming, and a reproach to my medical understanding and Christian beliefs.

To gain a fuller understanding, I attended healing meetings to observe for myself what was happening. I watched a Brother Ted Whitesell lengthen a woman's leg, and wondered what might be the purpose of this. But there were others who claimed healing from serious illness, and no amount of reading or observation, it seemed, would resolve the matter.

People spoke of a "Baptism in the Holy Spirit" as a second blessing to conversion. This was not compatible with my Christian understanding. I found it confronting and spoke out against it whenever the opportunity arose.

But there was no doubt in my mind that Christ spoke clearly of the Holy Spirit. He had told his disciples, "I am going away. Unless I go away, the Advocate will not come to you; but if I go, I will send him to you" (John 16:7 NIV).

Eventually, partly to satisfy my own curiosity, but driven by hunger to satisfy a deeper spiritual need, I asked a friend, an Anglican minister, to pray for me for the infilling of the Holy Spirit.[5]

As we stood in the sanctuary of a downtown Anglican church, afternoon sun streaming through the windows, it was as though the heavens opened. Instantaneously a sense of power and wellbeing came over me. Returning home, I turned the television on, turned the volume to loud, and threw myself down into a lounge chair. Beside me was the manuscript of a research paper that I had been battling with for several months. With a pencil I completed the paper longhand in about an hour. It was accepted by the prestigious "Green Journal" the *American Journal of Medicine*, almost without modification, and became the definitive article on the investigation of cerebral abscess.[6]

Later, I came to understand this intense spiritual experience not as a second blessing to conversion, but as an on-going experience of any Christian who invites the Holy Spirit to become part of their life.

It was while these events were unfolding in my spiritual life that I began to manage the after-hours locum service with my friend Bill, a radiology trainee at Royal Prince Alfred Hospital. As mentioned earlier, together with colleagues we provided night cover for fifty general practitioners in the inner western suburbs of Sydney at $4.00 a call. One of my patients was Mrs. Mac of Hurlstone Park, whose inexplicable recovery recounted in chapter 1 challenged my rationalist understanding of God's involvement in modern life. But I was to discover that God's miraculous intervention wasn't limited to direct healing of individuals. He was also at work behind the scenes, developing the techniques, and even the political structures of the healing profession.

3

The Silent Partner

When you stand on the spiritual battle field you will hear God laugh and if you listen carefully you will hear Him say, "It's not a fair fight, it's simply not a fair fight."[7]

Graham Cooke

The corridor of the old pie factory was, at best, difficult to navigate. With the absence of an inpatient waiting area, patients—radioactive and otherwise—were parked end to end along its length, allowing just sufficient room for two people to pass. If two trolleys were abreast, nobody went anywhere. Late one morning in 1974 as I hurried back to the reporting room, my boss sidled past in the opposite direction.

"Ultrasound," he growled over his shoulder. "Find out about it."

I had no idea what he was talking about and soon forgot his cryptic comment, only to be called to account the following week.

"Well, ultrasound. What have you found out?"

"Nothing."

"Kossoff," he said. "Go talk to Kossoff."

I was to learn that George Kossoff, director of the Commonwealth Acoustic Laboratories, worked in downtown Sydney just a couple of miles away. He was in fact the father of contemporary ultrasound imaging, having discovered the means of generating grey-toned images which were to replace the black and white line drawings of existing technology. This was an extraordinary development which the multinationals—

Toshiba, Siemens, General Electric and Phillips—would spend years and millions of dollars trying to emulate.

George was a most obliging and encouraging man. With his support, I was able to produce and publish the world's first grey scale images of the thyroid gland and of the parathyroids which lie just behind it and control calcium metabolism. In the following year, 1975, I was awarded two similar Travelling Fellowships by both the Royal Australasian College of Physicians and the New South Wales State Cancer Council to continue this work in Europe and then travel on to Philadelphia to complete advanced training in nuclear medicine. I accepted the latter.

Returning to Sydney in 1976, I applied for the position of founding Director of Nuclear Medicine and Ultrasound at the newly built teaching hospital at Westmead in Sydney's western suburbs. The hospital had been a pipe dream of visionaries at Sydney University and State Government for many years and was finally about to materialize.

My application was successful!

Here now was an opportunity to serve God in a most practicable way in what was to become perhaps the finest university medical complex in Australia. With a space allocation of one quarter of an acre, a budget of $1 million, and a hard hat, I set out to design a department capable of delivering the world's best practice in diagnostic nuclear medicine.

One of the first tasks was to generate a "wish list" of potential staff. This was easily done, but after many months I had managed to employ very few of the people on my list. The administrators were beginning to ask questions, and after twelve months I took the matter before God.

"OK," I said, "I'm not having any success. You do it. You choose them."

Almost immediately, applications began to materialize. A radio pharmacist applied who it was said had submitted the finest ever PhD in his field to the University of NSW. At the same time, a PhD physicist applied who in later years would be appointed Professor of Nuclear Medicine at Sydney University. Both became good friends of mine and highly valued members of staff. I was learning...but it was a slow process.

My learning curve became steeper. I was beginning to understand what it meant to have God as a Partner.

At one stage I urgently needed a piece of equipment, a digital gamma camera worth in excess of $100,000. There was no money to be had and my contacts in the state departments of Health and Public Works told me that no equipment was available. But God knew we needed that camera. I prayed about it and He gave me an assurance and an inner peace that one would be provided. I told my secretary, Barbara, about this. She was astounded and, I think, somewhat taken back at my admission. But then, late on a Friday afternoon in the last week of the financial year, there came a call from the NSW Health Department. If I could find a few thousand dollars that day, there was a camera available. The money was acquired that afternoon, and we took delivery of a new General Electric digital gamma camera. Both my secretary and I were overwhelmed by God's provision. Twenty years later, that camera has only recently been decommissioned.

But I was to find that partnership with God required courage—raw courage. The business plan set by my "Silent Partner" would take me far beyond my comfort zone.

Most doctors in academic and administrative roles at some stage find their professional territory challenged by others. I was no exception. There was always the general turf war over budgets and space. But some of the challenges were deadly serious. On one occasion my opposition was formidable, and I could see little hope of resolution in my favor. I was summoned before a committee of key administrators and academic heads to show cause as to why I should not surrender some of my equipment and staff to another department head. My department would be fragmented.

I knew instinctively that this was wrong. It couldn't possibly be God's will. He had placed me in this position for a purpose, not to surrender it to another. As I sat in my office preparing for the meeting scheduled for 1 p.m. that afternoon, God brought to my mind these verses from Isaiah: "No weapon forged against you will prevail, and you will refute every tongue that accuses you. This is the heritage of the servants of the LORD, and this is their vindication from me,' declares the LORD" (Isaiah 54:17 NIV).

This was God's *logos* or written word, but I also discerned it as His *rhema*, His spiritually revealed word for me at that moment.

We assembled at 1 p.m. in Administration. Pleasantries were exchanged but, glancing around, I saw that I was hopelessly outgunned. My opponent was fashionably late. Perhaps he would not show. But my hopes were dashed as he blustered in sporting surgical greens, face mask hanging around his neck and clenching a cigar in his teeth. Making his apologies for being late, he hunkered down, facing me across the table. He was first to speak and did so convincingly and with conviction. I began to lose heart. His arguments were strong, and those around the table were nodding sympathetically. He was winning hands down.

Then it was my turn. I stated my case with candor and without emotion. As I did so, my opponent became noticeably uncomfortable. Something was working in my favor, but I didn't understand what it was. There was a growing tangible sense of impending victory as I leaned forward across the table to take the advantage. He drew back and sank lower in his chair. I was winning, but had no idea why. Finally I offered him all of my support, offering to train his staff. For various reasons he declined. Meeting over.

I walked back to my office simply astonished at what God had done. I was never again challenged from that quarter and, in time, that man became a personal friend and confidant. That day I rediscovered God as my rock, unchanging, immovable. He was my "high tower."

A tower is a place to retreat to in difficult times, a place to find protection, encouragement, and inner strength. It is also a place to find weapons and armor to face a challenge. Perhaps most of all, it is a place to climb high enough to gain an overview, to see the problem in perspective, and to see the solution beyond the problem. Finally, when prepared, we can leave that tower to meet the challenge. Graham Cooke is a speaker and author based in California. He says, "When you stand on the spiritual battlefield you will hear God laugh and if you listen carefully you will hear Him say, 'It's not a fair fight, it's simply not a fair fight'."

My growing understanding of God as healer came not just through my own experiences, but also through my interactions with other

Christian health professionals. There were many international visitors to the Nuclear Medicine and Ultrasound department at Westmead hospital. Some came to help, others to learn, and some out of sheer curiosity. Our diagnostic techniques helped us to understand the natural world, but they couldn't account for the supernatural dimension. One of the first visitors to the new unit was a man who would challenge my certainties.

4

By His Stripes

To those who are called, sanctified by God the Father
and preserved in Jesus Christ: Mercy, peace, and love
be multiplied to you.

Jude 1:1-2

T he first thing I noticed about Don Tredway was his finely tooled
American cowboy boots. The second was his accent—which I
placed as Midwestern.

His reputation preceded him. He was a specialist obstetrician and
reproductive endocrinologist, a pioneer in the field of in vitro fertilization. A quick review of his CV revealed him to be an eminent professor.
He was an editor of specialty journals, and a Board examiner of young
doctors entering into his areas of expertise. There were numerous published papers and chapters to his credit.

He had been invited to Sydney to address other specialists in his
field. A meeting had been scheduled in the ballroom of the Sydney
Hilton hotel, and I had been asked to introduce him to his peers.
The more time I spent with Don, the more I liked the man. Despite
his exalted background, I found him to be humble with a great sense
of humor. But there was more to it than that, something I couldn't
put a finger on. There was something "special" about this guy. I
knew little of his personal background, but after several meetings
and many cups of coffee, I began to understand what made him so
different.

In the early 70s, he told me he had lived in Los Angeles with his wife, Donna, and their daughters. He was an obstetrician/gynecologist with the United States Navy. One day while consulting, he fell to the floor with excruciating back pain—to the astonishment and dismay of his patient! Investigations revealed a prolapsed disc. Surgery would be essential to relieve the pain. The operation was performed, deemed successful, and the pain did resolve.

Soon after, Don and family moved to San Francisco, where as a navy specialist he established a training program in microsurgery. This involved long hours of standing on the granite floors, back hunched, peering through a magnifying loupe. Before long, the pain returned with a vengeance. Further surgery was performed for another herniated disc but this time, the symptoms were not relieved.

Working became near impossible. He sought further advice, the best he could find, to be told that his back had become unstable, causing pressure on spinal nerves. A neurologist, an orthopaedic surgeon and a neurosurgeon recommended spinal fusion. At best, they suggested, there was a 50 percent chance of success.

For a year Don did not work, hoping the pain would subside. Unable to sit for any period of time, he spent hours flat on his back. Though not a religious man, he was descended from a long line of Methodist ministers and did occasionally attend church. But he had no concept of a personal God, and he dismissed the concept that God might play a part in his healing process.

Eventually, in despair, he picked up a Bible and, paging through it, found these words: "My son, pay attention to what I say; turn your ear to my words. Do not let them out of your sight, keep them within your heart; for they are life to those who find them and health to one's whole body" (Proverbs 4:20-22, NIV).

Now this caught his attention, especially the word "health." But the pain did not ease, and finally he agreed to spinal fusion.

Post surgery, the doctors were optimistic for a good result. Don was placed in a plaster hip spica cast which extended from his chest to his knees, and which remained in place for six weeks. He related the misery of immobilization and the sheer helplessness of being so restricted. Then came the long-awaited day. The cast came off and he was fitted with a long-term fibreglass brace. With the support of the brace, he returned to limited work, mainly in administration. He was weak and had lost about 55 pounds. But each day he regained a little more strength, and with strength came hope. Buoyed on, he began to pray for small things at first, and he saw these prayers answered.

Quite unexpectedly, a letter arrived from the Medical Faculty of the University of Chicago. It was an invitation to join the academic staff as a reproductive endocrinologist. He was delighted. This was one of the finest centers of learning in the United States, producing a high number of Nobel Laureates. This would be the pinnacle of his career. He and Donna flew to Chicago to investigate.

To take up the position, Don would have to resign his navy post. His friends were cautious: "What if the pain returns?" He would also lose the possibility of a disability pension. But Don believed that God was leading him. His mind was made up, and he put the family home on the market. It sold within three days.

"Another confirmation," he told me.

Finally, the surgeons recommended that the brace be removed. But then, the unexpected. Pain returned, and it was extreme. He also noticed some loss of movement in his lower limbs. The neurologist found muscle wasting and a significant neurological deficit. The opinion of the navy surgeon was that he would never work again. He recommended discharge on a disability pension. This would provide only one sixth of his normal income! Don was devastated and angry. Where was God in this?

He told of sitting in the car in the driveway of his home, deeply depressed. He had a family to support and he was in the prime of life. The move to Chicago would have provided a wonderful life for himself and Donna, and outstanding educational opportunities for their children. He was able to operate only under the most limited circumstances and required regular painkillers. But worst of all, he said, "God had let me down. God had failed me."

A few months earlier Donna had been visiting friends in Los Angeles, who spoke of the power of the Holy Spirit. They had witnessed personally the power of God to heal. She mentioned this to Don. He told her, "Shut up, woman. If I can't explain it, it doesn't exist!"

But as he said, "The hounds of heaven will not easily be put off." He was constantly confronted by references to God's ability to heal. He was given books on the subject and saw and heard promotions for healing ministries on TV and radio. One day he went to a basketball game. Unable to sit through the game, he returned to the car and switched on the radio to take his mind off his worries.

"You need a miracle," were the words of the announcer.

"Yes, I guess I do," he replied.

Don had been planning to attend a medical seminar program in Los Angeles, flying down in a private jet with colleagues. But even this posed problems because the pain was now intolerable.

Finally, reluctantly, he asked Donna to speak to her friends in Los Angeles to see if there was some way they might be able to help. As it happened, their church was to sponsor a healing service at the exact time of the medical conference, and it was close to the conference center. Don decided to attend—but no one must know.

On the first morning of the medical conference he excused himself, supposedly to rest. But he had other plans. He drove across town to the healing service, having sworn Donna to secrecy. There, he was met by her friends who escorted him into the service and sat either side "...to prevent a quick getaway," he said. The service began with music and singing. Never had he felt so uncomfortable and out of place. To make matters worse, the senior pastor had sent an apology that he would be late. This angered Don. He'd come to hear from the big man, not his deputy.

As the service continued, people were claiming to be healed. But Don was unconvinced. The pastor said that twenty would be healed from back problems. That got his attention. He observed that as people were prayed for they were apparently healed, touching their toes and thanking God. But he remained skeptical. Finally, the senior pastor arrived.

There were others with bad backs who would be healed, he said. Don had been keeping a running count.

Finally, in extreme pain, and with little to lose, Don stood on his feet and walked towards the front of the church. He received prayer and laying on of hands, an entirely new experience for him. Immediately, he said, he knew he had been healed. He has no memory of returning to his seat, but told of going out to the men's room where he removed the brace. The pain had gone and he could actually touch his toes. He returned to the auditorium holding the brace, astounded that God was able to provide instant healing where the very best of medical minds had been unable to help.

The next day he operated for two hours, and the following week took on a full surgery list. He was weak, he said, "But the more I praised God, the more my strength returned." There were some leg cramps, but the back pain was gone. Soon he was able to resume a normal working life.

The meeting in the Sydney Hilton ballroom went ahead as planned. The room was packed to capacity and, as I scanned the sea of faces, I recognized several of my professors. Don was introduced. In his own quiet way, he spoke of his medical background and discussed his infertility research. Then he went on to relate the circumstances of his healing experience. No hype, no loud voice, just a quiet, intimate presentation of what God had done in his life.

Towards the close of the meeting, those present were invited to receive prayer and to ask God's blessing on their lives and their practice of medicine. There was a tangible sense of God's presence in the hotel ballroom that afternoon. It was clear that many people's needs were being met. I had been wrestling with an issue of my own for some time and, that day, God put it to rest.

Don and I became good friends, and in the ensuing years visited China to participate in medical teaching programs. The seminars were rigorous and demanding. Each lecture, with translation and time for questions and discussion, took up to three hours. After the lectures there were often demonstrations, television interviews, and official dinners. Don managed these with ease, and I saw for myself that he remained completely free of back problems.

Today he remains well, and is based in Boston where he continues to work in his specialty field of infertility. Don once puzzled as to why God didn't also remove the surgical scars. His conclusion was that they remained as a reminder of what God can do when men have given up.

Through my growing friendship with Don, I began to understand that I worshipped a supernatural God and that I could expect Him to intervene in my life also, in supernatural ways. There welled up within me an excitement and an anticipation that God would lead me into new areas of service, areas where He would demonstrate His power and strength. But how to proceed?

The answer came early in 1980. I was invited to speak at a house party organized by the Medical Evangelical Union at Sydney University. One of the other speakers was to be a young eye surgeon in training, who had just returned from Youth With a Mission in Hong Kong. (Rob's story is told in chapter 7.)

His love for the Chinese people was contagious, and as a result I was encouraged to volunteer my services to Asian Outreach based in Hong Kong. A response came from a Dr. Donald Dale, newly appointed co-ordinator of the Jian Hua Foundation. Would I be interested in participating in a medical seminar program in Changsha, Hunan Province, and could I suggest other participants? I responded by return mail. My spiritual understanding of God the healer was about to be further honed by a multitude of fresh challenges.

5

Open Door to China

Who shall separate us from the love of Christ? *Shall* tribulation, or distress, or persecution, or famine, or nakedness, or peril, or sword? As it is written:

"For Your sake we are killed all day long; we are accounted as sheep for the slaughter." Yet in all these things we are more than conquerors through Him who loved us.

Romans 8:35-37

D r. Li reached into the pocket of his blue Mao jacket to produce a small Bible which clearly had seen better days. I glanced around and counted at least twenty Chinese soldiers with semi-automatic rifles. Several were taking an unhealthy interest.

We were standing in the departure lounge of an airport in central China. It was a square room of moderate size, furnished with rattan and the occasional Chinese rug. Twenty minutes earlier we had arrived by minibus. We had walked past the formal gardens of roses, foxgloves, and hollyhocks, a reminder of earlier occupation. We had noted the rows of Russian MiG fighters flanking the runway. It was rumored that few were serviceable, but they made a formidable impression.

We had been invited to China to speak at a medical seminar program hosted by one of the provincial medical associations. But now it was time to leave. The meeting had been a success but, in retrospect, it was a miracle that we made it into China at all, let alone managed to complete the program.

Before the journey, we had met in Hong Kong to prepare, and arrange visas. There were four of us in all: Professor Don Tredway, a cardiothoracic surgeon named Jonathon, myself, and our coordinator, Dr. Donald Dale. I first met Dr. Dale on the steps of the old military hospital on Hong Kong Island, the base for Youth With A Mission (YWAM).

Donald Dale was tall, lean, sandy-haired, and bespectacled. With quizzical expression, he had looked me up and down.

"You'd better find more suitable attire," he said with a wry smile and more than a hint of British accent. "You'll never survive here in a tie and jacket."

I was to discover Donald had an aversion to dressing up, second only to his aversion to Chinese opera.

He was on his way to a Chinese wedding and had dropped by to welcome me to Hong Kong. "You can come along with me if you wish," he said. "But I strongly advise you not to. It'll go on for hours."

The next evening at 6 p.m. we met in Donald's office. We were fired up and ready to go! Then came the telegram from China: "Unless you have made all the appropriate arrangements through official channels, please don't come." This was confronting enough, but not nearly as disturbing as a second telegram one hour later which simply said: "Do not come!"

What to do? We were set to go the next day. Donald sent a telegram in reply: "Doctors in Hong Kong. Are proceeding. Please advise." There was no response.

That night, as I packed for the flight the next day, I pondered deeply God's real purpose in this trip. Clearly there was more to come than I had anticipated.

I had been given a bundle of Christian literature to take along, "just in case." There were Gospels of John in the new Chinese script, together with copies of a booklet, *Streams in the Desert*, which I understood were much sought after in China. Never was a forbidden cargo more painfully obvious among my socks and underwear. If my suitcase were to be opened by the authorities it would likely be confiscated, and perhaps the whole venture compromised. But something told me to push ahead.

At midnight there was a call from Sydney. It was my wife, Lynne. She had pleurisy and was so breathless I could scarcely hear a word she said.

All of the children were also ill, and Brook, my older son, was very short of breath. My father, who lived nearby, was unable to help because he was experiencing angina. Sydney was in the grip of wild wintry weather.

"Oh, yes," Lynne added, "and a tree has fallen on the house, demolishing the pergola. But it's OK, the state emergency service has already been to clear the debris."

I had no idea what to do. In a few hours I was to fly into China. From that point on, there would be no opportunity to call home.

"We have friends in Sydney who would help—Noel and Phyl Gibson," suggested Gary Stevens, the leader of YWAM HK. I didn't know these people, but at 1 a.m., we called. They spent an hour on the phone with Lynne, counseling, advising, and praying for the family. By morning all was well. The crisis was over.

With an overwhelming sense of peace and a new respect for my Father God, I flew with the others into China, knowing that all at home were in safe hands.

It was evening when we climbed down the metal steps onto the tarmac at Guangzhou airport. It was August, and the air was hot and steamy. Military music drifted across from a speaker somewhere in the darkness, and silhouetted by the light of distant spotlights, I saw armed soldiers guarding several of the planes.

We were escorted with our luggage into the arrival lounge, where unsmiling immigration officers peered suspiciously and checked our visas. High on the wall, an enormous portrait of the "great helmsman" Mao Tse-tung watched over all. We walked a gauntlet of red-starred customs officers, who silently scrutinized our every step, and then out into the darkness. At no time was my bag examined!

We regrouped by a stand of giant bamboo outside the terminal, astounded, and thoroughly relieved that all had gone so well. There were no taxis, so we walked to the airport hotel nearby, dragging our suitcases and an overhead projector. (The overhead projector was a gift to the provincial medical association, but we carried it out again when we left. Nobody, it seemed, had sufficient authority to accept it.) After climbing eight flights of steps, we slept soundly that night on our bamboo mats, despite the constant drone of the martial music from the airport nearby.

Bright and early next morning, we boarded a two-engine turboprop for our destination in central China. We had been told that no seats were available, but as the time of departure approached, tickets materialized and we were ushered to our seats. On boarding, we were issued with a paper fan (air-conditioning, I assumed) and a few pieces of preserved fruit wrapped in waxed paper. As the plane gathered speed for take-off, the pilot, without warning, brought the plane to an abrupt halt, throwing passengers and baggage violently forward. The flight crew disembarked, and there followed an animated discussion with much pointing at one of the engines and shouting. But as quickly as the discussion began it ended, and we were soon airborne.

Heading north, I was uneasy about what might lie ahead. Would we be welcome? Would there be anyone to meet us? Would the meetings be able to proceed?

At the airport, an official party made us welcome. With much hand-shaking, smiling, and exchanging of business cards, we were hustled into a minibus and taken to a downtown hotel. Among the party was Dr. Li, a local surgeon. He remained aloof during formalities, but once behind closed doors he gripped our hands and wept openly.

"Thank God you've come," he said.

It was he who had sent the telegrams telling us not to come, but this had been necessary to keep faith with the authorities. He had been praying daily for four months that we would come.

Reaching into his blue cotton jacket, he took out a battered copy of a book by A.W. Tozer and read aloud from a chapter on the love of God. After each line he paused and gazed attentively at each of us in turn. Did these words mean as much to us as they clearly did to him? He had been criticized and persecuted for his beliefs, losing many of his civil rights, including the right to practice medicine. Most of his time was now spent translating foreign medical journals into Chinese. "God is doing wonderful things here," he said. "I saw a woman cured of uterine cancer. But we must be so careful."

Dr. Li told us how he loved music. His favorite pastime was to sing hymns. But the only way he could achieve this without unwelcome attention was to row out into the middle of the lake, out of earshot of others. It soon became clear that one of the major reasons we had come was to support and encourage this wonderful man.

Later that night, Dr. Li told us his story. His father had been a Christian pastor and he himself had become a Christian after reading his father's books in 1942. After school he studied medicine, and two years out of medical school had been asked to start a hospital for the People's Republic. It soon became apparent that through his inability to comply with the political demands on his life, he would be unable to continue his job.

In 1956 he was jailed for fifteen months by the Red Guard "for investigation" and, after release, was permitted to practice medicine in a restricted fashion. He had been forbidden to witness to his family, who were told that he was a traitor. They had been warned by authorities that the Bible was officially classified as pornographic literature. At the time of our visit, somewhere out of town he was running a small Bible-study group. But we would never venture there or meet these people in respect of their own safety.

The following day, we received our lecture schedule. Each lecture with interpretation would run for three hours. There would be demonstrations following and question times.

Don Tredway, familiar with China's one-child policy, had come prepared to speak on birth control. Ironically, the Chinese wanted him to speak about treatment of infertility. I had come prepared to speak on practical aspects of clinical nuclear medicine and ultrasound. The Chinese, on the other hand, wanted lectures on positron emission tomography (PET Scanning).[8]

This was a super specialty, which would not be relevant to China for twenty years. But it was clear that the requests were in line with Deng Xiaoping's Four Modernizations program, and we had little choice but to comply. We were also told that if lectures were too simplistic, the meetings would be cancelled. If they were too complex, we would not be asked to speak again. So it was back to the drawing board for us both.

The program began with speeches from dignitaries and party representatives. Donald Dale was interviewed on local TV. The lectures were long, and interpreters were not always fluent in English. The most difficult task was ensuring that the interpreter understood clearly what was said. It was important not to speak too quickly, as interpreters suffered great loss of face if they were unable to keep up. After one session, I made the mistake of asking for a more able interpreter. "We will discuss that in our criticism meeting," responded an officious young woman. In a later meeting, my interpreter was so limited in her understanding of English that I finally said, "We will forget the interpretation and just watch the slides." She responded, "What?"

The program proceeded well. Ever so slowly, we were winning the confidence and respect of local doctors, and developing rapport with the ever-present political observers from the scientific bureau. During breakfast one morning, an interpreter paid us a visit. He was surprised to see our simple fare of tea and pastries, which we offered to share with him. That evening he related this to a large group at dinner. They were delighted, expecting us as foreigners to eat lavishly. One of the party observers spoke out: "Ah, the simple life and hard work. That is good."

I soon became aware that the medicine practiced locally was quite different to that practiced at home in Sydney. As an example, intrauterine contraceptive devices were localized by X-ray rather than ultrasound. This was because an X-ray cost 50 fen (US $.26) whereas an ultrasound study cost 20 yuan (US $8). The patient did not pay of course, but the hospital unit was charged. I was asked to perform an ultrasound study on a local dignitary with a pelvic tumor. The heat and humidity in the room were extreme, and I was fanned by one of the nurses as I worked. After squeezing a normal amount of contact gel onto the patient's abdomen I was gently tapped on the shoulder. "You have just used a month's supply," I was told.

It was fascinating to meet people in the street. One man had never heard of Christianity. Another approached us directly and asked, "Why was Jesus nailed to a cross?" He expected that, as foreigners, we would know. Another asked where we had come from. When Don Tredway responded, "The United States," he replied, "Welcome anyway."

On Sunday morning we were accompanied by a Mr. Wong to the local Three Self Church, a freestanding brick structure next to the original church building, which was now used as a factory. Members of the congregation were in their late 70s and 80s, and many peered through large magnifying glasses. We learned that it was possible to purchase a Bible through the church, but to do so required divulgence of a great deal of personal information. This included answers to such questions as: "Are you a Christian? How long have you been so and through whom did you make your decision to convert? Also, are your family members Christian?" Understandably, many were cautious and preferred to obtain their Scriptures by other means.

The officially appointed church leader spoke on the Lord's Prayer. When he came to the words, "Give us this day our daily bread," he said, "We can ignore this section as our government provides all the bread we need." There was no offertory, and the service finished after one hour, to the minute.

From day one we had asked to visit the local hospital but this was always a problem, although no reason was given. And then, unexpectedly, on the last day permission was given. We were taken on guided tours of our specialty areas. Outside the main hospital gate was a large handwritten sign in Chinese: "Closed Today." I visited the nuclear medicine department to find it fully equipped with brand new equipment. The corridors were littered with packing cases. The others reported similar findings. Clearly the equipment had been shipped in for our visit.

That night we were invited to Dr. Li's home for a banquet, together with local dignitaries and party representatives. It was a four-bedroom house, large by local standards, sparsely furnished with heavy, dark, wooden furniture. A black and white television sat in pride of place on a white lace cloth. There was no running water.

Dr. Li's bedroom served also as the living room and dining area. The banquet, served on a large round table, was sumptuous. It would have cost the family dearly. There were speeches and many toasts proposed, and after the meal all were invited to entertain. Some sang, and Dr. Li played his ancient harmonium, accompanied by his son on the violin. Dr. Li's son-in-law, a heavy-set man with a florid face and a mop of black hair, sang a traditional song in a deep bass voice. Then it was our turn. We looked at one other blankly. Only one song came to mind with which we were all familiar— "The Battle Hymn of the Republic." As we made our shaky discordant start, the Chinese stood to their feet as one. "You are singing our song," they said. "Solidarity Forever," it seemed, could be sung in Chinese to this tune. And so, in full voice and with hearts brimming over, we sang to the glory of God as the Chinese sang to the glory of communism. I have to admit that the hairs on the back of my neck stood up.

But now we were leaving and our plane was ready to board. As we stood in the departure lounge Dr. Li opened his Bible, gazed into our faces, oblivious to the score of soldiers looking on, and proceeded to read from Romans 8:35-39:

> Who shall separate us from the love of Christ? *Shall* tribulation, or distress, or persecution, or famine, or nakedness, or peril, or sword? As it is written:
>
> "For Your sake we are killed all day long; we are accounted as sheep for the slaughter." Yet in all these things we are more than conquerors through Him who loved us. For I am persuaded that neither death nor life, nor angels nor principalities nor powers, nor things present nor things to come, nor height nor depth, nor any other created thing, shall be able to separate us from the love of God which is in Christ Jesus our Lord.

I never saw Dr. Li again. Word later came that he had lost further privileges and had moved to the north country. He is one of the bravest men that I have ever known. His family members, also Christian, remained cautious in their witness. They later managed to leave China.

I made several subsequent visits to China. On a later journey to a city in the far north, my interpreter was a local professor. At the conclusion of the meeting as we were saying our goodbyes he said, "You know, Dr. Crocker, I have to be as wise as a serpent and as gentle as a dove." This reference to words from Matthew 10:16 indicated clearly to me that this man was a Christian. This was the only reference he made to his Christian belief over several days, knowing full well my position.

On another occasion a different professor took my hand and said, "It has been a privilege working with you."

I thanked her.

Then she said, "You don't understand, Dr. Crocker. I am a Christian." And her eyes filled with tears.

At the outskirts of that city were posted lists of the names of people scheduled for execution. After executions, the lists were marked with a large red tick. This action was supposedly an attempt to rid the country of criminals. It was common knowledge that the term "criminal" was loosely interpreted. Many Christians, especially those involved in the house church movement, disappeared never to be seen again.

One remote city that we later visited was said to have no Christian church at all. As much as we wanted to attend church on the Sunday, we were told this would not be possible. On the Saturday afternoon one of our party, who was fluent in Mandarin, went walking with another. Their aim was to find the church they knew must exist in an area as large as the Sydney central business district.

A young girl on a bicycle stopped them on the road and, without speaking, beckoned them to follow. She led them to an old shop front, and then was gone. In the shop an aged man and his wife stood behind a counter, and behind them, on the wall, was an open cross. This was the local underground church. The couple warmly greeted my friends, and invited all of us to return the next day for a service.

We decided that it would be prudent to send only a few and to travel by an indirect route. In the back room that morning we found people who had not known contact with the outside church since before the Cultural Revolution thirty years earlier. They welcomed us with great joy, and were overwhelmed to hear that people from the West were actually praying for them. The hymns they sang were very old, not sung in Western churches for many years.

I learned a great deal about my Silent Partner in China. First that much more is achieved when we stop trying to do things in our own strength and allow God to take control. We were enthusiastic to share our faith and impatient to see results. But little happened until we were able to let go of the situation and release it back to God.

Secondly, China was my "boot camp" in learning about spiritual opposition, not only against the Chinese believers, but also against us as visitors. I had not understood that simply going there placed us and our families at home in jeopardy. But God, my Silent Partner, was there too as Protector and Shield to us and to our families.

My lasting impression of China is of those brave men and women who have maintained their Christian faith under the most difficult circumstances and often at great personal cost.

On the way home from church one day, we were approached by a young man on a bicycle who volunteered his services as guide for the afternoon. This was not unusual, as many people wished to practice their English with foreigners. He would meet us after lunch and take us for a walk on the local mountain.

"But first," he said, "I will take you to meet my professor." He led us into the university compound to a small dimly lit room of raw concrete, adorned only with the stains of many years. Here we met one of the most remarkable men that I have ever known. He was in his eighties, tall and lean, dressed in navy blue and with jet black hair. Surprisingly he spoke with a broad American accent which he had acquired as interpreter to General James "Jimmy" Doolittle during World War II. A brilliant man, now an emeritus professor, he had been sent to the countryside to farm during the Cultural Revolution.

But now he lived alone in this small room where he bred rabbits. As we spoke he held one and stroked it lovingly. Learning of our plans for the afternoon, the professor volunteered his services and proceeded to lead us at a cracking pace up the mountain path that led from the university. And then he stopped quite abruptly and turned to face us. "I am a Christian," he said, "and I am not afraid." He lived in isolation, and knew of no other Christians living in his area. We talked for a long time. I gave him my Bible and was able to encourage him. What a privilege to meet this man.[9]

6

Donald

For to me, to live *is* Christ, and to die *is* gain.

Philippians 1:21

To survive in China, infinite patience, a sense of humor, and language skills are essential. Happily, Dr. Donald Dale possessed all three.

On one occasion in central China, he led us up an ancient wooden staircase, stained and scarred by generations, to an expansive dining area bursting with patrons and filled with the happy sounds of people eating, and drinking the local Hunan beer. As we entered a hush came over the room. Every eye fixed on us, the only Westerners in town. A flustered young lady with grey trousers and white blouse ushered us to a private room. But Donald would have no part of it. "We'll sit outside with the others," he insisted in Mandarin.

He had his way, and we were seated in the main body of the restaurant. Donald scanned the English language menu.

"These prices are outrageous," he said, after conversing with people at tables nearby. "At least twice what the locals are paying." Donald was not able to pay these inflated prices reserved for "rich tourists." At the time he and his wife, Penny, were living in a one-room apartment on the roof of the Anglican church hall in Nathan Road, Hong Kong.

Eventually the young lady returned to take our order to be told that as we were poor travellers, we would order two portions only. The response from the kitchen was predictable, and explosive. To serve us

41

with two portions would result in a great loss of face. We were treated to a banquet, far more than we could eat. The chef attended us personally, serving his specialty honey, mandarin, and fungus soup. To my memory there was minimal charge.

On another occasion, we attended a formal dinner with local Chinese doctors and the ever-present Mr. Wong from the scientific bureau. (There was always a "Mr. Wong," a local party member, to keep an eye on matters.) Mr. Wong apologized profusely for his wife who was "indisposed" and unable to attend. Several attempts were made to present him with a small box of candy as a token of our appreciation. But each time he politely declined. He simply did not have the authority to accept the gift. Finally Donald intervened.

"No, no, Mr. Wong, the gift is not for you. It is for your poor wife who is unable to be with us tonight."

The gift was gleefully accepted.

"Oh," Donald added, "and perhaps she will share some with you, Mr. Wong."

He blushed deeply.

Donald was a man of action and not one to procrastinate. Keeping up with him was always a task as he walked quickly with long strides. An asthmatic, he was heavily dependent on his inhaler and would often be seen scurrying off to take care of some pressing matter clutching his Ventolin and titrating the dose to his rate of travel. But despite his haste, he learned to wait on God for direction, and to trust him implicitly.

Donald Dale made an indelible impact on my life. Having met him, I would never be the same again. Not only did he invite me to make my first medical tour of China, he became an inspiration to me—personally, professionally, and spiritually.

He was born July 18, 1923 in southern China, in a small town at the foot of the mountains, where his father worked in the English Presbyterian Hospital as a doctor. When asked his nationality he would say, "They call me White Chinese." But in some circumstances, because both his parents were Scottish, he would be proud to call himself a Scot.

He was only five when his parents fled to Taiwan to escape the communists who were creating havoc in the south.

As a boy, Donald rebelled against his parents' faith and recalls throwing his Bible to the floor and storming out of the room during family devotions. "I suppose I had the problem of being a missionary's child," he told broadcaster Kel Richards during an interview for Australian television. "I had to come to a point of total desperation. I had a pretty good estimation of myself. But one day I discovered what I was really like."

"If you think you are nothing, how can you offer yourself to God?" asked Kel.

"You are offering God a total wreck and asking Him to make something decent out of it," said Donald. "It's amazing what he can do."

"Why do you have such a fascination with China?" continued Kel.

"I've often wondered myself," he replied. "Remembering nothing of my early life in China, it's a bit difficult to understand. It all stems back to God, really. Right from the moment I came to know Him, I knew that China was in my future."

While completing his medical residency in the UK he met Penny, who was completing her nursing training. They shared a common love for China and the Chinese people and, as their relationship developed, there grew a conviction that they would serve there together one day. However, Donald's severe asthma precluded acceptance by missionary societies.

This verse was given them at the time of their marriage: "Trust in the LORD with all your heart, and lean not on your own understanding; in all your ways acknowledge Him, and He shall direct your paths" (Proverbs 3:5,6). Again and again they were to learn the wisdom and truth of these words.

One day, a letter arrived from the mayor of a small town in western China. Donald prevailed on a friend for a translation.

"This is our way to China," he said. "Tell us where we are going."

The letter was from the mayor of Beipei in Sichuan Province offering work in the new municipal hospital. "Come quickly," the mayor wrote.

"You will be free to share your faith, accommodation will be provided, and Dr. Dale will receive the salary of ten sacks of rice per month." This meagre-sounding pay was to be providential, and inspired the title of Penny's story of their life: *Ten Sacks of Rice: Our Way to China*.[10]

On the night of October 9, 1948 the young family was prayerfully bidden farewell from Euston station, north London to begin their seventeen-week journey to Beipei, Sichuan Province, western China. They boarded the *Rhexenor*, a small cargo ship that took only twelve passengers. The weather was bad. The news was worse. The communists were advancing on Shanghai and Nanking, and American and British citizens were advised to leave without delay. The captain was tempted to divert to Hong Kong. Finally he docked in Shanghai early on New Year's Day 1949, unloaded his cargo and passengers, and was away by nightfall.

Twenty-one days after the Dales arrived in Shanghai, General Chiang Kai-shek resigned and the political situation deteriorated further. It was now too dangerous to travel by ship along the Yangtze. The communists had arrived at the north bank and were shooting at boats going upstream.

Finally, by light plane and bus they completed the challenging journey to Beipei, and were welcomed into their new home with the few possessions they had been able to carry. It soon became apparent that their monthly salary of ten sacks of rice was a godsend. Local paper money was worthless and the only stable currency was rice.

Before long, their two boys began to run high fevers. And then the communists crossed the Sichuan border. "Leave now, for your own safety," the Dales were advised. They had been in Beipei just three and a half months! The plan had been to stay for seven years.

Back in Chongqing, they discovered that their luggage had finally arrived by steamer from Shanghai. Donald sold much of it for silver dollars. In Shanghai they had been told, "You are not real China missionaries until you have lost at least one child and all your possessions three times." Their response to these sobering words was to recall others spoken over them at their wedding: "Trust in the LORD with all your heart…"

The decision was made to go to Hong Kong, where the boys could receive medical attention. Almost as soon as they arrived, they were approached by a woman from Taiwan.

"Please come to Taiwan," she pleaded. "You are needed, urgently." But Donald and Penny were reluctant. They had been hoping for a quiet period in Hong Kong to consolidate their family after the rigors of China.

But more invitations to Taiwan followed, and with their boys now recovered from Sichuan fever, they finally yielded. Donald would run the Mackay Memorial Hospital operated by the Canadian Presbyterian Mission; the only foreign doctor for the entire expatriate population of Taiwan, about 500 in all. The hospital was in a sorry state. Medicine was scarce and pathology testing was not available. Donald curtained off one end of a corridor and, with the help of his medical books, set up a small pathology lab.

When western staff members were asked to leave the hospital, Donald and Penny remained in the city to create what was to become known as Christian Clinic. It would operate for twenty-eight years. The clinic was designed with a free section for the disadvantaged and a private practice which paid the bills. While patients waited, Brother Chang, a close friend of Donald and Penny, would preach the gospel. Many became Christians.

A Lutheran evangelist visited Taipei. After the meeting, Donald asked for prayer for healing of his asthma. He remained completely symptom-free for three months, but after a severe chest infection the symptoms returned. Later he was to say that with greater spiritual insight he would never have accepted the return of symptoms, which he interpreted as a spiritual attack.

On another occasion, Donald was to be keynote speaker at a leadership conference in central Taiwan. On the first evening he found, to his frustration, that the interpreter would not be available. Not yet fluent in Mandarin, he asked God for help. That night he spoke freely in Mandarin for an hour. The next evening his interpreter was available and translated. "Why didn't you speak in Chinese?" the students asked, afterwards. "It was much better last night when you spoke in Chinese." From that point on, Donald was ready for God to do anything in his life.

In the late 70s, both Donald and Penny sensed that God was telling them to move on to something new, even though they did not want to leave Taiwan. There was a growing refugee problem in Hong Kong as Vietnamese boat people flooded the colony, overwhelming local resources and infrastructure. For two years Donald worked side by side with Vietnamese health care workers who were able to practice under his supervision. Many became Christians.

In 1981, Donald was approached by three Chinese businessmen who had established a new charitable institution, known as the Jian Hua Foundation (meaning To Build China). The plan was to send Christians into China to assist in the Four Modernizations program established by Deng Xiaoping in 1978. This referred to the modernization of agriculture, industry, science and technology, and defense. Those sent under the sponsorship of Jian Hua must respect the Chinese constitution which forbade them to propagate their faith publicly. However, if personal questions were asked, they were free to respond.

Donald was appointed as Jian Hua Coordinator. His role would be two-fold: to identify Christians around the world who would be willing to work in China, and to identify areas of need in China where these people could be deployed.

At first teachers were sent and later medical teams to lecture across China starting in Changsha, Hunan Province. I was on the first of those medical teams. Later teams went on to Beijing, Tianjin, Ningsha and many other cities. Experts in engineering, agriculture, and computer technology followed the medical teams. Camps were established where Chinese young people majoring in English were able to live side by side with young Westerners through their summer vacation. This enabled many young people to gain valuable experience in part-time missionary work.

Donald officially retired in 1992. He was sixty-nine. By that time, Jian Hua staff in Hong Kong had increased from one (himself) to six. Eighty adults were serving full-time in China, and there were representatives in Australia, the UK, Canada, and the US.

Donald and Penny moved to Austin, Texas to be close to family, and for several years continued to travel widely, visiting friends, bringing encouragement, and promoting the work of Jian Hua around the world. In February 1998, Donald began to experience what was thought to be indigestion and then, early one morning, passed away quietly in his sleep. Shortly before he died, Penny had been aware of the Lord saying to her from the words of Genesis 5:24, "Donald, as Enoch, has walked with me many years, and now he is no longer with you. I have taken him." Donald's sudden death brought sadness to family and friends around the world. But they were comforted that the Lord had taken him in his own perfect timing, without pain or suffering.

My most enduring memory of Dr. Donald Dale is the night he spoke at our church in Baulkham Hills, Sydney, Australia, sharing his experiences and vision for China. He spoke of the great need, of the spiritual vacuum, and of the abject poverty in some provinces. He told of the families where poverty was so extreme that a family might possess only one respectable pair of trousers. One went out to work while another slept. When that one returned, the other took the trousers and went out to work.

He spoke also of a young girl with the *Little Red Book* of Mao Tse Tung. She had based her life on this corrupt gospel, and with tears in her eyes had come to realize that during the Cultural Revolution this man had turned the children of her generation into murderers. As he spoke to us he was overcome with compassion and had to pause for several minutes.

At the conclusion of a trip to Southwest China, Donald was driven to the airport for the flight back to Hong Kong. As he left the car, and stepped out of earshot of the driver, a Chinese friend said to him, "When you return, would you please bring me a Bible?" Sadly that was never possible. In later years whenever he recalled that incident, Donald would pray that someone else would take that man a Bible. As far as I know, that prayer remains to be answered.

7

China Syndrome

If I take the wings of the morning, and dwell in the uttermost parts of the sea, even there Your hand shall lead me, and Your right hand shall hold me.

Psalm 139:9,10

It was dusk as the massive steam locomotive ground to a reluctant halt at Beijing Railway Station. The carriages, weary of their load and the long journey north, stood motionless, anchored in a swirl of smoke and steam. The platform came alive as hundreds swarmed from the coaches to coalesce with waiting crowds. The scene was chaotic, the noise an assault to the ears.

Rob, a young Australian eye surgeon, his wife, Jenny, and I, with few resources and limited Mandarin, had traveled by plane from Hong Kong to Changsha and then on to Beijing by train. We had come to participate in a medical seminar program but, as is often the case in China, our plans were not evolving as we had hoped. We had the choice of returning home or pressing on. We chose to press on.

Swept on by the crowds into a nearby street, we paused to take stock of ourselves and gather our baggage by the failing light. Unwashed, tired and hungry, we were not a pretty sight, and I was quite ill with a chest infection.

The doctor at the Australian Embassy, a tall, pleasant-faced man from Brisbane with a shock of white hair, offered us shelter. After a hot shower and a meal of Western food, we settled down for the night. I slept on his examination couch.

But tomorrow was to be a new day in every sense. As it happened, our time in Beijing would be successful beyond our imagination, not in the manner that we had anticipated, but in terms of meeting colleagues and encouraging local Christians.

By this time, I had been to Beijing several times previously and the experience had always been remarkable. There were visits to the Beijing Hotel with its bizarre multinational architecture, prayer meetings in apartments where names were not mentioned because the "walls had ears," and unfamiliar food served with water in gin bottles with the labels still affixed. But on this visit it was not the process or the protocol that was extraordinary, but my traveling companions.

As a medical student, Rob had interrupted his studies to travel to Hong Kong where he and Jenny helped to establish the Youth With A Mission (YWAM) base. But it became clear to them that more would be achieved if they had medical qualifications. They returned home so that he could complete his studies and Jenny, a trained nurse, her diploma of tropical medicine. I had met Rob in Sydney while he was studying eye surgery, and he had been one of the catalysts for my increasing interest in China. It was his passionate speech at a Medical Evangelical Union house party in 1980 about the needs of the Chinese people that spurred me on to volunteer my services for the first time. Over the course of our friendship, he has also helped deepen my understanding of the healing God.

Once qualified as an eye surgeon, Rob, with Jenny and their two boys, moved back to Hong Kong. He established a practice specializing in corneal laser surgery.

Though a busy surgeon, he often traveled into China to teach surgical technique. On one occasion he was invited to demonstrate corneal transplantation. As he prepared, it became apparent that no corneas were available for the next morning's demonstration. Bringing this to the attention of the person in charge, he was assured that this would not be a problem. The next morning, four corneas were presented to him. The authorities had executed prisoners during the night to make this possible. He never again made himself available for such a demonstration.

After my first trip to China, I invited Rob and Jenny to accompany me on a subsequent teaching tour. Together we traveled to Changsha and Beijing, and with Donald Dale and others to Tianjin and north-west by train through Mongolia to Ningsha. Ningsha in northwest China is just a short distance from the Russian border. ("Four hours by tank," a local told me.) Traveling with Rob and Jenny was a memorable experience, as Rob described God's involvement in his everyday medical work.

A German lady who visited his surgery had previously suffered from cataracts and had been treated by lens extraction and intraocular implants. To his dismay he found that each lens had dislocated downwards, giving what he called a "rising sun" appearance. The only treatment was surgical correction. Rob explained this, inviting her to return after discussing it with family members. When she returned, the lenses were normally located. She told him that she had asked God to heal her—and He had.

With Rob, it was impossible to predict what might happen next. One morning I found myself with him in the change room of a shop on Nathan Road, praying for a Buddhist shopkeeper who had chronic liver disease. The man was overwhelmed with emotion and wept openly.

On another occasion I was invited to a day of cruising on Victoria Harbor in a boat owned by a Hong Kong banking corporation. Smart young waiters in short white coats served crustless cucumber sandwiches and Pimms, an English drink, on scrubbed decks in the morning sun. And in the afternoon there was sailing and, for the stout-hearted, swimming in the dark waters off Lantau island. (I declined.)

On one visit I was invited to sleep over on Rob and Jenny's boat, *Far Horizons*, a 65-foot launch moored in Clearwater Bay. It was their new home since they had sold their house on the eve of the Chinese takeover in 1997. This would facilitate transfer back to Australia if the political situation deteriorated.

Staying on a boat in Clearwater Bay sounded appealing. But I was not prepared for what followed. I discovered the boat was in dry dock, suspended 30 feet above the ground and tenuously supported by bamboo poles. Apparently the boat, with its fibreglass hull, had a bad case of osmosis, salt water having penetrated the hull. Access was by extension ladder. The only power was a single power cord for lighting and refrigeration. No air-conditioning!

The next morning, an animated crew of Chinese workers arrived. With much shouting they skirted the boat with canvas shrouds and placed large gas heaters below the hull to dry it out. The breeze from the South China Sea through my porthole was very welcome that night as we slept.

Through Rob and Jenny, I encountered other extraordinary people. One was Jackie Pullinger, a young British expat, who had begun a ministry to heroin addicts and Triad gang members in the Walled City of Hong Kong. This was a forbidden area for law-abiding citizens. Formerly a fort and watch post for pirates in the early nineteenth century, it was retained by the Chinese after the ceding of Hong Kong to Britain in 1842. Located in Kowloon near the old airport, on a small tract of land about 6.5 acres, it consisted of tall tenement houses stacked side by side, filled with an estimated 30,000 to 50,000 inhabitants. It was considered the most densely populated spot on earth. Abandoned by the Chinese after World War II, it became a lawless area controlled by Triad gangs. The police were reluctant to enter, creating a haven for organized crime and illegal business.[11]

Rob and Jenny arranged for me to visit the Walled City with Jackie. Walking along what seemed a very ordinary street in the morning light we turned and stepped down into a darkened passageway, lit by naked incandescent bulbs powered by illegal wiring that snaked sinuously from building to building. The stained walls of ancient tenements towered above us. A rat scuttled past and faceless men sat in doorways. Unlicensed dentists plied their trade behind showcases of grotesque *prêt-à-porter* dentures, which sat like spiders ready to spring. The machinery of home industry droned away behind closed doors.

As we made our way through the maze, Jackie introduced me to a colorful assortment of people: Triad members, heroin addicts, a man keeping watch outside an opium den. She knew them all. They were the residents of the city. Eventually we reached a small dimly lit room which

Jackie and her girls had leased from the local powers that be. This was "the Well," an oasis in a spiritual desert, where people could come to find love and acceptance, and receive help. And many did.

That afternoon, with Rob and Jenny, we shared a meal with people who had been helped by Jackie's ministry, leaving hopeless lives of addiction and crime to find life and a new beginning.

Later, we visited a room high in an apartment block overlooking Victoria Harbor. Here, behind locked doors, were about ten young men who, with Jackie's help, had recently overcome their addiction to heroin or were in the process of doing so. I glanced around at the sallow faces and rotting teeth, scars of opiate addiction. Yet there was something different about the eyes. They were clear and full of hope. These men were not as they seemed.

It was then that I learned I was to spend the night in this apartment. My other accommodation was no longer available, but I was welcome to stay the night with Jackie and these young men. One condition: I would be locked in until dawn.

There was an uneasy peace as I settled down to sleep that evening. Placing my passport and travelers checks under the pillow, I genuinely wondered whether I would survive the night. And, in the early hours, unable to sleep, I sat with Jackie as she watched and prayed over a young man withdrawing from his addiction—cold turkey.

In the morning after breakfast of congee (rice porridge) and Chinese tea, there was a time of prayer and Bible study led by Jackie. And afterwards, the young men gathered around to pray for me, yes for me, one of the most extraordinary and touching experiences I have ever known!

Through their involvement with Jackie's ministry outreach, called "St. Stephens," Rob and Jenny became intimately aware of the desperate needs of the disadvantaged of Hong Kong, especially the children.

"We'd often said that lots of families could make room for a needy child," said Jenny. "God was listening."

They were asked if they could foster a four-year-old girl whose mother, a heroin addict, had shot through—disappeared without a trace. Two weeks stretched to six months. Jackie's team eventually found the mother, who was unable to take the little girl back and requested they keep her.

During this time, Rob and Jenny met people who challenged their thinking: two elderly Japanese gentlemen who in 1946 had given up their US citizenship to adopt thirty-nine post-World War II orphans and a widow with two kids living on a garbage heap in Manila who found an abandoned child and didn't hesitate to take him into her home.

Rob and Jenny decided to adopt their little girl, now almost five. The Welfare Department opposed them initially, but with help from a local lawyer the adoption proceeded. Their own boys, Mitchell and Caleb, were now seventeen and fifteen. Their new little girl should have a sibling more her own age, a local one!

Again they approached the Welfare Adoption Unit. "We asked for an older child, three years plus," said Jenny, "but the Adoption Unit chose Peter, who was six months old. Born to a mother sixteen years of age, he had severe unilateral cleft palate and was deaf. They wanted a medical family for him and we fitted the bill. They also felt that our little girl, who was a very tough five-year-old, would be kind and gentle to a child with obvious needs. It worked, and she showed tremendous compassion and protectiveness to her new brother, offering to "punch the lights out of whoever done that to him"—referring to the big hole in his face. It was difficult for a five-year-old to comprehend congenital anomalies."

Peter underwent extensive reconstruction surgery in the Hong Kong Children's Hospital, followed by speech training. He has now developed into a fine, able-bodied young man, and commenced an engineering degree in Tasmania in 2010.

In 1992 Nancy Steinkamp, who ran an adoption agency called Crown, stayed with Rob and Jenny after touring orphanages in China. She told of the masses of unwanted children in Chinese orphanages, largely as a result of the one-child policy.

"Her stories had great impact on us," said Jenny, "and we became a Crown agency in Hong Kong, to facilitate adoptions from China."

Over the next six years they found homes for about sixty Chinese orphans, many of whom bore some kind of handicap.

In 1995, Jenny was invited by a province in northern China to liaise with their welfare department. There she visited an orphanage in Changun, a bitterly cold town that reached 40 degrees below freezing and saw desperate poverty. She recalls seeing a couple riding on a donkey swathed in rugs to avoid the blistering cold.

At this orphanage, Jenny met a six-year-old girl. "You must adopt this child," she was told by a staff member. The young girl spoke no English. She had been found by an itinerant worker in a cardboard box at the local railway station five years earlier. It seems that she had been abandoned when her left tibia (shinbone) broke after only a slight accident. It was not known at that time that she had Type I neurofibromatosis. This is a genetic condition which causes tumors in nerve tissue which can create unsightly swellings on the skin, but also exert pressure on nearby tissues, including bone, causing deformity. The tibia fracture had not healed, but had formed a false joint in her leg.

Jenny named the child, Holly. It appears that Holly had been led to the Lord by another child in the orphanage. She recognized God as her heavenly Father and had begun to ask Him for an earthly mother and father.

Adoption proceedings were complicated, but finally successful. Holly underwent surgery to lengthen and stabilize her leg, with excellent results. As I write she has developed into a fine young lady, now training in hospitality in Sydney, Australia.

In 1997, Rob and Jenny adopted another child, four-year-old Esther. She could neither speak nor walk properly because of previous ill-treatment.

"She's now a pretty good athlete," said Jenny, "and never stops talking."

Deep waters and turbulent seas were no strangers to this young family. But none so deep or turbulent as those which occurred off Costa Rica in January 2001. *Bobby*, a steel-built Canadian trawler was the successor to their fibreglass home, *Far Horizons*. Jenny, with their four young children, flew to Canada to take delivery. She had an Offshore Yacht Masters qualification, and with a volunteer crew, planned to sail the ship back to

Hong Kong. On the passage from Havana, Cuba to Panama, at the stroke of midnight of the new millennium, the engines failed.

"The sea conditions were very rough with steep 15- to 20-foot seas and 20-knot winds," said Jenny. "The boat rolled badly. A crew member issued a pan alert to shipping and we hove to, putting the rudder to windward with the bow at about 40 degrees to the wind and waves. We were about sixty nautical miles from Isla De Providencia, a volcanic jewel off the coast of Costa Rica. We drifted with the wind and eventually got moving again about forty-five nautical miles out. Just then we were joined in celebration by two dolphins surfing on the same wave, at about the height of the pilot house windows. We felt that this was a confirmation that we were OK."

With assistance from another boat they made their way through the reef to anchor safely in the shelter of this beautiful little island. All four children slept and watched movies during the entire saga, as if nothing had happened. "We prayed and thanked God for the safe journey," said Jenny.

Later that year, Holly, her two sisters Grace and Esther, and brother Peter, were baptized in a small church in western Hong Kong. One hour earlier they had written their sins as they remembered them on pieces of paper. They burned them, casting the ashes from the jetty into the still, clear waters of Clearwater Bay. There was not a dry eye as young Holly recalled her thoughts as a six-year-old girl in an orphanage in Northern China. "If God is my heavenly Father," she said, "surely He will give me an earthly mother and father."

These four adopted children had all been adopted under the most extraordinary circumstances. All were loved, all had a future.

I recently caught up with Rob and Jenny, now living in Australia. "An important Scripture for me," said Jenny, "is Proverbs 16:9, 'A man's heart plans his way, but the LORD directs his steps.' You never know what's next from day to day, so you have to be ready to go with the flow no matter what happens. God never changes; He is the only constant. Without that knowledge I'd go nuts. I gasp at how our children have made a family when they had no one, and how they've taught me so many things. I think my life has been richer than most and often wonder why God organized it that way."

"God is not a cosmic servant," added Rob. "He is above all, and has His agenda, which He will fulfill. He does allow bad things to happen to us, yet for a purpose, even though we may not see that purpose at first."

I asked Rob what was the biggest lesson that he had learned from God.

"Not to worry," he said. "He *will* do it, with or without my help."[12]

8

From Mundane to Extraordinary

"Now My soul is troubled, and what shall I say? 'Father, save Me from this hour'? But for this purpose I came to this hour. Father, glorify Your name." Then a voice came from heaven, *saying*, "I have both glorified it and will glorify it again."

John: 12:27,28

It was beginning to dawn on me that the intervention of God into the affairs of men and women transforms lives from the mundane to the extraordinary. It was also becoming clear that we have a choice: to continue our personal pursuits, or to submit to God's will and unlock the potential that He has for our lives.

In the 2007 film, *August Rush*, a young musical prodigy alone in New York says that the music is all around us. All that we have to do is open ourselves up...and listen. So with God. We can tune out and switch off, or we can tune in to the plan that He has for our lives. In the pressing rush of contemporary life it is so easy to switch off or, sadly, never switch on at all.

During my residency at Royal Prince Alfred Hospital (RPA), Dr. Russell Clark was one of my supervisors. Russell was forthright about his Christian faith and, to his credit, he also "walked the walk." On completion of his time at RPA, Russell was appointed as chief of medicine at the United Christian Hospital, Kwun Tong, Hong Kong.

En route to China, I would often visit Russell and his wife, Kay. During one such visit, I had lectured to his residents. Afterwards, we lunched in a local restaurant where they introduced me to local delicacies: Phoenix feet (chicken feet) and deep fried whole pigeons piled high on a large plate. "You must eat the heads whole," they insisted. During the meal, Russell shared a remarkable story that would remain with me over the years. While researching this book, I asked him to tell it again.

"We had a young lady come in to our Emergency Department, pregnant and extremely ill," he said. "She was the wife of one of my Burmese doctors." The woman had several blood disorders.[13] "She developed chest pain, and when we did an ECG we found evidence of an acute MI (heart attack). What's a young pregnant Asian woman doing with a heart attack?" It got worse. She went on to develop a deep vein thrombosis (blood clot) and then blood in her urine. Russell diagnosed a serious condition called TTP which causes low levels of platelets, formation of blood clots and nerve damage.[14]

"We arranged to have her transferred to the university hospital," he said. "But before this happened God put this thought in my mind: *I should pray that the lady should recover completely.*"

The woman's life was undoubtedly in crisis, but Russell faced his own professional and spiritual crisis. "I was emotionally affected by this lady's problem," he said. "Of course I would like her to get better. But to pray and to believe it? We looked up the prognosis of TTP in pregnancy. At that time no one had ever recovered."

God put another thought in Russell's mind: *Tell her that she's going to get better.* He argued with God about it. "Well, I said, I'm not sure I can do that. That's not professional. The prognosis is the opposite. This seemed like a breach of professional ethics."

But Russell obeyed. "I went in especially on the Saturday afternoon and told her, 'I want to tell you that I believe God is going to heal you. I am praying that it will be so, and I believe that it will be so.' And I began to believe that she would be healed. When the university hospital staff aborted her pregnancy, I thought, *they shouldn't have done that; I believe she's going to get better.*"

The result was extraordinary. "To the amazement of everybody," said Russell, "the young woman did recover, completely, and in later years went on to have children."

Russell now works as a physician at the Kilimanjaro Christian Medical Center (KCMC) in northern Tanzania. Catching up with him in Sydney, he was happy to talk and I was eager to listen. He eased back in his chair, sipped pensively at his Earl Grey and reflected. Drawing a deep breath he told the story of the women he now looks after in Medical Ward 2.

"A great many have HIV/AIDS, and you cry out to God how unfair it is," he said. "At times they are good Christian women, faithful to their husbands, doing everything that the Bible teaches them to do. Their husbands, who are unfaithful, pass the HIV on to them. And they die. You think about it and get angry, but there is nothing you can do." Many of Russell's patients come in the advanced stages of AIDS and have somehow managed to find money for the drugs, but it is too late.

He also told me about a young man called Francis who came into the clinic with advanced kidney failure. "He was a fine young man, a social worker in an orphanage," said Russell. Francis was close to death. The level of creatinine in his blood, which indicates kidney failure, had reached 2,000—excessively high. The medical team commenced peritoneal dialysis, where fluid is run into the abdominal cavity to absorb toxins and then allowed to drain. Russell had to improvise. "The man in the hospital who makes peritoneal dialysis fluid was away," he said, "so I put in normal saline with 5 percent dextrose. We saved his life. We saved his life!"

It wasn't a permanent solution, however. "He got peritonitis," continued Russell, "and it was desperate. A rich lady from Moshi decided to have him transferred to Nairobi." When Francis arrived at the hospital in Nairobi he suffered a cardiac arrest. He was resuscitated and put on hemodialysis (filtering of the blood). By now, his creatinine level was 2,500! The Nairobi hospital established Francis on CAPD, a form of dialysis that he could do at home, and sent him back to Moshi. His brother then donated a kidney for transplantation, the surgery took place, and Francis recovered well.

"Last week they brought him into hospital...dead!" said Russell. "We wrestled with God. Why did it happen?"

It had been Russell, thirty-five years earlier, who had restored my faith in the practice of medicine as a worthy pursuit and, indeed, as an art form. I had come under his supervision as a blood-spattered intern battling to recover from the rigors of a general surgical term. Having gained the University Medal for surgery, I had fully intended to pursue a career as a surgeon. But three months of arm wrestling with a Deaver's retractor,[15] pumping antibiotics into dying patients and sucking purulent fluid from sump drains had led me to a rigorous revision of my decision. Internal medicine was a far more attractive alternative and Russell, as a young physician and proponent of the specialty, embodied all of the elements that appealed to me in medicine. He was informed and competent. He was patient and long-suffering with his interns, and caring with patients and staff. He was a raconteur and refreshingly avant-garde, a renaissance man of the 1970s.

I had lost track of him completely after residency, catching up briefly in the 1980s during his stint in Hong Kong as Director of Medicine at the United Christian Hospital. And I had been aware of his return to Sydney when he accepted the position of founding Director of Geriatrics at St. Vincent's Hospital, Sydney. I recall his words at that time as he searched for new direction: "What does a retired missionary do?"

But now he had re-emerged from a posting as medical practitioner and teacher at the Kilimanjaro Christian Medical Center (KCMC) in northern Tanzania.

"How do you cope?" I asked.

"Cope!" he said. "I have to say to God every morning: 'the Africans don't want me here as I'm a bit of a nuisance. I know I'm not important to them, and I have to accept that no one else wants me here either. But, God, You obviously do, so help me.' There are disappointments with people dying when they shouldn't die, with mistakes on my part.

Sometimes I get it wrong! What I've been asking God lately is that I might have the right balance between pity for suffering and professionalism."

This was a different Russell to the one I had known. No less competent, no less able, but far more experienced and in touch with harsh reality. He had moved well outside his comfort zone and was dealing on a daily basis with the most difficult of situations. Sometimes there were breakthroughs, sometimes not. Sometimes there were clear answers to prayer, sometimes not. But there was always hope.

"Let me tell you an amazing story," he continued, still sipping his Earl Grey. "We have lots and lots of patients with valvular heart disease. We do what we can to help them, but many need surgery. Five years ago the government decided they would send patients to India, as there were good surgical teams there. There was a young man who needed surgery desperately. He went down to Dar es Salaam (Tanzania's largest city) and presented himself at the clinic every day for a month. But nobody would put him on "the list" for India.

"It was impossible to understand," said Russell. "Finally, he resolved that, as he was a Christian man, he would see God earlier than others. To put it simply, he would die prematurely."

But suddenly, everything changed. The young man was called into KCMC and told to prepare for surgery the following week. Russell continued, "It seems that twelve months earlier a cardiac surgeon whose wife had been part of a missionary family in Tanzania had visited our hospital. He had decided to bring a team of ten from Leesville, Florida to perform cardiac surgery. This wonderful team came with a container-load of equipment, and performed cardiac surgery for two solid weeks. They paid all expenses. There was no local cost. An extraordinary gift of grace."

As I listened to Russell tell these stories, I was puzzled. Here was a man whose strength had always been in anticipation, planning, control, development, and execution of proven strategies. He was committed to rationalism. But how did rationalism operate in his current situation?

"I wonder whether my greatest impact is to challenge the students and doctors to be rational," he conjectured. "Rationalism is a gift from God.

And science is a gift from God. We should rejoice in them. We should use God-given ability." He discourages guessing. "We need reasons to do things. The younger doctors are responding, and that's good. Some of the older doctors feel threatened. There have been disappointments, but I seem to have developed a temperament to deal with these things."

In Tanzania, Russell encounters patients with conversion disorder, sometimes called hysteria, where symptoms such as paralysis appear without any physical basis.

"Sometimes they exhibit neurological signs such as clonus (sustained muscle contraction)," he said. "It's hard when they're totally unconscious and won't respond to any pain stimulus. You can't find anything else wrong with them. You do a lumbar puncture of course and, if they can afford it, a CT scan which costs about $80 (1990s). You have to feed them through a nasogastric tube and eventually they wake up. There was one young lady who they said was cursed. She died! But hysterics are not supposed to die. So maybe she wasn't hysterical after all. She was a young woman, and it was hard."

Diagnosis can be difficult across the cultural divide. "There is so little health knowledge in the community," Russell said. Local people have a poor understanding of whether something is serious or trivial. "The number of symptoms they understand is about ten. 'General weakness' is one. Everyone is weak! That could mean quadriplegia, or that they've been in bed for a week. And the time factor is hopeless. Everyone says they've been sick for about two weeks. They also find it hard to relate the severity of their symptoms such as whether pain or shortness of breath is severe or mild. Another symptom is awareness of heartbeats. A lovely phrase...awareness of heartbeats. I don't take the histories, but I have to analyze those taken by my doctors. They find it hard to be analytical and there is a remarkable similarity in their histories. Basically everyone has 'weakness and awareness of heartbeats for two weeks.'"

By this time I was completely perplexed. What had led Russell into this extraordinary situation? Why had he left an academic posting in Sydney with tenure, security, and job satisfaction to take up a position in a remote region of Tanzania fraught with frustration and laced with danger?

Malaria in its most dangerous form was a constant threat, together with HIV/AIDS, and a whole brace of virulent infectious diseases.

Two weeks passed before I saw Russell again. I spent that time considering his words and praying over where our next discussion might lead. What was the "key" to this man? I approached our next meeting with an open mind, anxious to see what God wanted to say through Russell. To this point I really had no idea.

It was a cool evening, drizzling with rain, the Tuesday before Easter, in fact, when we met again. He hunkered down into the old leather lounge and began. Perhaps he sensed my frustration, but his tack tonight was quite different. He took me back to his time as a final-year medical student.

"I felt that God was saying to me, 'I don't want you to study on Sundays.' But I'm competitive. I like doing well. This was final-year medicine and I needed to study on Sundays. 'OK,' I said, 'I won't do it.' And I came second in the year and sixth in surgery," he added, showing me his Year Book. "That's really quite remarkable! I wanted to do well. But I'd never done that well before."

"What did you learn from that?" I asked.

"If you feel constrained and you feel you are talking with God, then you have to do it."

In 1970 as a medical registrar, Russell rotated through specialty terms at Royal Prince Alfred Hospital, Sydney (RPA). He sat the Royal Australasian College of Physicians exam in September, but with his many commitments found himself not prepared, and failed. No pass meant no senior gastroenterology post at RPA. Subsequently he did pass, and after discussions with his mentor, Professor John Reid, made alternative arrangements. He set off with his wife, Kay, for the United Kingdom to work with Dr. Roger Williams in the liver unit at Kings College Hospital London—a better option.

His last rotation at RPA before leaving for London was psychiatry. "No one actually tells you what to do," he said. "You spend lots of time with the patients, talking to them. I had this hysterical woman with torticollis (painful neck spasm). I had to find out what psychiatric problems were giving her torticollis. I couldn't find anything! But I can remember God putting this thought in my mind: *I want you to pray that this lady will recover, and I want you to pray aloud that she will be recovered before she comes back to see you on Monday. I want you to do it, and I want you to believe that if you pray that prayer, it will happen.*

"I said to God, 'It's not a real illness, and it's a silly prayer. I don't want to do it.' So I wrestled with God all Friday night and Saturday. But by Saturday night about nine o'clock I couldn't put it out of my mind any longer. I said, 'All right, Lord,' and I prayed."

The woman came back to see him on Monday morning. "Her neck was straight!" said Russell. "I asked her: When did that happen? 'Saturday night,' was the reply! What was I to learn from that? I think that God was telling me that I could trust Him. The disappointment of failing my exams and missing the post at RPA did not mean that God was not guiding me. I was getting new direction."

God again touched Russell's life in a major way during his tour of duty at the United Christian Hospital, Hong Kong in the 1980s. Life was good. His responsibilities included a happy mix of teaching and clinical medicine. He had introduced a program of Chronic Ambulatory Peritoneal Dialysis (dialysis that could be performed at home) for patients with kidney failure. These were often the poor of HK: truck drivers, manual workers, and the unemployed. With his help they were able to return to useful, productive lives.

"I was having a good time there," he said, "but Kay and I felt the need to go home to Australia to educate our children. The powers that be in Sydney were interested in what I was doing, but made no promises. Were there jobs? No, they were closing hospitals. I was very conscious that I was a general physician without procedural skills."

Geriatrics was recommended to Russell as a discipline with a future, and it was one in which he had experience, despite no formal training. When he first arrived in Hong Kong, the hospital established a department of geriatrics. "By the grace of God an English physician who had arrived a week before me had worked in geriatric medicine," said Russell. "Together we actually started the first geriatric unit in the Far East, and I ran it for ten years."

The need to establish an Australian home for his family was weighing heavily. "It was my earnest prayer that God would provide a solution."

It was at this time that the pregnant young lady was admitted under Russell's care with TTP, a condition that no one in her situation had ever survived. As well as placing the thought in his mind that he should pray for her healing, God also said to him, "This will be a sign to you that there will be a job for you in Sydney." The two issues were connected: if Russell would pray and believe, there would be work for him in Sydney. The further implication was that if she did not get better, there would be no job.

Russell was obedient and the young woman did recover completely, to the surprise and delight of all.

"After that, we went on a family holiday to Lantau Island," said Russell. "But I had to come back for a day to farewell one of my doctors." He found a letter from Sydney. It contained the advertising section from the Medical Journal of Australia and the note: "You might be interested."

"I opened it up, and there was the position of Director of Geriatrics at St. Vincent's Hospital, Sydney." The closing date for applications was that week, but Russell was scheduled to return to Lantau at 5 a.m. the next morning. "There was no time to prepare a full curriculum vitae so I sent a letter saying I was interested in the position, with details to follow. The rest is history."

Russell became Director of Geriatrics at St. Vincent's and remained in that position for ten years. By September 1995, he and Kay were once again considering missionary work. The education of their four children had put missionary dreams on hold for a time, "But nothing got in the way like Kay getting breast cancer," he said. "Basically I spent two years praying. Whatever I was doing, I was constantly in prayer and anxious."

In January of 1996, God once again spoke to Russell. "The thought came to me, *Trust me. When Kay survives five years that will be the sign that I want you on the mission field again, that you should go. Trust me!* I wasn't sure. I had felt that God was going to heal the lady with TTP but I didn't have the same confidence that He would heal Kay. But I did have the assurance that whatever happened, it would be all right."

Kay expected to die. "She would say, 'We must watch the Olympic Games because I won't be around to watch the next ones.' She coped with her cancer by expecting to die. That was helpful to her, but I wasn't so happy about it."

Five years passed and Kay remained well. They remembered God's words: "That will be a sign that I want you on the mission field again." With some trepidation Russell realized the implications. He would have to give up his job. "I wouldn't get another staff specialist job at my age," he said, "and I'm not a private practice kind of person. What if the cancer came back after I resigned? 'However, God, You said five years and I trust You.' So I had to give notice and finish up. And I did."

Both Russell and Kay were professional people. They needed to find ways in which they could both be gainfully employed. "This was a challenge!" said Russell. "A geriatrician and an ordained deacon!" But he had links with China in geriatric medicine and had been to Beijing twice. Together they searched for a position where they could be based in HK and have missionary outreach into China. They liked Hong Kong and felt confident there.

Full-time employment was arranged in HK with an apartment. But then came the news: problems with the visa. "They wouldn't allow me to get a full-time job as they didn't want full-time foreign doctors. They would permit part-time work, but this would not provide sufficient money for an apartment. And, although it had looked as though the Anglican Church in Hong Kong would employ Kay, they reneged. All doors were closed. We thought, *God, what are You doing to us?*

Then a visitor from Southwest China arrived in Sydney. "She was an underground Chinese-American Christian who had been living in Kunming," said Russell. "She visited the Church Missionary Society to ask if there were people who would be prepared to go to China. She wanted me to go. I was terrified. I don't have strong linguistic skills, and without a clearly defined Christian community I didn't think I could manage, I really didn't. What would I do? I wouldn't be a doctor in a hospital. And what would Kay do? But this was a new day for China. The government wanted to be pro-West. This was a way to help Christian growth of China."

Russell said he found this time very difficult. "God was exposing me to the reality of what it would be like," he said, "forcing me to see that the ideas I had for myself were probably not His. Finally the lady said, 'I don't think we have a position for you.' That brought closure on China for us, and allowed God to open new directions."

These pivotal events which occurred in Russell's life had not been initiated by him but, in a sense, had been thrust upon him. When we become Christians we enter into a relationship with God. But it is a two-way relationship. We may have our plans, but God also has His own plans and purpose. We are on His agenda, and when He does intervene in our lives we can expect to be extended beyond our own means.

God challenged Russell in those areas which he regarded as his personal strengths: his competitive nature, his clinical acumen, his professional attitudes, and his security. Each of us has certain strengths, natural gifts, and learned abilities—talents, if you like. It is right that we exercise and practice these talents. But just as they may be our strengths, they can also limit our progress.

Dependence on these gifts may reach a point where they impede and obstruct our progress altogether. Their true potential can only be realized when we submit them to God in an act of trust. At that point I have found that He will intervene, supplementing our abilities, and revealing true potential for ourselves, our families and, more importantly, others. God is not so much interested in our ability as our availability.

Russell and Kay have flown back to Tanzania for what may be their last period of service. Russell will resume his duties as physician at KCMC. Kay will resume her teaching responsibilities at the Munguishi Christian Training Center, where she will train young pastors and evangelists. God most certainly did have a place for "a geriatrician and an ordained deacon."

This current placement is the one they have trained for all their lives. There is much to learn and a great deal to do. Russell has plans for a medical teaching complex and an affordable plan to provide CAPD to the many people with chronic renal failure who will otherwise perish. As they go, they do so with the sound assurance from Ecclesiastes 4:12, "Though one may be overpowered by another, two can withstand him. And a threefold cord is not quickly broken." With God as their Silent Partner they cannot fail.

$$9$$

New Horizons—
Deeper Waters

Seven kilometers from land...straight down.

The captain of the Marina Svetaeva

In 1986, after a great deal of soul-searching, I resigned as Director of
Nuclear Medicine and Ultrasound at Westmead Hospital, a position
that I had held for ten years. Friends challenged the wisdom of my
decision.

"You are set for life," they said. "Why walk away from tenure, salary,
excellent prospects, and all that accumulated leave?" But God was telling
me that it was time to move on to something new. I was a builder, not a
landlord. The work at Westmead was done. I would either spend the rest
of my professional career defending it, or move on. I had seventy journal publications. Did I really need another seventy?

My plan was to leave the public system and enter private practice. This
would allow greater freedom for outreach into China. The decision was
precipitated by the fact that we were busy, so busy in fact that we were
not coping with referral from the population of western Sydney, which
was increasing at an astounding rate. There was no money in the hospital budget to expand. The hospital board had a strong left wing bias at
the time and would not countenance the prospect of a private practice

to assist with the workload. And so, together with Tony my business partner, I decided to establish a small department in the medical center across the road from Westmead Hospital.

On my final day I was presented with a gold medal by the executive and academic staff in the boardroom, after a serving of dry white wine and devils on horseback appetizers (a prune wrapped in bacon—a hospital staple which appeared on all auspicious occasions). After this I returned to my office for the last time, checked the shelves and drawers for personal effects and then left, shutting the heavy door after me. As I did so, the words of a farmer friend returned to me: "Son, what does a farmer do when he leaves a paddock? He closes the gate." There was no turning back. This was it!

The following day I sat in doctors' waiting rooms scanning through dog-eared magazines, waiting my turn to shake their hands, and encourage their referral to my new practice. But it soon became clear that I had lost more than my position at the hospital. I had no title, the freedom to come and go at will was no longer available, and instead of a budget I had a bank facility. What upset and surprised me was that without a prestigious title I found myself less in demand as a public speaker. My professional identity had vaporized overnight. God was teaching me one of the biggest lessons of my life.

After the first week I was having serious doubts about the soundness of my decision to quit the hospital. The past was gone, the future was uncertain, and the present was tenuous to say the least, as my home was on the line. I had been comfortable and secure in my work. But in a matter of days my security blanket had been snatched away.

Then came the opportunity to hear an American speaker, Jack Hayford, who was visiting Sydney for a few days. Somehow I knew that I needed to hear what that man had to say.

For years I had prayed that God would give me spiritual eyes and ears to discern his will. That night Jack said: "I want you to understand that as Christians we *already have* spiritual eyes and ears. Tonight we are going to ask God to open them." At his invitation, I stood to my feet with others and joined silently in a corporate prayer. And then, something happened, something wonderful. God spoke directly into my spirit, completely out of left field. I knew it was God. The words were simply these:

"You are Ern Crocker, very much loved son of Father God."

The understanding of that simple but profound truth became reality in my life from that night on. It replaced all the secondary identities that men had placed on me and that I had claimed as my own. It has wonderfully supported me through twenty-five years in private practice and unambiguously defined who I am and where I am: in an ongoing relationship with Father God.

From an identity in God there grew in me a deeper understanding of God's character and nature. As a child I had known Him as Jesus. As a young doctor I had experienced His presence as Holy Spirit, witnessing his power to heal and His presence as Advocate and Strengthener. Now I also knew Him as Father. From this grew a working relationship with God in my personal life and in business. He became my Silent Partner, present at every board and committee meeting and in every aspect of my work as a doctor. When there was success, I rejoiced with Him. When there were decisions to be made, He was always there to consult. When there were bad days, I found strength in Him.

And there were some bad days...

"You'd better sit down," Tony said. "I have something to tell you."

Sensing the bed behind me I sat down and pressed the phone to my ear, not knowing what to expect.

"We've had a murder in our Blacktown rooms, but it's OK, everything's under control."

It was November 1992. I was transiting in London after a conference in Innsbruck, and had decided to call Tony from my hotel room to catch up on news and events.

A sessional psychiatrist had been accosted by one of his patients in our waiting room. Words were exchanged, the patient drew a home-made machete from his jacket and killed the doctor outright, in full view of patients and staff. He then walked calmly to his car and drove home to the New South Wales central coast. A quick-minded patient recorded his car registration number and he was soon apprehended.

I returned home to find the rooms in disarray. Patients failed to keep appointments, staff were distressed. The news media continued to run TV updates nightly. People would walk by, pointing, and whispering. The ambience in the rooms also was different. There was a continuing sadness and heaviness. No one wanted to be alone there, especially in the morning and after dark. Staff became ill. Several developed shingles, and a flu-like illness plagued staff well into 1993.

No amount of cleaning, new carpeting, staff lunches or pep talks seemed to help. Finally I determined that the problem may well be of a spiritual nature. I called two friends. Peter Irvine is a friend of many years and co-founder of Gloria Jeans Coffees International; Zahir Ahmed, a local pastor, is a converted Muslim. We would meet after work one day and pray over the rooms.

It was about 7 p.m. on a Wednesday evening in the winter of 1993 when Peter and I met in the street outside. The rooms were in darkness and I had a deep sense of foreboding. We entered and stood in the deserted waiting room where the murder had occurred. It was quiet, and the darkened rooms beyond were intimidating. There was a knock at the door. It was Zahir. But he was not alone. He had brought along his Wednesday night Filipino Bible study group. This was not as it was supposed to be!

In they streamed, clutching babies, and guitars. Small children were soon playing on the floor exactly where the body had been. Rather than formal prayer there was singing, clapping, and strumming of guitars. Then as the music and prayers continued, it happened. Quite tangibly the coldness and heaviness lifted like a cloud, to be replaced by physical warmth and a sense of peace and wellbeing. People were aware of what was happening and began to praise God and rejoice. They moved from room to room and then circled the building to the astonishment of neighbors, praying and giving thanks.

The rooms were never the same again. The business grew, people remained free from illness, and the sense of fear and foreboding that had literally haunted the place never returned.

It is not uncommon to find ourselves in deep water. On a recent trip to Antarctica, I overheard a passenger ask the Russian captain how far we were from land. We had just left Cape Adare heading south into the Ross Sea.

"Seven kilometers, Madam," he growled, "...straight down."

It was just a few days later that we found ourselves in a Force 10 gale. Frozen sea spray encased the ship in ice inches thick. The vessel pitched as mountains of water exploded over the bridge of the ship and growlers;[16] large pieces of ice punished the ice-toughened hull. Two Aussie pilots struggled to secure the helicopters which were lashed to the deck. Against advice, I stood on the leeward deck anchored to the rail, curiously without fear. The seawater was at 28 degrees Fahrenheit, and to fall overboard would have been fatal. But there was a beauty and a richness to this awesome spectacle and I was not about to miss a moment of it. As I stood there on the deck, peppered by the icy spray and despite the storm, I felt an inner peace of God's presence in my life.

It is often in deep water that the greatest riches are to be found. "Launch out into the deep and let down your nets for a catch," said Christ to Simon (Luke 5:4), and it was only then that the fishing nets were filled to the point of breaking. Much of our life is spent in the shallows, splashing around looking for answers. All we manage to achieve is to get wet. When we venture into the deep by choice or by happenstance, we are placed in a position where we must entrust ourselves to others. When that trust is placed in God we can expect not only to be delivered, but also to discover a richness of life never imagined, let alone anticipated.

When we accept Christ into our lives, God gives us a measure of faith, sufficient to move on from a life of nomadic wandering and into the wonderful plan and presence that He has for our lives.

We may be led along paths that we would not choose for ourselves into situations that challenge and test our faith, but that will eventually bring us into His rest. We may also be rescued from paths ill-advisedly chosen by us, or imposed upon us by circumstances, that may have led us into desperate situations. He is able to lead us, teach us, and share our burden.

Whether we are able to enter into the plan that God has for our lives will depend upon whether we accept His invitation. Whether we are able to rest in His plan will depend upon whether we are prepared to submit ourselves to Him completely and allow Him to live through us. And that rest does not imply retirement or resignation. Neither does it imply the absence of external threat or internal conflict. Rather it implies the possession of adequate resources through His inner presence to meet any agenda.

Such has been the case with a number of my Christian medical friends. In each situation, God has met them at their point of need and brought them through to solid ground, rejoicing. In the section that follows, accounts are recorded of doctors who have found themselves in circumstances that they would never have anticipated, let alone pursued, and often in peril of their lives. In each case, God has been faithful. In each case, He has led them step by step, sometimes from the absolute depths of despair and discouragement to higher ground and into His rest.

As I injected the dipyidamole into the patient's arm, his blood pressure fell and the heart rate increased as expected.

"You know I had a heart attack two weeks ago?" he gestured.

"Yes," I assured him.

"As I lay there in the emergency room," he continued, "Christ came to me and put His arms around me. I knew that He loved me."

He paused and tears filled his eyes.

"Doctor, I now know Him who once I only believed."

— 10 —

Knowing Jesus

But as for me, I trust in You, O LORD; I say, "You are my God."
My times are in Your hand.

Psalm 31:14-15

This was exactly where it happened. From this very spot Bob was washed out to sea on that dark night so many years ago. Sun filtered between high-rise apartments, spotlighting a police vehicle tracing a lonely course along the high-water line. Signs warned people to stay out of the water: STINGERS, NO SWIMMING. Several joggers lurched past as I walked along the wet sand, remembering what had happened right here in the summer of 1973.

Dr. Bob Batey had been attending the Annual Scientific meeting of the Australian Society for Medical Research at Surfer's Paradise on Australia's Gold Coast. I was his resident at the time, in the Clinical Research unit at Royal Prince Alfred Hospital.

It was the night of the conference dinner at the Chevron Hotel. The formal gathering had gone well, and someone suggested a swim. As they made their way down to the beach, Marcus, one of Bob's colleagues, remarked, "If I don't come back, will somebody make sure my belongings are on the plane to Sydney tomorrow?" A curious throwaway line to be sure, but eerily pre-empting events to follow.

At 10.30 p.m., the air was warm, the water inviting. Just an ordinary night, really. No wind, and the sea was calm. Bob stood in water to his knees, the waves lapping his legs. Then, without warning, the sand beneath him was swept away. He was in deep water and out of control. A riptide had washed away the sandbar, and Bob and his friends were being swept out to sea.

It was wrong to swim against the current. He knew that. But what could Bob do? He must make it back to shore, yet the harder he swam, the farther out he was taken by the rip. There was absolute darkness, except for the receding lights of Surfers Paradise.

Drowning seemed inevitable. Desperate now, Bob prayed for help. But nothing happened. He was chilled to the bone and tiring rapidly. *This must be what happens when people drown*, he thought, and recalls bobbing his head into the dark water to see what it would be like. "I knew it was only a matter of time."

Just as all seemed lost, a man on a surfboard called from further out. It was a colleague from Royal Prince Alfred Hospital—the neurology registrar, in fact. He had managed to recover one of the other members of the party, a young woman who lay draped across the board. But there was no room for another. Grasping Bob with one hand he managed to tow him back toward the shore, but eventually had to release him. "It's over to you, Bob," he said. "You'll have to swim for it." With the help of several large waves, Bob made it back to the beach to be dumped unceremoniously onto the sand. One of the professors who had been watching came to his aid. "Bit of a Lazarus act, Bob!" he said.

Together with others they attempted to resuscitate the young woman on the beach, but to no avail. Bob called home. "I'm all right!" he said. But no one knew what he was talking about. The news of the tragedy had not yet reached Sydney.

The *Sydney Morning Herald* reported that Dr. Claire Campion died one week later in Princess Alexandra Hospital having never regained consciousness. The body of Dr. Marcus Ma was recovered several days later.

As I walked along the beach and thought on these events, I knew this had not been the only time that God had intervened to save Bob's life. Nearly thirty years after this event, Bob and his wife, Adrienne, had been staying at a guesthouse in the Blue Mountains west of Sydney. They loved the charm of this wonderful old home with its four-poster beds, warm rooms, and caring owners. It was one of their favorite spots. But today they would drive to the mountain village of Blackheath.

They packed the car and headed west. But conditions deteriorated. Wind howled and snow blanketed the windshield. After a quick walk in the falling snow beyond Blackheath, they turned the car and headed back to the safety of Katoomba.

It was approaching noon as they turned south into the main street. With a welcome parcel of hot fish and fries they made their way down to the popular scenic spot of Echo Point, and parked next to the old pavilion. Wind buffeted the car, and before long the windows were fogged. Small branches and pine needles struck the windshield menacingly as wind and sleet lashed the car.

Then, without warning, there was a mighty impact. To his horror, Bob realized that he could no longer see Adrienne sitting next to him in the front passenger seat. She was silent. He feared the worst.

"Are you OK?"

She answered, but her voice was muffled.

"Can you move your legs?"

She replied that she could. Still not knowing what had happened, Bob sounded the horn to attract attention.

Sirens screamed. Rescue and emergency vehicles appeared, seven in all, and an unfamiliar face appeared at the driver's window.

"Aw, mate, you are gonna need a chainsaw!" said the stranger.

Only then did Bob learn what had happened. A 99-foot radiata pine had fallen directly onto the car, and a massive branch had crushed the roof between passenger and driver. The impact had been so powerful that the front windows had blown out.

Adrienne had been struck on the head. She was conscious, but had chest pain. It was nearly an hour before Bob was pulled out through the back door on the driver's side, and another forty minutes before Adrienne was carefully extracted from the passenger seat by the emergency crew. She was hypothermic, and later it was confirmed that she had a crushed fourth thoracic vertebra and a fractured first rib.

Adrienne made a complete recovery, though shorter by one vertebra, and Bob was unscathed. But the incident had a profound impact on them both, and also on the local town council. Visitors to Echo Point will have noticed that all of the large radiata pines have been removed, and the car park has being completely remodelled.

Bob and Adrienne knew that God had spared their lives. What might have been a tragedy became cause for rejoicing, and a time to remember God's protection. Each year on June 24, the anniversary of the accident, they buy fish and chips for lunch and take time with their family to thank God for His mercy and protection.

Such incidents have the potential to be life-changing. But the response of each individual will depend upon values, expectations, and faith. Some buy a lottery ticket. Others turn to a life of good works. Most will be thrown into a period of introspection and self-assessment, attempting to re-evaluate their purpose and direction in life, maybe for the first time.

Is it remarkable that Bob survived these two events? Yes it is, especially considering that others had perished. Was he just lucky, or was it a matter of fate that he survived? I believe that it was neither. Bob had been a practicing Christian for many years. He knew that God had a specific purpose for his life, and that he would live every day that God intended to achieve that purpose.

But what was Bob's purpose in God's eyes? His career spanning forty years had been prestigious from the outset. He had graduated with honors from Sydney University, had been appointed clinical superintendent at Royal Prince Alfred Hospital. As a young gastroenterologist, he had worked with the late Dame Sheila Sherlock, doyen of hepatology, at the Royal Free Hospital, London. After completing his MD at Sydney University, he was appointed to the Medical Faculty at Westmead Hospital, where he held the position of Director of Drug and Alcohol Services.

Subsequently, Bob was appointed conjoint Professor in Gastro-enterology and Hepatology to the University of Newcastle, Deputy Dean Faculty of Health Sciences University of Newcastle and Director of Gastroenterology at John Hunter Hospital. He is currently Professor of Medicine and Dean at the University of New South Wales, based at Bankstown Hospital.

His publications to this date include 150 abstracts of papers presented at national and international meetings, 130 papers in reviewed journals and numerous chapters in books.

Bob has been involved in numerous national and state health department committees, and is currently chair of the Hepatitis C subcommittee for the Ministerial Advisory Committee on Aids, Sexual Health, and Hepatitis, a role he has held for six years.

Surely this was sufficient for any man. Surely his purpose had been fulfilled. But God had other plans. What had gone before was preparation for what lay ahead.

"Knowing God" has been one of the great quests of Bob's life. As a young doctor studying in Britain, he had asked a close friend, later to become president of the Baptist Union of the UK, "What does it mean, to know Jesus?"

The answer had been, "Bob, I think it's a reality that grows with you day by day. But it is a journey, and one day we'll meet Him."

Bob's life *has* been a journey. Often the destination has been unknown, but always the direction assured and confirmed. His trust in God has allowed him to follow the path that God has set before him.

I asked him how God had led him over the years. "As a young person I was self-conscious," he said. "Public speaking was difficult for me. But God said to me, 'stop looking at yourself and try Me out.'"

Over the years Bob has done just that. God has helped him to walk through the loss of a parent, difficult professional decisions, and personal situations. "God gives me the capacity to get up and get on with the day," he said.

It was with this attitude of trust and gratitude that Bob and Adrienne recently decided to find some practical way to thank God for His goodness. Whatever they did would be a token gesture, but it would be a way of acknowledging God's merciful interventions in the life of their family.

Bob was aware of how easy it is to slip back into the system of daily routine, and was determined not to let this happen.

For years he had held a fascination for India, having been there twice before. He had helped establish a gastroenterology service in the Baptist Christian Hospital at Nellore, and had facilitated the training of doctors to perform gastroscopies and colonoscopies. On a later trip to Vellore, he had been a guest of the Indian Institute of Science, representing the Australian Academy of Science, and had lectured on hepatitis C at Bangalore and Vellore.

In late 2003, the opportunity presented itself to visit Nellore, in the southern-most coastal region of Andhra Pradesh. This large agricultural center is a three-hour drive north of the thriving industrial city of Chennai. For many years it had been an important center of learning for the region, and was the only education center in Andhra Pradesh during the British rule. The Baptist hospital in Nellore had been experiencing difficulties, and Bob planned to help in whatever way possible. Flights were booked, and Bob and Adrienne set out for India in February 2004.

Bob was able to address some of the financial and administrative problems. But following this, he and Adrienne set out with a Christian friend to visit several of the surrounding towns and villages, eight in all, ranging from mud-brick villages to thriving towns of tens of thousands of people. Always they were well received. They spoke in churches and chapels, and were overwhelmed by the warm acceptance of the people and their positive response to the gospel. They saw people accept Christ as their Lord and Savior. Families were restored and lives changed.

Bob returned from India challenged and encouraged. He had seen the impact of a loving God on people in dire need. He had also experienced, in a new way, how God was prepared to use him as he made himself available.

Since returning from India, Bob now also serves in an advisory capacity to state and federal departments of health, where his opinion is greatly respected. One thing is certain, Bob will live every day that God has preordained, and he will do so with the assurance of God's continuing presence.

11

Fire by Night

I was five months pregnant and completely out of my depth. I had been running and jumping fences and I just wanted to go home...but I was the embassy doctor that day, and I just had to do it.

Anna

It was the morning of September 9, 2004, another busy day in the streets of Jakarta, a bustling, cosmopolitan city of 12 million people. Anna sat in her rooms across the street from the Australian Embassy talking to the clinic manager. History would record that at 10.15 a.m. local time, a mighty explosion shook the building, shattering windows, and showering them with shards of glass. A one-ton car bomb in a Daihatsu delivery van had been detonated in the street outside the Australian embassy, and the terror group Jemaah Islamiah had claimed responsibility.[17,18]

"We didn't even know where the bomb was," said Anna. "We ran out onto the street which was not the thing to do, of course. People were screaming and running. There was smoke everywhere and total confusion."

The scene was one of utter devastation. The blast had blown windows out of at least ten office blocks around the embassy up to the thirty-story level, and damaged others within a radius of over 1600 feet.[19] Glass was everywhere. Trees down the center of the street were stripped of foliage. "We ran to the small hospital behind the clinic, but then I received a call: 'Go to the embassy! The bomb was at the embassy!'"

The street outside the embassy was littered with bloodied bodies. The iron fence had been flattened and there was a large crater near the gates where people had been waiting in line shortly before.

As the building was heavily fortified, none of the people inside had been seriously injured. The level of preparedness at the embassy had been excellent, as staff had received emergency training just a few weeks earlier. There were people with lesser wounds for Anna to tend, but most of the casualties had already been triaged and dispatched to hospital.

In the street, the situation was different. Nine people lay dead, including two security guards and Indonesian nationals; 139 were seriously injured.

Anna worked relentlessly throughout the day and late into the night, in the emergency rooms and intensive care units of the local hospitals. Her Australian qualifications allowed her to treat expatriates under the sponsorship of the Australian embassy, but without Indonesian medical registration she was unable directly to treat locals. But she was able to advise, and to arrange transfer of patients to Singapore.

In ICU, one of the patients brought to her attention was Manny, a five-year-old girl whose mother had been killed instantly. The little girl had been seriously injured and was in a coma, with injuries to her brain, her abdomen, and her right side.[20] It was Anna's responsibility to assess her condition and suitability for departure to Singapore. Her mother had been visiting the embassy to obtain a passport for her daughter, whose biological father was an Australian citizen. The mother's partner however was an Italian citizen, and there ensued a great deal of discussion between the Italian and Australian embassies as to the girl's future. The little girl survived her injuries and was eventually repatriated to Italy.

"I couldn't have made it through that day in my own strength," said Anna. "I was scared. I was five months pregnant and completely out of my depth. I had been running and jumping fences and I just wanted to go home. I'd had nothing to eat, and maybe a couple of bottles of water to drink. But I was the embassy doctor that day, relieving the regular doctor who was away on leave, and I just had to do it."

What extraordinary sequence of events had led to Anna's involvement in this bizarre situation? What circumstances had taken a young doctor in her second trimester of pregnancy and placed her squarely in the wake of a terrorist bomb? Only eighteen months earlier she had been working as a general practitioner with special interest in women's health, in the leafy Hills district of north-western Sydney. She had enjoyed working in Sydney. But in retrospect she is able to recognize the hand of God moving in her life at that time. Somehow she had known it was time to "up stakes" and move on. "It was like when the Israelites were led in the desert by a pillar of fire by night and a pillar of cloud by day" (Exodus 13:21), she said. "Well, my pillar was on the move."

In Sydney she met Peter, a young business executive. He had recently returned to Sydney from Jakarta to report to his Board on the Bali terrorist bombing of 2002, which killed 202 people, eighty-eight of them Australians. Anna and Peter planned to marry. As Peter had a contract to work in Indonesia and was soon to return, Anna had to face a tough decision. Was she prepared to live in Indonesia?

Absolutely! Moving to Indonesia was like going home for Anna. Born in the United States to missionary parents, she had spent much of her childhood in Indonesia—four years in Java and six years in Northern Sulawesi Province, where her parents had moved in 1969. This was a remote area with few Western residents and strange customs. Her father had led *National Geographic* teams researching the elaborate death rites of the people in the region. Anna had become fluent in Indonesian and regarded Indonesia as home. On her few trips to Australia as a child, she admits that she had found the country strange and unfamiliar.

But life in Indonesia as a child had posed its own problems. "There were no doctors and very few medical supplies. Prayer was all we had. My brother was accident-prone. I remember him falling face down, nearly ten feet onto a concrete slab. He was horribly smashed up, but survived, and God healed him. I also remember people getting their sight back after prayer. But I was quite young at the time."

In March 2003 Anna and Peter were married in Sydney and, with great expectation, moved to Jakarta. Anna could not register as a medical practitioner unless she undertook extensive retraining. But she did not want to assume the traditional role of an expat wife. "It can be a good life, but it can be very boring." Encouraged by Peter, she sought work. There were no female expat GPs in Jakarta at the time, and she received three job offers.

Women's health had always been Anna's special interest, and she developed a vision to establish what was to be the first specialized women's health clinic in Jakarta. Being unregistered, she was unable to practice as a doctor, but acted in the capacity of technical officer. She counseled and advised Western women on health issues, and supervised Indonesian doctors caring for local patients. She also had a background in palliative care, and found this helpful in counseling patients according to their deeper needs.

Anna lectured, wrote articles for news media, and arranged evacuations from outlying areas. She also introduced the new "thin-Prep" Pap test to Jakarta. This was a new improved means of examining cervical cytology without the need for the attending doctor to prepare a smear with all its associated practical limitations. Patient samples were obtained in Indonesian clinics and sent to Singapore for analysis.

As a Christian she was able to speak to others regarding her beliefs, one on one, but was very much aware that proselytizing was not permissible. "Muslims can pray for themselves but they can't pray on behalf of someone else," she said. "But they acknowledge that Christians can do that. So if a Muslim has a sick child they can't pray directly to Allah for that child but they know I can pray in the name of Nabi Isa (the Prophet Jesus) and they just love it. That's OK because you are not proselytizing, just showing your love and concern."

A Christian couple was asked to pray for a sick child with a high fever in a remote hospital. "The child immediately recovered," said Anna. "The patient in the next bed who had been watching with interest called them across. 'Can you pray for me?' she asked. One thing led to another, and the couple spent the entire day in that hospital praying for one patient after another.

"The supernatural is very much in evidence in Indonesia," she said. "Everyone believes in the supernatural, whether it's evil or good. I can remember Dad casting spirits out of people. Horrible things happened, like people vomiting nails. Back here in Australia we seem to be able to ignore the spiritual side of things. But I think this is just Satan's method of cover up.

"The verse that tells us to 'pray without ceasing' (1 Thessalonians 5:17) is very important to me," said Anna. "It's easier to stay in touch with God in Indonesia because the spiritual side is always there. So I'm talking to Him all the time."

Anna spoke more of her "pillar of cloud and fire" (Exodus 14:24) which led her out of daily routine in Sydney and into her present situation. But the pillar served many functions with the Israelites and so too with Anna. It led her through spiritual darkness, bringing wisdom and understanding in times of confusion. That same pillar would also protect her in times of abject danger:

> And the pillar of cloud went from before them and stood behind them. So it came between the camp of the Egyptians and the camp of Israel. Thus it was a cloud and darkness *to the one*, and it gave light by night *to the other*, so that the one did not come near the other all that night.
>
> Exodus 14:19-20

Although Anna was directly exposed to the events and the aftermath of the Embassy bombing, and apparently had also been within just over one mile of the Marriott bombing, she was unscathed and her baby had come to no harm.

The last time I spoke with Anna, she was in Sydney for the birth of her first child. A few weeks after that, she was to return to Indonesia to rejoin Peter and resume her professional responsibilities. She did so at a difficult time—only six weeks following the 2004 Tsunami which killed 232,000 Indonesians. She could have expected that there would be much to do in the wake of that disaster.

But she may be assured that God will never test her beyond her means. He will never send her anywhere that He has not gone before, and He will never leave her or forsake her. Her Pillar will be a constant witness to others: "They have heard that You, LORD, *are* among these people; that You, LORD, are seen face to face and Your cloud stands above them, and You go before them in a pillar of cloud by day and in a pillar of fire by night" (Numbers 14:14). It will also be a sign to other believers and a cause for worship and rejoicing that our God is a personal God and that He meets with us in times of need: "All the people saw the pillar of cloud standing at the tabernacle door, and all the people rose and worshiped, each man in his tent door" (Exodus 33:10).

12

A More Excellent Sacrifice

The unluckiest man in the world is he who rides the lion
or he who rules Yemen.

Old Yemeni Proverb

A biting southerly gusted up from the nation's capital as the tires of my four-wheel drive cut into the loose gravel of the car park. I glanced around to see if my guests had arrived. It was August 2004. Ken Clezy, an Australian surgeon, and his wife, Gwen, had just returned from Yemen. Lynne and I had arranged to meet them for lunch at historic Lynwood Café, in the bushranger town of Collector, New South Wales.[21]

His was a story that must be told. It had weighed heavily on me for almost two years. But every time I tried to make headway, doors closed. I wrote a draft; put it aside for nine months. Nothing. More closed doors. But then one night Ken was on *Foreign Correspondent*.[22] I knew this was the man I had to talk to about what had happened.

Ken was already inside, engrossed in the menu. "Food to die for," I had told him on the phone some days earlier, "especially the roast chicken." He was wasting no time researching my recommendation.

We made our introductions. Here was a man that I might have known all my life. Already I liked him. Despite his years abroad, Ken remained a true Aussie in the best sense of the word. At seventy-four he was a big man, slightly stooped, with a rugged but gentle face radiating a love and a peace that this world simply does not comprehend. His voice was deep and gravelly, and as he spoke in a broad Australian accent he measured and weighed his words.

"When you have three close friends gunned down while you're having breakfast, that shocks you like nothing else can," he began. At 8:15 a.m. on December 30, 2002, a fundamentalist Muslim extremist walked calmly into the administration offices of the Baptist Hospital at Jibla, Yemen. He shot dead physician Dr. Martha Myers, administrator Bill Koehn, and purchasing officer, Kathy Gariety. The gunman wounded Don Caswell, the hospital pharmacist, and shot at several others. Finally he pointed the gun at the radiographer and pulled the trigger. There was a click, but no shot. The gun had jammed. He dropped it to the floor and surrendered to security guards.

Ken had been at the early chapel service and then reviewed some patients, but now he was having breakfast with Gwen. There was a phone call. "Yemenis...Mr. Bill!"

It appeared that a man from some miles away had arranged for his wife to see Dr. Martha Myers in follow-up that morning. He waited till 8:00 a.m., but then went to Administration where he found Dr. Myers.

Pretending to reach for his wallet, he pulled out a Kalashnikov, AK-47 assault rifle, which had been cradled like a baby in a blanket, and shot Dr. Myers in the head. He then entered Bill Koehn's office where he found both Kathy Gariety and Bill Koehn. Both were shot in the head,[23] Bill apparently as he rose from his chair. The gunman then fired two bullets into the abdomen of the pharmacist. (No vital organs had been hit, and he was OK.) Finally the gunman dropped the gun and was heard to say, "I feel cleaner. I've cleansed this place."

The *Wall Street Journal*, reporting the incident in its Eastern Edition on December 31, 2002, claimed the gunman, Abed Abdul Razzak Kamel, to be an associate and student of Ali Mohammed Jar Allah, a radical Islamic preacher who, two days earlier, had shot the deputy secretary-general of Yemen's secularist Socialist party.[24] The journal also reported that this was the second killing of missionaries to the Middle East over a period of two weeks.

Four months later, *The New York Times*, in its late East Coast Edition April 22, 2003, reported that the suspect had told court officials that he had moved from Sana, about 125 miles to the north to Jibla, after he had heard about missionaries working there in the Southern Baptist Hospital. At the commencement of his trial he said he had acted out of a religious duty to take revenge on people who converted Muslims. The man has subsequently been tried, convicted, and executed.[25] His defense lawyer is quoted as saying, "You couldn't hang someone for killing infidels."[26]

Prior to the incident, hospital staff had been preparing to return the hospital to Yemeni administration. Two weeks earlier, Bill Koehn had actually painted out the word "Baptist" on the hospital sign. (After the incident, Yemeni newspapers referred to the hospital as the Hospital of Peace.) Staff members who were leaving had decided to give their final six months' wages to the 160 permanent members of staff who would be staying on. The money had been allocated and placed in envelopes. It was to have been distributed that very morning.

Dr. Myers was buried the day after the shooting in the hospital grounds. It was estimated that 40,000 Yemenis lined the streets to pay their respects. She was greatly loved. She was an obstetrician/gynecologist who had given herself unreservedly to the Yemeni people over a period of twenty-four years. After first working in the hospital as a medical student in 1971, she had returned to work there permanently in 1978.

Her obituary published in *The Lancet* said that she had a compassion for people that was insatiable, especially for people who were in need.[27] One of her Yemeni patients is quoted in *Christianity Today* as saying that every day Martha Myers took care of her, she used to visit her house until she was able to stand up and walk without causing any danger to her pregnancy. She said that without Martha Myers, she would not have her child, and that she had been more of a friend than a doctor.[28] Ken, referring to her ceaseless efforts on behalf of her patients said that Martha had not had any idea of time, but had had a great idea of eternity. A hand-painted board placed over Dr. Myers' grave carried her obituary in English and Arab script. The English words said simply, "She loved God."

The chicken was excellent, and later the espresso was perfect. But I don't remember dessert at all. As the afternoon moved on, I became progressively engrossed in Ken's words. Why had he been opening chests in a missionary hospital in Yemen at age 74, a time of life when most doctors are happy to recline in the comfort of family and personal pursuits? Just before he left Yemen in June, Ken had operated on a six-day-old boy with a tracheoesophageal fistula, a congenital deformity allowing food to pass into the air passages. I wondered how those big hands had brought healing to one so small and debilitated. What was the measure of this man? I asked him how he did it.

"If you are a surgeon and you have the right books, you can do it," Ken said. "The buck stopped there at Jibla. You did what you had to do. I had to operate on patients who had failed biliary surgery. In Australia these patients would go to hepatobiliary surgeons. But if you have to do it, and do enough, you can." As we sat talking, I began to explore Ken's past.

Born the son of a farmer in South Australia, Ken knew two things for sure. Firstly, he would never be a farmer. "Nothing about the land interested me," he said, "and, wise man that he was, my father perceived this early on and didn't try to persuade me to go on the land."

But Ken was also aware that he was a child of God. "By the time I was twelve I had a clear understanding of the gospel, and knew that it had claims on my life. There was a painting by a famous lady from Ballarat on our dining room wall, and under it the words, 'In all your ways acknowledge Him and He will direct your paths.'"

In his final year at school, Ken was challenged by the message of a missionary speaker at a South Australian Christian Endeavour convention. Ben Butcher had established a mission on Goaribari Island in the Western District of Papua after the Scottish missionary James Chalmers was killed there. Known as the Greatheart of New Guinea, Chalmers and his colleagues had been clubbed to death, beheaded, and eaten by natives on the Fly River on Easter Monday, 1901. Chalmers had been a man who made an impact. His traveling companion, the author Robert Louis Stevenson, had written these words to Chalmers' wife:

> He is away up the Fly River. It is a desperate venture, but he is quite a Livingstone card! He is a rowdy, but he is a hero. You can't weary me of that fellow. He is as big as a house and far bigger than any church. He took me fairly by storm for the most attractive, simple, brave and interesting man in the whole Pacific. I wonder, I wonder if even you know what it means to a man like me— a man fairly critical, a man of the world—to meet one who represents the essential, and who is so free from the formal, from the grimace.[29]

The life, passion and sacrifice of Chalmers impacted heavily on Ken as a young man and would be a beacon, leading his uncertain steps along the path which lay ahead.

Ken was encouraged to study medicine by Gwen's uncle, a South American missionary. "He was a pastor, but he pulled teeth and did other minor procedures." Ken's experience with doctors had been "limited and all negative," he said. But as he put it, he "felt the call of God to pursue a career in medicine."

As a medical student, he completed an elective term in Papua New Guinea (PNG) in the summer of 1952-53. He was immediately sold on the idea of going to PNG but realized that the prospect of performing general medical duties there would be daunting. There was a severe lack of skilled surgeons. And so Ken decided to pursue a career in surgery, something he had not previously considered.

In 1959 he attended a Church Missionary Fellowship Conference in Great Britain. The speaker was Dr. Paul Brand, the British surgeon from Vellore Medical College, India, who had revolutionized the understanding and management of leprosy. Ken was deeply moved by the life and work of Paul Brand and, after prayer and a great deal of soul-searching, made application to study with the great man.

In 1963 Ken was awarded a fellowship from the World Health Organization to work with Dr. Brand in Vellore, India. He and Gwen packed their belongings and, with their four children, traveled to India to work with lepers. He recalls passionately, and with affection, the privilege he shared being present at Brand's last teaching session. Brand devised a series of tendon transfers to treat the "claw hands" which badged people as lepers and made them outcasts. He also modified previous techniques to get good results with foot drop and facial paralysis. But more importantly, Brand established that people experience ulceration and loss of tissue in their hands and feet because they continue to use damaged, numb parts. "He devised microcellular rubber insoles, which for a long time were the only way of protecting anaesthetic feet," said Ken.

He remained a humble, gracious Christian all his life, according to Ken. "When we were in India he led the weekly staff Bible study for months, and at the Orlando leprosy meeting in 1993 he conducted an early morning prayer meeting for all comers."

Later, Ken was to spend five years in Madang working as a surgeon, where much of the work involved reconstructive surgery with lepers. In all he spent twenty-eight years in New Guinea working as a surgeon, finally returning home to Burnie in Tasmania when one of his trainees was able to take over his responsibilities. After ten years as a surgeon in Burnie he retired from his practice, turning it over to a new man.

In 1999, Ken applied to the missionary organization Interserve to work as a general surgeon, and was offered a temporary position at Jibla, Yemen as locum for one of the surgeons who was on leave for language training. The placement was to be for six months, but he was still there at the time of the massacre in December 2002.

Ken makes two major points of which he is emphatic.

"The first is this: "If you are willing to do the Lord's will, He will not let you blunder down the wrong alley. He opens doors and closes them." This has been a recurring conclusion of many of the doctors interviewed. So many have told me that they have found themselves in the most unlikely, and at times, seemingly irrelevant life situations. Many have questioned God's purpose and sought clarification and confirmation. Sometimes, only in retrospect have they been able to see His greater wisdom and purpose. Ken grew up in a rural setting where he learned to make do or improvise. How useful that training was to his later life on the mission field, and in particular in the Middle East. Also his early experience as a student in PNG taught him of the need to study surgery. How wonderfully God used that skill in his later years.

Ken's second point, he says, "is one of life's lessons. If you don't walk the walk you may as well forget about talking the talk. All I can do is display grace and peace. They'll say, 'Clezy, he either fits the mold or he doesn't.' They download the Scriptures from the Net so they know what to expect. We had one lady, a poor widow, who had a sick child needing surgery. We treated her like a lady. No one else had ever done that. The surgery on her son was successful...This is the best way to witness in a Muslim community."

But why did that tragic massacre at Jibla occur? The question must be asked: "Was God oblivious?"

Early on the morning of the shooting, Ken had been scheduled to speak at morning devotions. The roster had been published *one month* prior. He had carefully and prayerfully chosen a reading from Hebrews 11:4: "He being dead still speaks." The words refer to Abel, who had offered to God a more excellent sacrifice than his brother Cain, who had murdered him in a fit of jealousy for doing so.

Ken had been giving serious thought as to what he might say. The hospital was due to close the following day. What could he offer to all those unhappy people?

"We don't know much about Abel," he said to those gathered that morning, "but he offered God the best he had. He still speaks today. If you've been offering God the best you have, don't be downhearted."

The words from Hebrews were prophetic. They applied to the impending demise of the hospital, and also to the greater role that it was to play in the life of the community and in the lives of those who would continue to work there. But the words would also apply to those who were to perish one hour later, and to their friends and loved ones. The seed of their "more excellent sacrifice" was to yield a harvest far greater than would ever have been anticipated.

On the day after the shooting, the hospital was effectively closed down. Many staff members including Ken and Gwen left to return home. Ken said, "I thought the hospital was finished…The embassy staff and FBI could not get us out fast enough." But this was not to be the end. The government of Yemen was so distressed and ashamed that they took over the hospital, opening it again on February 1, just a few weeks later, to be funded by presidential decree.

Some staff remained, and new local doctors were employed. Ken and Gwen returned to the hospital despite the looming threat of the Iraqi war. "There was a clear need to go back," he said. "I'm not a brave man, but I have God's protection over me all the time. We had left without even the opportunity to say goodbye to friends. It looked as though we had run away." And then he added, "When so many people in the Arab world think Christians are ogres of Caucasian origin who drop bombs on you if you are Muslim, it seemed important to show that this wasn't so."

Ken and Gwen joined Bill Koehn's widow, together with the pharmacist who had survived several bullets in the belly.

"We had been through the fire together," said Ken. "New warmth grew in many relationships, and it was clear that God was bringing good out of what had seemed to be total disaster. We saw the situation as abject devastation, but if you believe God is in control there must be good coming out of it."

Now the hospital is a Yemeni government institution. "Nobody can say it is an American enclave," said Ken. "Now it is multicultural and in the context of the recent Iraqi war, this is more acceptable. We now have Americans, New Zealanders, and Indian staff members, and there are more Yemenis than foreigners living in the hospital compound. The new chief medical officer is a local man who studied medicine, and later surgery, in Baghdad. He has been joined by another local surgeon trained in Syria."

The outreach to the local towns and cities has also been maintained, including support to one of Mother Teresa's hospices and visitation to a local women's jail. Evangelism is now effective by means of the silent witness of those present.

Why did God not intervene at the time of the shooting? Did He play any active role in modifying the sequence of events or the outcome? It seems that members of the Yemeni government were to meet with administrators on December 30, the day of the shooting, at 10 a.m. The government had been asked to assist with finance. An American plane had recently bombed an al Qaeda transport, killing six. "The government wasn't saying much about it," said Ken, "but they weren't happy." One can only guess at the negative attitude the Yemeni government may have had towards the project at that stage.

"Al Lindholm of Yemen Baptist Mission was to have met with us at 8 a.m., two hours before the meeting with the government. But he had a car accident and broke a wheel. If he had been there on time he may well have been killed. Also, a staff member involved in finance and distribution of funds to remaining staff had planned to be in administration at 8 a.m. to finalize plans for distribution. A 'chance' phone call from a friend about a personal matter ensured that she would not be present."

I spoke recently to another of the doctors present at the Baptist Hospital on the day of the shooting. He remained saddened by the events and continued to mourn the loss of his friends. But there had been no quenching of his spirit or passion. He spoke lovingly of the Yemeni people and of the urgency of their need. There was an expectation in his voice as he contemplated continuing outreach to the peoples of the Middle East.

When we submit ourselves to the Father, we take on the love that He shares with us. It becomes part of our persona and allows God to reach out through us to those around. This love is not love, as the world knows love. It is God's agape love that enables us to say, with others before us, "Though He slay me, yet will I trust Him" (Job 13:15).[30]

I'm standing Lord:
There is a mist that blinds my sight
Steep jagged rocks front, left and right
Lower, dim, gigantic in the night
Where is the way?

I'm standing Lord:
Since Thou hast spoken Lord I see
Thou hast beset-
These rocks are Thee!
And since Thy love encloses me
I stand and sing!

Written by Betty Stam who at age 27, with her husband John, 28, was beheaded by the communists for her Christian beliefs on a cold hillside in China, December 1934.

13

A Very Present Help

I learned how to seek God's face rather than His hand. I learned to seek God for Himself rather than His healing. I had to ask myself: Will I be led by Him? Will I trust Him?

Linda, general practitioner

Linda was at her lowest ebb. Everything was black. Just a short trip to The Gap, a cliff edge at the southern headland of Sydney Harbor[31] would end it all. And it really didn't matter.

Things had not been going well for her for some time. She had reached a point of total despair. The court case didn't help either.

"I would have jumped The Gap," she said. "If someone had driven me there I would have jumped." But this was not to be. And with the help of a psychiatrist—not a Christian man—she withdrew from the prospect of a sudden and violent death. "After that I had a lot of help from psychiatrists. But I still had a great deal of guilt which plagued me day and night."

I sat in Linda's surgery as she told me her story. It was 6 p.m. on a Friday night. The last patient had gone and the receptionist had locked the front door.

Twelve months after drawing back from the brink of suicide, in 1997, Linda was busy attending house calls. She visited one of her older patients, Margaret, who was in the advanced stages of heart failure.

The patient, a remarkable woman of eighty-eight, was beautifully groomed. "She was a gorgeous lady," said Linda. Her husband had died some years earlier, apparently never fully recovering from a motor vehicle accident and finally developing depression and dementia. During that time she had been helped by the healing ministry at St. Andrew's Cathedral in Sydney, which she had attended faithfully for many years. She understood Linda's turmoil and was anxious to help.

"Linda, you have to let the problem turn you round to the answer," she said. "Stop looking at what you did to God. Start thinking about what He's done for you." Here was the remarkable situation of a terminally ill patient counselling her doctor. "I'll pray for you Linda," she said. Shortly after, Margaret passed away.

Impressed by Margaret's example, Linda began to attend the Cathedral Healing Ministry where she met Canon Jim Glennon. This was all new to her. "I was a paid-up Anglican, and had never heard of *healing*."

In May of that year, she traveled to a church in the Southern Highlands of New South Wales to hear a visiting speaker who reportedly had a healing ministry. That evening as she sat listening, she felt warmth on the back of her neck. Looking around, she could see no sign of a heater. She had scoliosis, a twisting deformity of the spine, and had suffered for years from chronic neck and thoracic pain. But that night, as she drove home to Sydney, she realized that the pain was entirely gone. For the first time in thirty-two years she was pain-free. "I didn't believe it," she said. "I was a church Christian and had never experienced anything like that before."

Linda had a general practitioner friend, Jess, who had been involved in a severe motor vehicle accident ten years earlier, sustaining a major injury to her sternum (breast bone) requiring hospitalization. What was not realized at the time was that she had also received a lower spinal injury. A few weeks after the accident she developed foot drop and pain in her left leg. Surgery was performed on three successive occasions, but the end result was a painful, wasted leg. She had a "dead" leg, and it had been that way for ten years. Doctors could offer no hope.

Buoyed by her own experience of healing, Linda introduced her friend to the man she had heard in the Southern Highlands, asking him to pray for her. During the time of prayer, Linda sat on the other side of the room thinking, "What a waste of time. I shouldn't have brought her here and given her false hope. She's had a dead leg for ten years."

At 2 a.m. the next morning, Jess awoke. She could feel pins and needles and tingling in the toes on her affected leg. A few days later she showed her doctor that she could wiggle her toes for the first time in many years.

Later, I met Jess, to verify the story of the healing and restoration of her leg. She has retired from medical practice now and works as a hospital chaplain. "I no longer have to make excuses for talking about God," she said. "People expect it of me."

We sat in the back room of her apartment as she told her story, Vivaldi's *Four Seasons* quietly playing in the background. She had been driving home from her surgery on a wet afternoon in April 1988, past The Kings School in north Parramatta.

"Without warning, the lights of an oncoming car were in my eyes," she said, "and I felt the impact. It was head on. It crushed my sternum and I had pain in my chest." Terrified that any movement would puncture a lung, she remained motionless until the ambulance came and she was transported to hospital.

After two weeks she was discharged.

"I had been concentrating so hard on my breathing that I didn't realize anything else was wrong," said Jess. "But then I noticed pain in my left leg and that I was dragging my left foot."

CT and MRI scans revealed that the backward thrust on the left femur had destroyed the L5/S1 disc, displacing fragments upward. (When we met, I viewed the CT and MRI reports and was able to verify the damage.) She had spinal surgery twice (laminectomy), but there was continuing pain and foot drop and progressive wasting of the muscles of her left lower leg. She limped badly and required a cane. "I had little movement of my foot and it was unstable," she said. "Even when I walked on the uneven edge of a rug there was excruciating pain." Eventually, after further specialist consultation, spinal fusion was performed but the foot drop, pain, and wasting persisted.

"I could only sit for short periods," she said. "I used to take a banana chair with me to church and lie at the back."

In 1998 she was invited by her friend Linda to a healing seminar at Sydney's Golden Grove where Linda's friend Tom would be speaking. But there were many people present, and she was so hindered by her pain that she decided not to ask for prayer.

Subsequently Linda invited the speaker to her home for dinner, and Jess also. As they sat eating, Linda asked Tom if he would mind praying for her friend. He took her into the next room and began to pray.

"I'd had a lot of prayer, but *this time* I felt that God was going to heal me," said Jess. As he prayed she felt warmth in her leg. Tom told her that he believed God was going to heal her, but in his own time. "Satan will try to take that healing away," he warned.

"I normally took panadeine forte (paracetamol plus codeine) at night to help me sleep," she said. "But that night, I didn't." As she lay in bed the thought occurred: *I wonder if He's healed me already.* She got out of bed and found to her astonishment that she could bend her toes upward and stand on tiptoes for the first time in ten years. She had full strength, which was very strange as there continued to be marked wasting. "I could go up and down on my toes." She leapt and bounded around the room testing her new strength and freedom.

The next morning the healing was still there. After several weeks the muscles grew in bulk and the wasting resolved completely with the resumption of normal activity alone. She did not enter a rehabilitation or physical therapy program. Her doctor, an atheist, was astonished and agreed it was a miracle, but one that had been caused by mind over matter.

I saw for myself that her leg was fully restored with no wasting or neurological deficit, and that she walked without a limp.

As I drove home in the rain after my meeting with Jess, I became aware that it was the evening of 11 September, five years to the day after the terrorist attack on New York's Twin Towers. It occurred to me then, and has since, that although men can restore earthly structures, only God can fully restore His most precious creation. My doctor friend Paul once said, "Ern, it is not until you have nothing left but God, that you realize that God is enough."

In spite of her friend's healing and the other positive events in her life, by December 2000 Linda was in real turmoil. She struggled daily with guilt and depression, admitting, "I was good on the outside, but not on the inside." One of her patients came to see her.

"You need deliverance, Linda," she said, "but you have to want it."

Linda's situation is not uncommon. The incidence of anxiety and depression in the medical profession is alarmingly high. A review published by the Brisbane North Division of General Practice examined the incidence of mental illness and suicide in the medical profession.[32] It reported an incidence of depression and borderline depression of 27 percent in general practitioners, and of anxiety and borderline anxiety as 55 percent.[33] The review also stated that the incidence of anxiety and depression has consistently been reported as being higher among general practitioners than in the general public.

The NSW Medical Board reported twenty-one known suicides in doctors in the five-year period ending 1997, an incidence of 19.1 per 100,000 registered doctors compared with a community rate of 12 per 100,000.[34] Nine anaesthetic registrars and specialists were known to have committed suicide Australia-wide in the four-year period ending 1997.[35]

In response to these horror statistics, The Doctors Mental Health Working Group was established to "Review available evidence and practice with respect to the mental health issues affecting the medical profession, the factors which contribute to these and the strategies for effective prevention and management."[36]

Despite efforts by government and associated bodies and from within the medical profession, stress, anxiety, depression, suicide and attempted suicide remain major problems within the medical profession.

By 2001, Linda had reached a stage of desperation where she was ready to give up medicine. "My patients were seeing someone in torment." She felt rejected by people, but worst of all she felt rejected by God. At this stage, a friend gave her a book called *Excuse Me, Your Rejection Is Showing* by Noel and Phyl Gibson.[37] This helped considerably—but there was yet a long way to go.

"I didn't think that God spoke today," she said. But on Sunday, March 26 of that year, she was to learn otherwise. She went to her church that morning, arriving an hour early. It was the end of daylight saving, and she had forgotten to reset her watch. Sitting in her car outside the church, she decided to read from her Bible to pass the time.

Turning to Isaiah 12, she read aloud. In the distance the choir was rehearsing. To her astonishment, as she reached verse 4, the very words that she was reading were sung by the choir, in the same translation, at precisely the same time, and with the same timing: "Give thanks to the LORD, call on His name; make known among the nations what He has done, and proclaim that His name is exalted."

Startled, she called out, "God, does this apply to me?" Reading the chapter again her eyes fixed on verses one and two: "I will praise You O Lord. Although You were angry with me, your anger has turned away and You have comforted me. Surely God is my salvation; I will trust and not be afraid. The Lord, the Lord is my strength and my song; He has become my salvation."

At that point the gates of her prison were opened. Linda moved forward into a freedom that she had never known. She sought prayer ministry and, with God's help, was able to work through the spiritual problems that had bound her for years. She rejoiced in her new freedom.

"I know what it's like to say goodbye to God," she said, "and go down to the path of the dead."

Linda's situation reminded her of an ancient Hebrew custom: "If you buy a Hebrew servant, he shall serve six years; and in the seventh he shall go out free and pay nothing" (Exodus 21:2).

"The Hebrew man sells himself into slavery for six years and the seventh year he is freed," she said. "I went for six years and six days. In 2002 we had a party here at the surgery," said Linda, "and seventy-five people came. Lunch was provided and a visiting speaker prayed for patients. I saw a woman stand from a wheelchair and walk normally."

However, Linda's own challenges were not over. In November 2005 she was diagnosed with Chronic Inflammatory Demyelinating Polyneuropathy (CIDP), a chronic inflammatory disease of the nerve cells. She had experienced numbness in her lower extremities for some time, but now developed severe symptoms in her upper limbs as well, including numbness, weakness, and tremor. "I was in free fall," she said. "They offered me steroids and plasmapheresis."[38] This new challenge in addition to her other problems was almost overwhelming. What would she do?

Linda again called the pastor, now her friend, whom she had first met in the Southern Highlands, to hear the sobering but encouraging words: "Linda, if you receive your healing, you have it."

"As he prayed for me it felt like a fire hose pouring down over me. It felt that strong," she said. "I learned how to seek God's face rather than His hand. I learned how to seek God for Himself rather than His healing. I had to ask myself: Will I be led by Him? Will I trust Him?"

When dealing with depression, peer support resulting from collegiality is an important factor in allowing doctors to share their concerns with others and hopefully to find help. But the pace and time constraints of busy clinical practice often produce forced isolation. Many doctors, even those working in group practice, may find themselves very much alone. And often the issues are so personal with implications so far-reaching, that they cannot readily be discussed.

A Christian doctor is in the fortunate position of having another partner, a Silent Partner, who completely understands his or her dilemma and is willing and more than able to help in those most difficult times when assistance may otherwise seem so far away. But the doctor must be prepared to draw close to God and to trust Him. An encounter with God will bring healing in itself; but God may also bring the doctor into a relationship with other people who are able to assist.

It was late and I made ready to leave.

"There is one more thing I must tell you. It was as though I had a ten-inch block of steel right here," said Linda, pointing to her chest, "between my heart and my head. In May of 2005, after prayer and counseling, that block of steel was removed." She explained that until that

104

time all her Christian experience had been head knowledge, purely intellectual property. But from that time on the knowledge, love, and experience of God in her life had become living reality.

I had one more question. It was a tough one, but it had to be asked.

"Why you, Linda? Why did God save you when so many others have died?"

There was a pause. She smiled.

"I don't know—I certainly didn't deserve it. But He did it anyway. He really is very kind, you know! I was a paid-up Anglican and had been for many years. I had been baptized and I even went to China to a mission hospital as a student. But I knew nothing about grace. I deserved nothing, but God saved me."

Later she called me at home. "My verse is Isaiah 12:2," she said. "The Lord is my strength and my song, and has become my salvation."

That time of depression didn't make sense. I wondered, *where's God in all this?* But God took me out. He was very good to do that. It actually took my problems to prize me out of my comfort zone....I'm a depressive and it doesn't take much to push me over. But I've found out when I am weak then I'm strong. It's not my backbone, but God's backbone. Before this I had doubts that I could sacrifice everything for God. But I've been there, done that, got the T-shirt. I know what it is to lose everything.

Michael, general surgeon

14

One Man's Walk

But one thing I do, forgetting those things which are behind and reaching forward to those things which are ahead, I press toward the goal for the prize of the upward call of God in Christ Jesus.

Phil. 3:13,14

"Well I'm going," he said. "On February 3 we leave—thirty-seven in the team, including seven doctors, nurses, an engineer and several photographers."

"Where?" I asked, expecting to hear Banda Aceh, Phuket, Phi Phi, or maybe Sri Lanka.

"Right up to the Thai-Burmese border."

"I hope you are good at amputations. I understand half of the surgery at this stage is amputation."

"Well I don't know," he replied. "We'll primarily be treating war refugees, most of them Burmese."

For years Michael had been a busy general surgeon, a solo practitioner in the western suburbs of Sydney. On call 24/7, he was never in a situation where he could count on a good night's sleep. The local "gun and knife club" often kept him busy through the night in the public hospital. And the next morning there would be routine lists, post-op checks, and rooms to attend. There were church, family, and community commitments. Life was busy. But he was strong and healthy and, somehow, he managed.

But like a shadow out of the night, there had come an unwelcome visitor, a black dog to menace and intimidate. Depression stood at the door and surreptitiously entered his life. At first, Michael was unaware of the gravity of the situation. But progressively he became more and more incapacitated and unable to cope with daily routine. For three years he struggled with this unseen destructive power, finally leaving clinical medicine until the situation resolved.

"For a year I sat doing nothing," he said, "and that's when I came to realize that the world went on without me." He considered suicide, seriously, and on several occasions. But personal experience of the impact of suicide in a friend's family prevented him from taking action.

Many refused him support, and some openly opposed him. They failed to understand the nature of his predicament. But there were those also who stood by him, and prayed for him.

Whenever there is a problem in our lives, there will also be a promise of God to meet that problem. "For He Himself has said, 'I will never leave you nor forsake you'" (Hebrews 13:5). It was this unerring sense of the presence of God that saw him through.

The provision of that promise came through the hands of expert medical practitioners, through the support of friends, and also from an unexpected quarter. Would he be interested in traveling to Jordan to visit a hospital there? He would not practice, but would share his knowledge with local doctors and counsel them both as a Christian and as a medical specialist. Tentatively he accepted the invitation. It was an expensive proposition, especially as he had not been working, but he knew it was important.

Michael relished the time in Jordan, returning home with a broader horizon and a new vision of where life may lead him. Then came the 2004 Boxing Day tsunami. Over 200,000 had perished in Indonesia alone, and an accurate death toll would never be known. His friends suggested they raise money to support the appeal. But Michael knew what he must do.

As a general surgeon with good all-round practical skills, he felt compelled to make himself available. The acute situations had been dealt with, but as time passed, wound infections, gangrene, and aspiration pneumonia posed increasing problems. But the regional needs of South East Asia were not limited to those imposed by the tsunami. He was soon recruited to a medical relief team bound for a remote area of the Thai-Burmese border, where civil unrest and border clashes presented imminent and continuing danger.

"The trip will be interesting," he said. "Fly to Bangkok, then air-conditioned coach followed by non-air-conditioned bus and then elephant. The elephants manage well, but the guys on top have to cope with the foliage. Apparently on the last trip one of the passengers struck a branch containing a nest of fire ants. Apparently this didn't bother the elephant at all."

"Are you worried?" I asked.

"I'm told it may be dangerous," he replied, stroking his chin and pausing briefly. "Many of our patients will be casualties from border fighting. The border is criss-crossed by an undulating river and it's often difficult to tell which side you are on. This can be a bit tricky. But I've looked death in the face before, and it doesn't really worry me too much."

We prayed together, claimed God's protection over the team, and he was gone. First news by mobile phone from Bangkok was spirited and enthusiastic. They had arrived safely, he had spoken at several local churches, and they were preparing to travel up-country. I waited patiently for news but, for several days, only silence. What little did come through I managed to glean from his wife, Glenda, who had remained home to manage the practice while he was away.

After two days in Bangkok they had made their way to Mae Sot on the Burmese border, a strategically placed town of 45,000 people often not shown on maps. Here they set up base camp and then moved on to Umpan.

The invitation to this town had come from a local businessman who, it seemed, was not on favorable terms with the hospital administrator. And so the team was not permitted to use the local hospital facilities. Undeterred, they set up a makeshift surgery in the local Buddhist temple, performing minor procedures on a small wooden bench used by the monks. This included suturing and excision of lumps. No pathology testing was available. "But at least I could check for tuberculomas," said Michael. "Tuberculosis is rife in this area.

"I wasn't thinking that I was saving lives," he said. "I was prolonging them, but what we had to share was far more precious than physical health. We couldn't hold an evangelical meeting there. That would have been a bit cheeky, but we did pray for every patient."

Many couldn't understand their words, but it became clear that the power of prayer for these people was not limited by their understanding of the spoken word. People were impressed by the medical team's caring attitude and sent others to inquire as to what they were saying. As a result, three people were converted.

I was concerned by their use of a Buddhist temple for Christian work, remembering my own experiences in China. I had often been invited to visit temples, and there had generally been a hesitation in my spirit preventing me from entering. These places were spiritual strongholds, surely not places for Christian service. Then I recalled how Elijah had called on God to demonstrate His power on an altar alongside one built by the priests of Baal, and how fire had fallen from heaven devouring the altar, the sacrifice, the drenched timber and even the priests (1 Kings 18).[39] I remembered also how John Wesley, forbidden to speak in church, had preached to thousands standing on his own father's grave. Surely God would use these people in whatever circumstances they found themselves.

From Umpan they moved back to Mae Sot, and again set up a clinic. "We took every opportunity to talk to people about the Lord," said Michael. Because of the number of dialects this was difficult, and they would often use a sequence of two or three interpreters to convey their words.

In this town, they encountered strong spiritual resistance. There was an almost tangible barrier between them and the local people, making it extremely difficult to communicate and, in particular, to minister God's love. But this occurred in business hours only, 9 a.m. to 5 p.m. The moment it turned 5 p.m., no problem. There seemed to be no logical explanation, until finally one of their local supporters said, "Did you see the shaman? Did you see the shaman?" In fact, a local witch doctor had stationed himself outside the building they occupied, 9 to 5, chanting and ringing his bell. While he was there, their efforts were impeded. As soon as he went home, the resistance melted away.

An older lady presented herself to their Chinese doctor for medical attention. She was illiterate and not mentally alert. He decided to treat her medically, but not to talk to her about God. It would be too difficult. In her notes he simply recorded the conventional symbol representing female, a circle with a cross beneath, together with her age. When he had finished his consultation he referred her along to the prayer support group. But these people, who were not medically trained, read the symbol as a cross with a halo above it and took this to mean that she was Christian. So they prayed for her with such enthusiasm that she called for an interpreter for an explanation. The interpreter, ironically, happened to be the Chinese doctor. He explained the gospel to her with great authority, after which she made the decision to convert to Christianity.

They presented her with a Bible which she carefully wrapped in a cloth as a sign of respect, and then placed on her head implying reverence and submission. She was the first from her village to accept Christ.

Finally came the day to leave Mae Sot. Before boarding the bus they were taken to visit an old man, the father-in-law of a prominent local businessman—a colorful character who sported a Rolex watch (genuine, he said) and diamond accessories. The businessman had converted to Christianity during their stay, but was concerned about his father-in-law who was senile, immobile, and had suffered a stroke.

Despite his feeble condition, the father-in-law was able to make a confession of belief in Jesus Christ. As they were leaving, one of the group members said, "Look, we believe in the power of prayer, let's pray for this man to be healed." They dutifully prayed over the man, boarded the bus and were gone.

Six months later, a follow-up team visited Mae Sot. They went in search of the old man only to find that he was now mobile, sound of mind, and walked confidently, taking large purposeful strides. They found that he had been restored both physically and mentally.

There is no rational explanation for what had happened. The medical team had made their assessment without the benefit of CT, MRI, cerebral perfusion scanning[40] or even a specialist neurological consultation.

But it was clear that something wonderful had occurred in the life of this man. Whether he had progressively recovered from a severe debilitating illness or whether he had been miraculously healed may never be known.

But now it was twelve months later, and my friend was preparing for another trip into South East Asia. This time, he and his colleagues would spend two weeks in Thailand. They would travel once again to Mae Sot to continue their work and follow up on the previous year's outreach. He would then lead a team into Cambodia. This would be untested ground and he was not sure what they would find. "I'm glad that he's going," said Glenda, "but I'm a bit worried. He'll be gone four weeks this time."

It was twelve months almost to the day since he had returned from the Thai-Burmese border. We sat at his dining room table contemplating the next trip into Cambodia which was imminent. In three days he would fly with the team to Bangkok and then on to Chang Mei. His home was littered with items still to be packed. A generator sat unboxed in the middle of the lounge room, and computer parts were stacked high on the front porch.

We sipped our tea without exchanging words as commentary from the dying moments of a one-day cricket match between Australia and Sri Lanka droned from the downstairs television. Australia was 7 for 308.

"How has this whole experience changed you?" I asked.

"Well," said Michael, "it's put my own problems into perspective. That time of depression didn't make sense. I asked myself: where's God in all this? But God took me out. He was very good to do that. It actually took my problems to prize me out of my comfort zone.

"I've come to understand my real purpose in life," he said. "Ephesians 2:10 tells me that we are God's workmanship and that He created work for me to do even before the world began. So the work I do now is a real privilege. The good thing is that God gave me a chance to do this. The fun, and I say fun because I am that sort of guy, is being part of His plan and saying "I was part of that." In Australia a lot of what we do is marking time. But this is what he made me for. It's putting flesh on my belief."

Michael has found that the experiences have made him stronger. "I'm a depressive and it doesn't take much to push me over. But I've found out when I am weak then I'm strong. It's not *my* backbone, but God's backbone. Before this I had doubts that I could sacrifice everything for God. But I've been there, done that, got the T-shirt. I know what it is to lose everything."

Before leaving, I shared with him words from Genesis in which God spoke to Abraham in a vision guaranteeing his protection: "Do not be afraid, Abram. I am your shield, your exceedingly great reward" (Genesis 15:1).

It was late on the Sunday evening when the phone rang. I was watching a one-day cricket match between Australia and South Africa on TV, a real nail-biter, and reached reluctantly for the phone.[41] Michael's voice was a little strained and he dispensed with the usual banter.

"What was that verse again, the one about God being Abraham's shield?"

I read it to him again: "Do not be afraid, Abram. I am your shield, your exceedingly great reward."

He listened carefully and then read me another given him by a relative. "And the LORD, He *is* the One who goes before you. He will be with you, He will not leave you nor forsake you; do not fear nor be dismayed" (Deuteronomy 31:8). The words of these verses he would "bind around his neck." He would "write them on the tablet of his heart." They would go with him and before him and, when he returned, they would remain with him still.

He flew out the next morning, on schedule, with one large suitcase, a backpack, and assorted cardboard boxes. He was confident and full of expectation, knowing that wherever he went and in whatever circumstance he found himself, he would not be alone.

"After all," he said, "this is what I was born for."

At some stage in the life of every man and woman there comes a time of impasse. This occurs whether they are Christian or not and doctors are not exempt. It may take the form of a serious illness, or a family or financial crisis. It may be a period of severe self-doubt leading to despair. In some situations it is life threatening. Occasionally it may have fatal repercussions.

In February of 2012, I arranged to meet with a group of Christian doctors on retreat in Kona, the big island of Hawaii. Several agreed to share their stories with me. Each despite his Christian belief had at some point in life reached a point of despair and spiritual isolation. One had spiraled down into life-threatening depression. One had sought professional success and spiritual fulfillment by his own striving. One had known extreme professional isolation in the US prison system.

At the point of desperation each of these men found purpose and fulfillment as they abandoned themselves to the empowering presence of God and His Holy Spirit. Their lives were transformed and they discovered the extraordinary plans that God had for each of them.

No Retreats, No Reserves, No Regrets[42]

I've lived thirty-five years. I have everything that I have ever wanted including a wonderful family. Do I keep going and live another thirty-five or am I supposed to die now?

Bob, primary care doctor

B ob was far from his family practice in Lancaster County, Pennsylvania. He eased back in his chair, poured himself another coffee and glanced out over the waters of Kailua Bay. The Hawaiian Iron Man triathlon was eight months away but several brave pretenders pitted themselves against the swell, and fading memories of past champions.

"We got into Bluefields Nicaragua just after Hurricane Mitch," Bob said. "We had two bags of medicine, a little money, and not a clue where to go. The local mayor said, 'You've got money and medicine. We'll give you a boat and send you up the river. You pay for the gas'."

The next morning Bob and his crew assembled on the dock to wait for their boat. They had two guards both armed with machine guns as it was just after the fall of the Sandinista regime. As they waited, two of the girls from their team spoke to the guards. Five minutes later Bob observed both of these men on their knees accepting Christ.

Bob was in Nicaragua at the invitation of his local pastor to brush up on his Spanish. "It might come in handy," he was told, in his new job as a prison doctor in Lancaster County.

But he got more than he bargained for in Nicaragua. One night the team held a mission meeting. A young man fell at his feet apparently dead and someone started CPR. But Bob examined his pulse and found that he was very much alive.

"He was drunk," he said. "I picked him up and put him on a park bench and began to pray: 'In the name of the Lord Jesus, come out of this man spirit of addiction.' The third time I prayed he jumped up off the bench and grabbed me.

"'Doc,' he said, 'who was that scary lookin' black figure standing next to you while you were praying for me?' He was speaking Spanish, I didn't know any Spanish at that stage but strangely that night I understood every word.

"I said, 'Son, I don't know who that was, but if you don't want to see him again you'd better run up there and give your life to Jesus.' He ran up, gave his life to Jesus and passed out."

Not all of Bob's days were so filled with drama. He had always had a heart for urban medicine. In the 70s he trained at Dartmouth Medical School in Hanover New Hampshire. "I fell in love with the idea of primary care and epidemiology," he said. "But at that time it was all very new and not at all fashionable." He first took advanced training in Primary care at Lancaster General Hospital but after several years changed direction to study emergency medicine.

In the mid-90s, he experienced what he described as a midlife crisis. "Something inside me said there must be more. I've lived thirty-five years. I have everything that I have ever wanted including a wonderful family. Do I keep going and live another thirty-five years or am I supposed to die now?"

Searching for meaning and purpose, he joined the US air force reserve as a flight surgeon and became actively involved in healthcare reform associating with such men as Jack Kemp, housing secretary under President George H.W. Bush and vice presidential running mate with

Bob Dole. But none of this was filling the void in his life. None of this was answering the question that gnawed away at his soul, what was his purpose in life?

He continued to work in Lancaster General where he had developed a successful model of care for the poor of the community. "Political support was important to us," he said. "The US government had to give its approval for our program and the governor had to be our friend." And then, in the middle of it all, one day God actually spoke to Bob and told him that he was on the wrong path. He said he heard an audible voice saying, "Do you know where you're going?"

To that point Bob had no belief in God and had not been a church attender. He had no interest in God at all. "But I knew it was God," he said, "Who else would be speaking to me in my house when I was there alone? And who else would ask such a question. I started searching for a Bible. I opened it, questioning, 'So what path does work? Where am I going?'"

And then it hit him, "You mean I'm going to hell?"

God's answer was a simple "yes." End of conversation. This left Bob in terror.

And so began a spiritual journey. Bob accepted Jesus as his Savior and began to seek out people to advise and counsel him. From that point on, his whole approach to medical practice changed.

As he encountered people in the emergency room with panic disorder, anxiety, depression, and addiction he began to discern the root causes or triggers that had brought them into this condition. He soon realized that this was his passion, to be able to help people in crisis and to do it from a spiritual as well as medical perspective.

One day a young man came to his clinic. He had run away from a juvenile detention facility. Bob shared the gospel with him. "His mother begged me to go with her to the judge to have him placed in a Christian program and I did. But soon after I had a call from her. She was in jail accused of trying to kill another woman. I knew I'd been used by this woman and it made me angry. But the Lord said that I was to go to the prison and visit her."

In the prison Bob counseled the woman on several occasions. One day he met the prison doctor who asked why he was there. "Long story short, he told me he could use some vacation coverage." Over the next year Bob seriously considered prison medicine as an alternative to emergency medicine.

He began to assist with volunteer medical work at a homeless shelter in Lancaster County and was helping them with their drug addiction program. He made connections with Teen Challenge and opened a post Teen Challenge home for men. Arrangements were made for him to meet with David Wilkerson.[43] On a Sunday afternoon Bob went up to Times Square Church where Wilkerson met him in a back room after the service. Wilkerson prayed with Bob and prophesied over him. "I don't remember a word of our conversation," he said. "But as I was driving home through the Holland Tunnel the Lord spoke to me and said, 'Whom shall I send?' A week later I quit my job and within the hour the warden called and offered me a full-time position as prison doctor. That was 1998."

Bob assumed that this must be the right place for him. He would be free to bring healing for addiction, and to share his faith without worrying what others might think. But that wasn't quite how it turned out. "I got a lot of flack, and was told that people didn't like Christians who prayed for people. One night I was sitting at home. The phone kept ringing about a man who was having seizures at the prison. I picked up a devotional book. It was a story about a man with seizures who needed demons cast out. I kinda let it go, thinking what a cute story. But the next morning, having had several more calls about this same man, I picked up a different devotional book and guess what? It was the same story." He knew that God was speaking to him.

He drove to the prison concerned about the man with seizures and at the same time having a large argument with God asking, "How come I'm not trained to do that stuff? I'm already in trouble at work." To top it all off he was half way to work when he remembered that this was the day the Jewish medical student from the local medical school would come to observe him!

Bob managed to convince himself that God really wasn't in this. It must be his imagination. Walking into the sick bay he prayed, "God I know you wouldn't do this to me. But if it's really you then make it obvious." He didn't even make it through the door before guards came running to tell him that the man was having another seizure. By the patient's bed were two guards and two nurses, to his knowledge none of them Christians. Every thought in Bob's mind was, *If I do this I'm fired.* So he tried whispering a prayer. No effect.

Bob realized now that there was no retreat. Looking up at the guards he said, "You're not gonna believe what I'm going to do—and by the way I've never done it before—but here goes: In the name of Jesus come out of this man, seizures." Nothing happened. The man kept fitting.

Eventually the seizures stopped. Bob went back to his office to find the Jewish student with his first patient of the day, a Muslim lady. "I had given this patient Scriptures the week before. She had asked for more and told me that she wanted to lose weight. I said there's a wonderful story in Mark 9 about a boy whose father brought him to have Christ cast out seizures and that some things only come about with fasting and prayer (Verse 29). About three lines into the story I got convicted by the words: Oh unbelieving generation how long have I got to put up with you? (Verse 19). My mentor called at that moment and said the Lord had told him to call me and to tell me that I just needed more faith."

Later that day the man started having seizures again. More confident now, Bob prayed the prayer of faith and the seizures stopped. "We discovered," he said, "that the root of it all was anger with his father who had put him in closets and beaten him as a child. He got saved that afternoon. Somehow I didn't get fired. The Jewish guy was very quiet."

Later an article was written in *Insider* magazine through Chuck Colson's ministry about the work Bob was doing.[44] The result was more persecution ending up in a confrontation with the warden, who told Bob that he would have to prove that what he was doing actually worked. He asked Bob to set up a controlled trial between inmates who choose to pursue mental health through his model, and those who didn't.

Two months into the trial, Bob and his friends decided to do a land-cleansing initiative for Native American issues in the Lancaster community. In December 1763 authorities had rounded up the remaining tribal leaders in the region. They had put them into jail for protection, only to have a bunch of self-styled vigilantes, the Paxton boys, show up on a Sunday morning. They broke into the jail and decapitated, scalped, and cut the Native Americans to pieces. The justice system had failed to protect them and the vigilantes were never brought to justice.

"In November 2003," he said, "we had a group of native leaders come to our community. For three days they prayed for the bloodshed and the broken treaties and covenants in our region. After this they came to the prison and released a blessing and a prayer over the prison and over our program. Within one month the cost of medication that I was prescribing dropped by two-thirds; not just the psychotropics drugs, but all medications."

For the next five years while medical inflation was running at 10-15 percent per annum, Bob's costs went down every year. People were healed and set free from emotional issues and addiction. "Eighty percent of the new inmates were addicts," he said, "and 6000 people came through each year. We were detoxing 2000 addicts per year without a single complication. So there was a clear spiritual connect between the cleansing of the land and the release of God's favor."

Bob now found real favor within the prison system. He worked twenty hours per week, had authority to hire and fire and freedom to take leave as required. This allowed him time to continue his mission work and he returned to Nicaragua on several occasions.

He had always worked with the concept that God wanted to renew the cities of America. "He assigned me to work in the urban context so prison was just one part of that." Bob's church in Lancaster was a deep inner city church where he remains a member today. "Most of our people had been addicts, street people, and prostitutes. We've been doing medical mission work with them for the past twelve years combining hip-hop and urban artists with medical teams around the world. The church was birthed out of the Jesus movement among gang leaders in Los Angeles, California.

Most of the pastors are ex-gang bangers. It's a David Wilkerson kind of story."

In 2005 the national body invited Bob to help in the Kurdish area of Iraq. "We went to Iraq to do our usual two-bags-of-medicine model," he said. "The director general of the Kurdish people wanted to meet me before I was allowed to do anything. He invited me to give a lecture on family medicine and to arrange a training course for their doctors in the spring of the following year." But Bob did not believe they would let him preach, and as he said, unless he could share his faith, he was unwilling to become involved.

He was invited to a formal luncheon with the director general and his associate, an austere man who stared him down and said, "Radical Islamists are proselytizing their faith by using bombs. You Americans and Europeans don't seem to understand what's going on or whose paying for that."

Bob interpreted this as, *Don't you dare proselytize your faith in my country*. So Bob asked, "What do you think of Christians who would come here to proselytize?"

The response of the director general was swift and emphatic, "My people's hearts are broken. If you help change people's hearts, you're welcome to do it."

Six months later Bob returned to Iraq with his team and taught twenty-one doctors how to practice family medicine and how to establish their own training program. The commanding general later visited them in the United States. They were now working with high-level officials to develop a Kurdish-American model with its core as a Christian witness.

During the years of mission in Iraq and Nicaragua, Bob continued to find favor in the prison system.

"It was a great job," he said. "The system took all the risk and paid out the prisoners' medical bills." But in 2006 a decision was made to outsource the prison medical program to private interests and late in that same year a Christian company was contracted.

But soon the politics shifted. The three county commissioners fired the company and hired another, principally to get rid of Bob. It was impossible for him to work in the new system and reluctantly he resigned.

The day he left the prison, he flew out to spend a month in Iraq. He found himself launched into faith living with no reserves and no income. As he put it, "There were some painful moments."

In 2010, God provided opportunity for Bob to work part-time in the urgent care unit at Lancaster General. "I would go to work and pray, 'Is this where you want me Lord? It pays the bills but what's the spiritual aspect here, forty patients a day with runny noses after Iraq and Nicaragua?'"

One day a friend called. "I don't know what this means, Bob," he said, "but the Lord told me to call you and tell you you're doing exactly what you're supposed to be doing."

Bob still works with his local church and this last year has been a time of going back to his first love, providing total health care at the urban level. "We use the same model," he said, "that we used in the prison for the community of Lancaster County. We've also been invited into a family practice where we can operate in the same manner and bill insurance companies for it."

In 2011, Bob met with Mark Anderson of Call2all[45] and told him of his passion for urban medical practice. Mark invited him to Long Beach to meet others with a similar passion. "I found," he said, "that there was a world of doctors out there that think as I do, and I had never met any before. My work had been regarded by many of my colleagues as insane, foolish. I had been isolated in the prison system and I had begun to think that I was the only one that thought as I did."

Subsequently, Bob has met with like-minded leaders of the medical profession internationally, and together they are currently developing a model that links different ministries across patient care. A patient might present with what appears to be a simple medical problem, but in fact there may be complicating family, financial, or other issues. Here finally was a way in which all might be addressed.

Another like-minded leader that Bob met with in Kona was Canadian doctor David Demian. David maintains that God is shaking the nations in preparation for the establishment of His Kingdom. The global financial crisis, the upheaval of world religions and challenge to the sanctity of marriage are all elements of this. Dr. Demian maintains that as Christians we must seek God's mind, to determine His truth and find our individual roles in His purpose. Like chessmen on a board we each have specific strategies to fulfill.

Through the course of Bob's life he has known the pain of isolation, not in a social or familial sense, but in the context of his profession. Such is the case with many doctors and healthcare workers. Yet God sought him out and called him to account initially in the privacy of his own home, and later in the course of his prison ministry. God then lifted him out of that lonely place, where no man or woman should dwell, and placed him strategically into a group of like-minded people of common purpose and direction.

"You've found your place then, haven't you?" I asked.

"Yes," he said, "and I wasn't even looking for it."

God's purpose for us as Christians is to relate and operate as family, while still seeking our own specific role for the fulfillment of His kingdom purposes. An analogy might be drawn to the game of soccer. Junior team players converge to chase the ball around the field—often to little effect—whereas pro-team players are strategically placed for maximal effect. Bob and David, as members of that Christian family, have positioned themselves to hear God's voice and to take up their roles for the next part of the story.

No regrets, I thought as I pondered this man's story and considered the impact that his life will continue to have on so many.

— 16 —

Letting Go—
Letting God

God showed me that He is the Great Physician and I'm just the assistant. He's the boss and I'm just...Oh wow!

Brad, Family doctor

"**I** came to know the Lord when I was seven years of age," said Brad, "and spent the next twenty-seven years trying to figure out what I was supposed to do with my life."

I was speaking with Brad, a pleasant-faced, softly spoken family doctor from San Diego. His dress, demeanor and facial expression signaled that he was a deeply sensitive and caring person.

As a young man he had struggled with his Christian commitment. "Mom and Dad were Christians and they really tried to live out their Christianity in the home. But I continued to ask myself, *Am I really committed to what I believe? Am I sanctified?* Y'know, I remember a time when I was walking near this rose garden. I said, 'It doesn't matter, God, what I do, I just need to be sold out to You. Don't care whether I'm a plumber or a doctor, I'd just give up anything for you.'"

Through college Brad developed a passion to become a medical doctor and serve on the mission field. But after fourteen letters of rejection from medical schools, he began to doubt his ability and his future. "My grades were OK," he said, "but in America you need stellar grades to get into medical school. I had a GPA of 3.6. I needed 3.7 or better. They look at the numbers but they don't look at the person."

But Brad was determined to become a doctor. If necessary he would apply to a Caribbean medical school. Just when all seemed lost there was a call from Loma Linda. Someone had dropped out of first year; would he fill that position? He was twenty-three.

Finally Brad had found purpose and direction and by graduation had met his wonderful wife-to-be, Phyllis. "She was in the mold for missions," he said, "and I knew this was the litmus test. If she didn't have a heart for missions, we couldn't form a marriage."

As a new graduate, Brad found that he was still striving to perfect his salvation. "And I knew I just couldn't do it in my own strength," he said. "We prepared for mission work and we stayed out of debt. Finally I came to the view that training and teaching was the only way to go. I had been to Africa and seen how medical missionaries could so easily burn out and I wasn't going to do that."

In California he entered a family medicine training program with the University of California San Francisco, and met senior members of the American Academy of Family Physicians. They were planning a training program for doctors in central Asia and invited Brad to join them.

"So in 1996, five years after the Soviet Union broke up, I went with a team of Christian doctors to Central Asia. We were basically teaching specialists to be generalists, as the Soviets had only trained specialists. Doctors were not trained to look after families. If you were to get chest pain," he explained, "you went to a cardiologist. If you got bone pain you went to an orthopedic specialist, and so on. We were taking care of everyone, including the local expatriates."

During that time, a retired US military man presented with chest pain. "He turned ashen grey in front of me," said Brad, "but I couldn't find anything wrong with him and his ECG was fine. The next morning God spoke to me in the shower. He said, 'that man has a dissecting aortic aneurysm.'[46] I called him and said, 'Jim, meet me in cardiology, *now*!' We confirmed the diagnosis." Ninety-six thousand dollars later, Jim returned from Germany with an aortic graft and a new valve. The survival rate from this condition is 15 percent, but Jim didn't just survive, he thrived.

"This was one of the first times," said Brad, "that I realized the whole medical thing in my life was beyond me. I was doing the job but God had *His* purposes. It showed me that He is the Great Physician and I'm just the assistant. He's the boss and I'm just...Oh wow! That was my revelation; that God could do things that I just couldn't."

Jim was a specialty language teacher. He had taught English as a second language to military officers from all over the former Soviet Union. He could now go back to meet with them and disciple them. Some became open Christians and others secret Christians. Some called God, Father, but had not gone all the way—yet. This man was pivotal in God's purpose. He had reached where no other man could. At that stage the Lord spoke to Brad saying, "I'm going to use *you* Brad, to keep my kingdom purposes going."

"I remember another expat," he said. "She complained of the worst headache that she'd ever known. With two other Christian doctor colleagues, I went to her apartment that night as our government clinic was only available during daylight hours. Straight away, we knew that a lumbar puncture was required. Sure enough the cerebrospinal fluid came out 'pink lemonade,' which is classic for a leaking cerebral aneurysm."

With that provisional diagnosis they took the patient to the American base where the diagnosis was not accepted. But they agreed to send her to Germany where digital subtraction angiography[47] confirmed the diagnosis to be correct. The aneurysm was clipped and the patient was fine.

"The other doctors didn't believe us," he said, "but we knew we were right because God had revealed it to us. I just felt His presence in that whole situation. It could have been so much worse."

Even so, Brad was still striving through struggles, challenges, and all sorts of spiritual battles. He finished ten years of medical service in central Asia finally publishing an article on family medicine development in third world countries, achieving one of his life goals. "But you know what?" he said, "Publishing that article had been a goal and I did it, but

I'm sorry, there was no God in it at all. It was just dry. I had seen it as the pinnacle of my career but it was completely empty." At that stage he turned away from academic medicine.

The local international school for missionaries' children needed a new director and Brad accepted the position. "I was in a whole different stratosphere working with kids' education." He said. "I was killing myself working even harder than when I was a doctor. I neglected my devotional life and my relationship with God. I was doing what I regarded as God's will but severely sacrificing my relationship with Him."

By 2009, he had become spiritually dry. "I badly needed help" he said. "I'd had a taste of a deeper intimacy with God but I needed to reboot my spiritual life and strip away a lot of the things that didn't need to be there. My organization was gracious enough to let me come here to Kona for a sabbatical. God provided the money for me to bring all six family members with me."

It was during that time that God led Brad along a different pathway. He was able to let all of the striving go. He received wonderful help from Christian doctors and leaders at Youth With A Mission. But as he said, it wasn't just the people that helped him, it was God Himself.

"I found my identity in my relationship with God my Father rather than in my own pursuits and accomplishments. I learned to experience God's love in my personal life. I finally came to understand that I needed to relax, to stop performing, that God's acceptance of me did not depend on how hard I tried or what I achieved."

Following this, Brad went back to Central Asia to pack up and say goodbye to the team. He returned to the States entering a family medicine practice in San Diego. He now practiced medicine in a different way. He began to listen to what God was saying.

"Before, I had practiced 'schizophrenic' medicine in America. I was a great Christian in the home and at church and I was a good doctor, but my Christianity never interacted with my medical life. The two were very separate," Brad said. "I can't believe the spiritual opportunities that God gives me in family practice now. I've come back to the place where I originally failed. God had to bring me back to show me that this is how it should be done. Now I get it, and I'm excited. As I approach each day I say, 'God, what do you want to show me today? What new opportunities do you have?' Sometimes He opens spiritual doors, sometimes He says hold back, your job is just to pray. When a patient comes to me and they're depressed, and they begin spilling their guts, they don't give the whole story, but they give me enough clues so that the spirit of God starts to show me what's going on."

A wonderful lady recently came into Brad's practice. She had a Down syndrome daughter and was the sole caregiver. She had severe abdominal pain and was full of fear. "Everyone in my family has died of cancer," she said, "and I'm the only one left to take care of my girl. My stomach's been hurting for two weeks and it's getting worse. I need an abdominal CT to see if I have cancer."

"'OK,' I said, 'but you are fearful and I want you to know that perfect loves casts out fear.'[48] She started to cry because she knew I was right."

On the morning of the test, God woke Brad and told him that the patient had a simple ulcer. The test result would be normal. "I could have called and cancelled the test but she needed to have it for her own peace of mind. I got to call her later and say, 'Your test is normal everything is going to be fine.'"

"Later she told me that when she woke early on the morning of the test, she was pain free and knew that she had been healed. She felt that I might be mad at her if she didn't keep her appointment, and had the test if only to please me. We both had a good laugh realizing that God was probably laughing too as we rejoiced in the healing and His way of telling us, "I told you so."

Brad now makes no distinction between his Christian and non-Christian patients. "I know that I must treat them equally. I thought I had special connection to my Christian patients, but now I think: *no, they're no different*. Sometimes God uses me in a proactive way and sometimes He just uses me as an intercessor for them acting on their behalf, standing in the gap."

Recently God placed a lesbian couple under Brad's care. His first impulse was, "'Why me God? Why do I have to deal with this?' But God has given me a tremendous love for this couple. I look forward to seeing them. It's a spiritual opportunity to love them where they're at, in a very needy place."

"In a sense God is priming me and showing me what He can do. Even when I'm striving He's always there and He's giving me a taste of His character. He can still use me even if I'm spiritually deaf and dumb. It's a great message of hope—just think how much more God can use me when my ears are unplugged. Now it's just me, God, and the patient."

17

Set the Prisoners Free

God said to me, "All truth comes from Me and all people can do is to distort that truth or discover it."

Paul, psychiatrist

In 1959, at ten years of age Paul and his mother flew from Cuba to Miami with a few dollars and one suitcase apiece, leaving the Marxist regime of Fidel Castro forever.

His family had fought in the resistance against Batista and later supported Castro, only to find that he was an oppressive tyrant far worse than Batista. Paul's grandparents had owned a beautiful farm in eastern Cuba. They were evicted by Castro's men, who sent them to live in a cheap hotel where they died.

As a small boy growing up in Cuba, Paul had attended several schools. At four years of age he was sent to a Catholic school run by nuns. This was typical of education in Catholic Cuba at the time. Paul often experienced their less charitable side and was threatened with being locked in a dark underground cistern as a form of punishment.

One day as he was being scolded he opened a can of tomato juice from his lunch pack and smeared it over the nun's white habit. He was promptly escorted to the school gate by the ear, never to return. His concerned mother enrolled him in a Methodist missionary school where they taught him the Bible. "Jesus became my hero," he said.

In grade six he was sent to military school where the Catholic catechism was taught. The priest told Paul that he alone was able to forgive sins, not Jesus. He was also told that he must not read the Bible as this required interpretation by the clergy. This angered Paul and he argued with the priest. "He told me that I was going to hell," said Paul, "and he kicked me out of school."

In Miami, Paul's mother—although trained as a teacher—worked as a maid. In school Paul was at first a good student, but in his junior senior year became involved with drugs and alcohol, and became a hippy. He embraced eastern mysticism and the occult. "I suspected that I would end up in prison, dead or insane," he said. At the time he remained at college in pre-med "but I had such a bad grade average that they put me on probation," he said.

In 1969 Paul met two young men from a local Bible college who led him to accept Jesus as Savior. "The irony was," he said, "that I argued with them about everything just as I had argued in Cuba with the atheists who said there was no God, and with the Catholics who said that Jesus could not forgive sins." He was saved but there was no purpose in his life and he saw it going nowhere. He enrolled in a Bible college where he spent four years studying. At that same Bible college, he met Cathy his wife-to-be.

After graduation Paul returned to pre-med with new resolve. He was accepted into the Medical University of Georgia and graduated with straight A's. His old professors were astounded.

During his years of medical training, Paul and Cathy had two children. To help support his young family Paul joined the US Army health professions scholarship program. After a rigorous internship at Madigan Army Medical Center just outside of Tacoma, Washington, he was sent to the Czechoslovakian border to command a medical facility. "It was an armored tank division," he said, "and it was the devil's playground. There was drug abuse, child abuse, and wife abuse. An officer had recently been murdered inside the post and there were German prostitutes roaming the base. I teamed up with the chaplain—a godly man. He was charismatic but didn't force his views on others. All the denominations came together under this one man. I respected him greatly but at that stage I regarded charismatics as too experiential, too emotional."

Paul had previously experienced the supernatural through his involvement with the occult, and drug abuse. But here in Western Germany he was to experience for the first time the powerful intervention of the Spirit of God in people's lives. "We had a lady who was always trying to commit suicide," he said. "Her husband would beat her, and her kids were always sick. She took drug overdoses and tried to jump out of a third story window. I didn't know how to help her. But then late one night she came to my office and poured her heart out. I said, 'Ma'am the enemy is sitting on your shoulder whispering lies.' At that moment a force came straight at me, but it dissipated before it hit me as though I was shielded by an invisible barrier. She was startled too.

"Then the Lord said to me, '*Witness to her.*'

"I argued, '*But she knows the gospel.*'

"He said, '*Witness right now.*'

"And so I did and she received the Gospel. I realized that the enemy had kept her blind and that now she understood for the first time. There was such a miraculous change in that whole family that the underlying problem had to have been demonic. Her husband who had been declared untrainable by the army became a model soldier. He went to Saudi Arabia and became an evangelist smuggling Bibles into that country."

Paul was encouraged by senior officers to remain in the army as a career soldier. "One day you'll be a general," they said. But Paul had other plans. His friend, a paramedic and pastor in Miami Beach, was heavily committed to the pro-life movement. He had set up crisis pregnancy centers and invited Paul to join him.

So in 1985 he returned to become an emergency medicine doctor working the streets of Miami Beach and training paramedics. But as he said, "It was a dead-end job going nowhere," and he soon applied to join the anesthesia training program at the University of Miami's Jackson Memorial Hospital. At the time it was the busiest surgical program in the southern US.

Paul worked one hundred hours per week, commencing at 6:00 AM each morning and was on nonstop anesthesia call every other day. The program had one of the highest resident divorce, drug abuse, and suicide rates of any in the country. "They were working the residents to death," he said.

Gradually he became stressed and depressed. He developed joint pain and localized swelling. Investigations revealed that his rheumatoid factor was 3000.[49] "My immune system had turned against me and I was spinning down into a deep depression," he said.

He told his supervisors that he desperately needed a break. Their response was to put him in charge of the surgical intensive-care night shift. "One case nearly broke me," he said. "An old black woman in congestive heart failure came in. They stripped her naked and put tubes in every orifice. I had to put in a central line. She turned to me and I could see she was terrified. I realized then that I had become a machine. I had lost my soul. I remembered the verse 'What good does it do a man to gain the whole world and lose his soul?' Well, I had lost my soul. I told the nurses to cover her up. I explained to her who I was and what I had to do. When I had inserted the central line I went into the bathroom and wept bitterly."

Returning from the bathroom Paul found that he could make no sense of the medical terminology in his own patient notes. "It was scary," he said.

"Are you OK?" the nurses asked. I called my wife, Cathy. She said, 'Paul, you need to come home *now*.' My backup said he could cover me through what remained of the shift. But this was a very punitive residency. You just couldn't mess up or you were finished. I thought to myself, *this is it*. Waiting in the rain for Cathy, I saw my reflection in a plate glass window and heard a voice say, 'You might as well kill yourself because you're finished.'

"I said, 'No, I belong to God.' The voice went away but the idea of suicide as an escape would return to haunt me."

The next morning, the chairman offered Paul six months leave on full pay. He asked for two weeks to give himself time to think. During that time the Lord made it clear to Paul and Cathy that this was not where he was meant to be. Each day his hands were becoming more painful and swollen and eventually the diagnosis of rheumatoid arthritis was confirmed. He was also depressed but wouldn't admit it to anyone. "That's not what doctors do," he said.

At that stage Paul quit the program to have surgery on his hands. The surgeon was not encouraging and said that he would probably not use them again in a meaningful way. Paul decided to have a complete break from medicine for about a year to recuperate.

There was a Christian retreat in Lake Placid, Florida and they needed an assistant administrator. "I knew the director," he said. "He was an old dog, a retired professor from Bible college. The pay was lousy but it was a great rest and in that time God healed my hands. As soon as I was able, I returned to part-time work in the ER to maintain my level of practice."

At that stage God renewed Paul's vision for teaching and missions. In 1986 he began part-time training of students in cardiopulmonary medicine at the Pacific and Asia University in Kona. But he continued night shifts in the ER and spent much of his time commuting between Hawaii and the Mainland. The stress once again began to build.

There was an insidious deepening of his depression and eventually he began to think about suicide again. "I couldn't see clearly," he said, "and I decided that my family would be better without me."

In the evenings he drove to the ER in an old VW camper van. There was a gas stove in the back which often leaked. He would make it look as though he had stopped for a rest and been overcome by leaking gas. It would be regarded as an accidental death and the family would not blame themselves.

With a firm plan in place there came a sense of release and as Paul shaved at home that evening in preparation for work, he reflected: *This is it. The pain and despair will soon be gone.*

It was then that he heard the voice of God from within. "Paul, what are you doing?"

"What?" he said.

"What are you doing, Paul? You're about to end your life...I gave you life not for you to take it."

There were tears in Paul's eyes as he continued. "I knew it was God," he said, "but I didn't want to hear this at all. I said, 'What do you want me to do?' He replied, 'Tell Cathy.'"

Cathy listened quietly. "Paul, it's about time you got over your pride and found some help," she said. He took her advice and sought help from a Christian psychologist. Soon he began to experience the healing power of God working in his life.

Paul quit his job in the ER and with Cathy and family, enrolled in a Crossroads counseling course at Youth With A Mission in Tyler, Texas. This was followed by a period of mission outreach into Eastern Europe in 1989. This was a pivotal year as the Berlin wall had just come down, and the team was sent to Poland, Czechoslovakia, and Eastern Germany.

During the outreach they experienced the Holy Spirit's guidance in powerful and miraculous ways. But they were not well prepared. The leader had little understanding of Eastern Europe and did not speak the languages. Cathy and Paul spoke survival German from military days and so the job of interpretation fell to them.

They found themselves in some difficult situations. One night they became lost in Eastern Germany with nowhere to spend the night. On a map Paul found the town of Wittenberg, the significance of which escaped him at the time. It was near midnight when they arrived. The town was dark and depressing.

"We stopped at a guesthouse," he said. "We told them we had families and children and needed a place to sleep, but they turned us away. 'We have sleeping bags,' we said. 'We can sleep on the floor and be out in the morning before the guests are up.' Again they said no. At that stage an old lady came out from the back room and spoke to me in a rapid East German dialect that I didn't understand. But as she spoke a vision began to crystallize in my mind. I saw an ancient courtyard of cobble stones. There was a stone archway and beyond that what looked like a deserted castle. I thought that one of my old LSD trips was coming back. *Wow*, I thought, *that's weird*. I'd never had anything like this happen before.

"Waiting in the bus outside, Russell, one of our guys had been praying. 'Paul,' he said, 'I've just had a vision,' and he described exactly the vision I'd had, stone by stone. Our leader was not the least bit interested, but as we drove off Russell and I both recognized the building from our vision. We stopped the vehicle and ran to the ancient iron gates only to find them locked—but there was a tiny light high up in a tower. A young man approached us across the stone courtyard.

"I heard the Lord's voice say, 'Speak to him.'

"'What's the use Lord?' I said.

"'Speak to him,' I heard again."

They told the young man that they needed a room for the night.

"You can stay here," he said, "but I'll have to get the key."

He returned with the key, unlocked, and led them up the winding steps. When the doors at the top were opened, they were amazed. This medieval monastery had been beautifully refurbished as a youth hostel. There were showers, beds, and cooking facilities. God had provided all that was needed.

In the morning Paul woke to find Russell shaking him.

"Paul, this is it!" he said.

"This is what?"

"This is it!"

"What do you mean?"

"This is where Luther nailed the theses to the door. The Wittenberg door! Let me show it to you."

And Paul said, "It was a beautiful door, the door to the reformation where in 1517 scholar and theologian Martin Luther had nailed his ninety-five theses." And the steps that they had walked up the night before were those which Luther had climbed on his knees in penance before he understood the meaning of God's grace.

Coming back from Eastern Europe Paul was spiritually on fire. He had seen God's intervention in people's lives and had developed a heart for missions. He also heard there was a need for a man to pioneer health schools in Latin America.

"I speak Spanish and I love teaching," he said. "I thought this must be what God wants me to do. We had sold most of our property and we were positioned to go full time. But with one phone call the door closed. The person responsible said, 'No, until the Lord tells me, the answer is no, and that's it.' I tried everything but no one could open that door. 'God,' I said, 'what do You want me to do?'"

Again the voice of doubt pursued and Paul fell into a deepening despair. After that disappointment Paul moved on. Before the mission outreach into Eastern Europe, he had developed a growing interest in psychology. But his Christian psychologist friends had encouraged him to train in psychiatry. "Then you could prescribe medication and do therapy," they said.

Paul learned that there had been a migration of faculty from Duke University's psychiatry training program to the University of Georgia, his old alma mater. He had interviewed for the course and been accepted into the residency training program. But he had put in a condition. He told them that he may want to do mission work and alerted them to his history of depression and suicidal thoughts.

They're going to think I'm nuts, he thought.

But their response was amazing, "We'll leave the door open."

When the door was closed to missions in South America, the Lord said, "There's only one door open, Paul, and you're going through it."

"I said, 'Lord, psychiatry is a godless wilderness. When I did my rotations as a student they laughed at me for being a Christian.'

"God said, 'I've got a reason for you to train in psychiatry.'

"I thought, *Well, God has shut the door on missions. How can I trust this thing about psychiatry? It's going to tear my faith apart.* As a medical student I had wanted to run away from psychiatry but now God was dragging me back. I began to question whether I was really hearing from God at all."

Shortly after Paul was given a book called *They Found the Secret*, written by V. Raymond Edman.[50] Edman wanted to know what made men and women great for God. Finney, Chambers, Moody, Hudson

Taylor, Amy Carmichael. What was the common thread? He was to learn that each began with a vision and a mission, but no spiritual anointing. Eventually each one hit the wall, reaching a point of total despair and surrender. It was at that point that God anointed each of them with His Holy Spirit.

"I was at that point of despair," he said. "I didn't have anything." He began to spend hours on his knees each day surrendering himself to God. "Here's my life, God," he would say, "do whatever You want. If You want to put me on the shelf, that's OK. It's up to You."

During that time there was a revival at the local church and Cathy encouraged Paul to go along. He attended faithfully each day but nothing happened. As he put it, "God remained silent and distant."

On the final evening he was impatient for the service to end. Then during the last prayer, he entered into an experience that would change his life. In his mind's eye he saw a light coming towards him. "I knew it was Jesus," he said. "He came to me and took over my entire being. Peace and joy as I had never known filled me." Cathy immediately sensed a change. "Something is different about you," she said.

"I said the Lord's always been in me and with me but this is different." It seems that Paul had experienced an infilling of the Holy Spirit. The experience eventually faded, but the memory did not.

"Looking back," he said, "I now know that God gave me a special anointing that night—an anointing that gave me tremendous clarity of mind and discernment and a peace that I had never before experienced. And He had a purpose for me—to go into psychiatry—a purpose that I would not fully understand until years later."

"I want you to go into psychiatry," God said, "and I want you to dig your foundations deep. I want you to dig a foundation of truth and *that* truth will be your foundation and anchor. I want you to see patients through my lens, my microscope, to understand how I made you and your patients and to love them as I do. All truth comes from Me and all people can do is to distort that truth or discover it. With that basis you can learn from Freud."

"But he was a godless man," said Paul. "He discovered things that are important and you can bring them back to My foundation."

Paul learned to integrate discovered truths in the field of psychology and neurology with God's Word. He learned to understand the true nature of the human spirit as the basis of personhood. God taught Paul to put himself inside his patients. And from that perspective he was better able to understand them in their individual struggles. He learned how that mental deception created by the enemy of humanity was able to enslave the human spirit.

"When I began my studies," said Paul, "my colleagues thought I was crazy because I had nine supervisors. I wanted to learn from everybody, psychoanalytic therapists, behavioral, and Gestalt therapists. He discovered that each theoretical school had a compartmentalized view of human nature and experience. He came to understand that man's fall from God's grace had fragmented the inherent unity of God's truth and that he needed to reintegrate truth in understanding and practice. His practice of psychiatry must be based on the unity of God's truth.

During psychiatry training Paul needed to moonlight to pay the bills. One of his professors had a job in a South Carolina prison. He was near to retirement and offered Paul his job. "Paul, do you want to take this on for a while?" he asked.

"I said, 'Prison? No way!' But he kept asking and eventually I agreed to try it for a month."

Paul loved the work and found that he began to have breakthroughs with some of the more violent men. Some had three or four life sentences. It was a maximum security prison, where violence was a way of life. He began to understand about the wounding of the human spirit and how people could so easily fall into spiritual bondage.

He also began to understand the nature of evil. "If you do evil enough, you become evil," he said. "I could see that some of my patients had completely gone over. They enjoyed hurting others. At that point all you can do is to contain them. They are sociopaths. But thank God they are a small minority. Most of the men and women that I have worked with over the years are certainly salvageable."

After psychiatry training, Paul practiced military psychiatry, private practice, and managed to take every opportunity to teach. He taught at the post-doctoral, graduate, and undergraduate levels. Eventually he went into full time prison work in Georgia and remained there for fourteen years. After the first seven years, Paul said that the state did the unimaginable: they converted the maximum security male prison in which he worked into a women's prison. "They did this virtually overnight," he said.

Looking back, Paul can see this change as the hand of God. "Over 90 percent of the women had been severely abused, most sexually in early life. Some had been shot up with IV heroin by nine years of age and were sold into prostitution." He said, "All were addicted to substances or self-mutilation and were involved in prostitution or toxic relationships with drug dealers or abusive men. Many had children with multiple fathers. Many had lost custody of their children to the state because they could not care for them from prison.

Their stories and lives were dismal. Yet time after time Paul saw these women healed and set free. "The Gospel story of Mary Magdalene is a powerful witness," he said, "because they see how Jesus treated the prostitute and the transformation that took place in her life. You can see tears in their eyes. They've been looking in the wrong mirrors all their lives.

"I ask them to think about how the prostitute felt about herself. She was dragged to the feet of Jesus. The men in town knew her and abused her sexually. They wanted to kill her. She wasn't a prostitute because she wanted to be. She was trained to sell herself by the lies that she'd heard and the indignities that she'd suffered.

"Something happened to Mary Magdalene which caused a miraculous transformation. She saw something in the Lord's eyes because the next time you see her she walks into a party of Pharisees uninvited. I can just hear the comments: 'She's the one who kissed His feet, washed them with her tears, and then used all her savings to pour ointment on His feet.' When Judas and the Pharisee criticized her, Jesus said that she was doing it because she knew how much He loved her."

At this point Paul's voice faltered and he had to pause. "You know who stayed at the cross?" he asked, "Only three—and she was one of them.

Who saw Him come back from the dead first? Mary Magdalene. When these women see themselves as Magdalene, there's a transformation that begins to occur in them which changes their lives."

Paul finally left the prison in September 2011. "It was tough call," he said. Until that time there had never been a complaint against him. But he knew there were people in the system that didn't like him because of what he stood for. The head of the state correctional medical service, a pediatrician, called Paul's employers and told them that if he continued to order Hepatitis C tests for his patients she would have him fired.

Paul said, "I deal with drug addicts and prostitutes and you don't want me to do Hep-C testing?"

They said, "No, you can do HIV but not Hep C because if they are positive, we will have to treat them."

Paul refused to comply with this condition and withdrew his services.

After thirty years of practicing medicine and psychiatry, God is sending Paul and Cathy on a new journey to counsel and train young people, something very dear to their hearts. Already, they have traveled and taught many times in the University of the Nations counseling school at Chatel, Switzerland. Recently, they returned to University of the Nations campus in Kona, Hawaii to staff a medical missions training course and outreach. After that, they traveled to France for training and back to Chatel to teach an advanced training seminar in counseling. This year, they will also assist others in the pioneering and staff training of a counseling school in Chile. Their vision is to equip others and train others to multiply.

Few men today experience the pain and opposition faced by Paul. Born of a Cuban family who resisted Batista and Fidel Castro, as a small boy he saw relatives suffer and die. As a confused young man on the streets of Miami, drugs and pursuit of the occult took a savage toll. But God had a wonderful plan for his life and not one of these experiences was wasted.

By accepting Christ, his life changed dramatically and he was able to resume his medical studies and to graduate as a doctor. But career stress, physical illness, and spiraling depression on two occasions brought him near to suicide. It was only at the point of utter despair when he surrendered himself to God completely that God anointed him with His Holy Spirit. From that point, his life was renewed and God introduced him to the specific plan that He had for his life. As a prison psychiatrist, he has been instrumental in changing the lives of thousands of prisoners and setting them spiritually and emotionally free.

Paul has found, as so many before him, that it is not sufficient to have a vision and that even well-conceived plans and strategies may not prevail. And so where does the power come from? Paul finds strength beyond himself by surrendering to God and by embracing His Holy Spirit. God gives him the strength and purpose to continue the journey that He has ordained. Every experience that Paul and Cathy have been through together only serves to build a stronger and more stable platform from which to launch themselves into His next adventure. And as the vision becomes clear they prepare to go!

It was like death and resurrection. I entered hospital on the Thursday to receive a death sentence that evening. Friday was all about dying. On the Saturday I slept for the first time in many weeks. But Sunday—that was resurrection!

Rosemary Bradford

18

A New Heart for Rosemary

Whom have I in heaven but You? And there is none upon earth that I desire besides You. My flesh and my heart fail; but God is the strength of my heart and my portion forever.

Psalm 73:25,26

It was dark at 9 p.m. when the cardiologist arrived. The lights in the Intensive Care Unit were dimmed. He examined Rosie thoroughly and reviewed her tests. His manner was grave.

"I'll speak to your husband," he said and left the room.

Philip will never forget the doctor's words. "I couldn't give you worse news," he said. "Rosemary has peripartum cardiomyopathy." He continued that she was in severe heart failure and would not survive heart transplantation. Furthermore, because of a pre-existing kidney problem, this surgery was not even an option. His considered prognosis: she would be unlikely to survive forty-eight hours.

The news was devastating. Family and friends were alerted.

"That Friday," said Rosie, "was all about dying." The cardiologist had given her no hope of survival.

It had been late at night some weeks earlier, when the call came through to our Strathfield home. The tone in Philip's voice told me immediately that something was dreadfully wrong.

He was calling from Auckland in the North Island of New Zealand where he and Rosie had been attending a conference. She had been pregnant with their fifth child but had become progressively unwell with a cough and increasing shortness of breath.

Towards the end of the conference she had gone into premature labor and had been taken by ambulance to hospital. Her labor was brief but extremely painful as there had not been sufficient time for staff to administer adequate pain relief. Grace Rebecca was born at just thirty weeks gestation and was immediately placed in the neonatal intensive care unit.

Each day, Rosie visited young Grace. But each day it became more of a physical effort.

"Are you always this short of breath?" asked a nurse.

The baby also became progressively weaker and finally, five days after the birth came the news: baby Grace was dead.

Rosie was given weekend leave from hospital to attend the funeral. It was a time of sadness, but also one of thanksgiving for the precious time spent with baby Grace. They had hoped that the funeral might bring closure, but this was not to be the case.

Rosie's health continued to deteriorate. Friends called in their local doctor who was alarmed at her condition. After running some tests he decided to hospitalize her "without delay." She overheard him talking on the phone to the ambulance booking clerk.

"She has heart failure, renal failure, anaemia, and pneumonia."

That couldn't possibly be me, she had thought.

And so Rosie was taken to the prestigious Green Lane Hospital in Auckland, a hospital renowned for its level of expertise in cardio-thoracic medicine. There she was diagnosed as having pneumonia, given antibiotics and, after a brief stay, sent home! Encouraged that the hospital doctors didn't seem overly concerned, Philip and Rosie resolved to remain with friends in Auckland while she regained strength for the trip home to Sydney.

But her health continued to fail despite antibiotics. She developed sharp, pleuritic chest pain and her breathlessness became worse.

In desperation the young couple turned to their book of daily readings, a book of God's promises compiled by the great preacher, Charles Spurgeon. The reading for the day was not familiar. It dealt with the appearance of the angel of the Lord to the wife of Manoah. The angel brought news that she would conceive and bring forth a son, Samson, who would deliver his people from the Philistines (Judges 13).

Awestruck, Manoah prepared a sacrifice and as the flames arose, the angel ascended with them. Manoah and his wife fell down in fear.

"We will surely die, as we have seen God," said Manoah. But his wife replied, "If the LORD had desired to kill us, He would not have accepted a burnt offering...nor would He have shown us all these things, nor would He have told us such things as these at this time" (Judges 13:23).

Philip and Rosie took heart. Here was a word of hope in a time of desperate need.

It was at that stage that Philip called me. I listened in dismay as he related the sequence of events and described Rosie's condition. He was extremely worried and perplexed. Why was she so ill? Why had the doctors not kept her in hospital, and why were they unable to help? What should he do?

My mind raced ahead of me. Pulmonary embolus (blockage of a lung artery) seemed the most likely possibility, maybe pneumonia. Under the circumstances, all I could do was to encourage him to seek urgent specialist medical attention.

Rosie's condition continued to deteriorate. Finally, they made a difficult decision. They would return home to Sydney as soon as possible, despite the local doctor's advice that she should not fly. At home, with family, and doctors familiar to them, surely things must improve. The doctor protested, but reluctantly gave his permission.

Once back in Sydney, they returned to the Anglican rectory in Manly where Philip was catechist (student minister) at the time. They arrived on Sunday. By Thursday, Rosie was gravely ill. Their neighbor, a general practitioner and friend, arranged for a chest X-ray.

"Rosemary, you won't recover at home," he said. "You must go to hospital!"

Bags were packed and Philip drove Rosie to the Emergency Unit of Manly District Hospital. She was admitted directly into the intensive care unit, and a consultant cardiologist was summoned from St. Vincent's Hospital with some urgency. It was later that evening, after examining Rosemary, that he broke the news to Philip. She would be unlikely to survive for forty-eight hours.

I had limited knowledge and no personal experience of peripartum cardiomyopathy, then called puerperal cardiomyopathy, so I turned to the books. My textbook[51] defined it as "a form of cardiomyopathy (disease of the heart muscle) developing in the last month of pregnancy or within five months of delivery in the absence of pre-existing heart disease."[52] The heart muscle weakens, the chambers become enlarged and failure of the left ventricle ensues. The left ventricle is the main pump of the heart. It pumps oxygenated blood from the lungs out into the systemic circulation of the body. The condition may be complicated by blood clots to the lungs or to the remainder of the body.

Patients fell into high and low risk groups depending on heart size.[53] Published mortality figures from three small series were in the range of 7–50 percent, with half the deaths occurring within three months of delivery.

Lynne and I had known Philip and Rosie for many years. We had attended youth fellowship with them and studied at university together. We had been at their wedding, a week before our own, and were godparents to one of their children. Philip had a degree in clinical psychology and had worked with people with impaired hearing before commencing studies at Moore Theological College to become an Anglican minister. He was currently the catechist at St. Matthews Church, Manly. These were good, wonderful, loving people.

I was incredulous of their situation, and my own faith was challenged. How could a loving God allow something so dreadful to occur in the lives of people such as these? Not only had they lost their beautiful little girl, but Rosie herself had been given no chance of survival. And what would happen to Philip and their four young children?

I excused myself from rooms next morning to visit Rosie in the intensive care unit. It was a beautiful day, the sky blue and cloudless, sun sparkling on the ocean. Rosie was in a private room with a window overlooking the water. She was sitting, supported by several pillows, on oxygen therapy. Her condition alarmed me. She had oedema (fluid swelling) of her limbs, and large amounts of fluid in the chest cavity. Her resting heart rate was about 115. Chest X-ray and echocardiography had demonstrated gross heart enlargement and very poor function of the left ventricle. I was disheartened, but prayed with her and encouraged her as best I could.

From the hospital I went straight to the family home. In Philip I found a strong, enduring faith. My purpose had been to encourage him but rather, he encouraged me. Many were there. Some had brought food, others prayed. Some had just come to show their love and support. The principal of Moore Theological College had just called to offer his support. As I joined my prayers with those of family and friends, it seemed that God gave us a common thread to our petitions: that God would give Rosemary "a new heart." Whether this meant by transplantation or restoration of her own seemed inconsequential. But we prayed for a *new heart* for Rosie.

Over the next twenty-four hours, people all over Australia joined in this prayer. Canon Jim Glennon and people from the St. Andrew's Cathedral Healing Ministry in Sydney interceded for Rosemary. We called our friend Pastor Noel Gibson in Melbourne, where he and his wife Phyl were leading a church retreat. The whole congregation joined their prayers with ours.

The concept of a "new heart for Rosie" grew like a wave gathering momentum and growing in profile as it approaches the shore. What had begun as a common focus for our thoughts and prayers became reality in our minds and spirits. It was as though God was saying, "This is what I intend to do, just believe and keep praying."

Through Saturday Rosie remained in the ICU. She sat semi-reclined to assist her breathing, arms clasping her thighs. "As I sat in that warm bed with the sunlight streaming through the window," she said, "it was as though I was cradled in God's arms." That night she slept restfully for the first time in weeks.

On Sunday morning, remarkable news. She was improving, rapidly in fact, far beyond the expectation of the medical staff. So marked was her improvement that she was transferred from intensive care to a general medical ward.

. The cardiologist returned that day to arrange transfer to St. Vincent's Hospital for terminal care. He was astonished to find how much improvement there had been in Rosie's condition since he had last seen her. Philip remembers his words, "There must be healing in this place." He decided against transfer to St. Vincent's. The conditions at Manly seemed to be "favoring the patient."

Rosie continued to make a rapid recovery. She was soon discharged and returned home, where she recovered completely. I visited her a few weeks later to find her out, cycling around the streets of Manly, symptom-free.

Eighteen years later, Rosie continues to have a sound heart, and actively participates in parish and local community work. She has recently undergone a successful kidney transplant for the pre-existing renal condition.

Recalling the events of that time she comments, "It was like death and resurrection. I entered hospital on the Thursday to receive a death sentence that evening. Friday was all about dying. On the Saturday I slept for the first time in many weeks. But Sunday, they moved me out of the ICU into the general ward. I was greatly improved. That was resurrection!"

If God could heal Rosemary's heart why then did He not heal her kidney condition at the same time? This is a valid question and there is no immediate answer. Paul the apostle struggled with his own "thorn in the flesh" which may have been a physical impediment (2 Corinthians 12:7). The Bible tells us that he sought the Lord three times regarding this and yet apparently was not healed. Kathryn Kuhlman, who had a much-publicized healing ministry in the United States in the 1970s, eventually died of long-standing rheumatic heart disease. It is understood that she said one day she would have to talk to God about this.

There is one possible answer. In Rosemary's case it was the pre-existing kidney condition that precluded a heart transplant, which allowed God's healing power to be exercised. And as a result, hundreds of people witnessed at first-hand the power of prayer and the intervention of Almighty God.

Yet the question remains. Why are some healed and some not? Is it a God factor or does it lie in our domain? Why was Rosemary saved and baby Grace was not?

Rosemary's story poses a major problem for the medical profession. Most doctors will have heard of similar events but generally have no ready, comfortable explanation. The response will often be "mind over matter" or "it must have been a miracle," but said without conviction. A dilemma such as this is often placed in the too-hard basket, where it remains. Such accounts do not sit comfortably with a rational approach to medical science.

Divine intervention in the healing process is not in accordance with our experience of conventional health care. Many of us accept the examples from the Scriptures in their historical context. But does God really heal today? Contemporary accounts are acceptable as long as they remain at a distance. But what happens when they impact on us directly?

19

A Gift of Faith

Call to Me, and I will answer you, and show you great and mighty things, which you do not know.

Jeremiah 33:3

The memory of Mrs. Mac and that night in Hurlstone Park has never been far from my conscious mind. The incident was a milestone of my Christian experience. But it was also a signpost of events to come.

We were holidaying at Fliske Milne, a working farm, in a remote area of the Snowy Mountains of New South Wales. My daughter, Sascha, had been unwell for several days with a chest infection. She had asthma which was becoming worse. One night Lynne called me to Sascha's bedroom. She had a fever and was extremely breathless. It was about 2 a.m. The temperature outside was sub-zero, a gale was howling about the house and it was beginning to snow. I decided to take her to the Base Hospital at Cooma, about 56 miles away, aware that driving under these conditions would be treacherous. But when I checked the car, it was almost out of gasoline and I knew the local filling station would be closed until 7 a.m. To complicate matters, we had no working phone.

There was little to do but keep a close eye on Sascha. But I was fearful. Her medication was having little effect and she was becoming more distressed. We prayed and I challenged God, "Why don't You help her? Why don't You put Your hand on our daughter and heal her?"

"Why don't you?" came a voice from within.

Lynne and I placed our hands on Sascha and prayed for her. Her condition improved, and by morning she was symptom-free.

As Christians we are entitled to say with Paul, "It is no longer I who live, but Christ lives in me; and the *life* which I now live in the flesh I live by faith in the Son of God, who loved me and gave Himself for me" (Galatians 2:20). When we lay our hands on someone and pray for them we are, in effect, ministering Christ's love. The Reverend Graham Miller refers to God's hand as "the hand that never lost a man."[54] What better partner could any doctor wish to have?

David is an impressive character with a long black beard and a broad grin. Trained in Sydney with postgraduate experience in Great Britain and Papua New Guinea (PNG), he now works in a Christian family practice at the foot of the Snowy Mountains.

"I've been a Christian for as long as I can remember," he said. "I grew into faith and I've never had reason to seriously doubt or question my beliefs." I related my experiences with Mrs. Mac and Rosemary. Had he experienced similar events during his years of practice? He listened thoughtfully.

"Oh, I have nothing to tell you," he said, "except maybe for that time in PNG." He told of how a man was brought into hospital after being bitten by a taipan. The Papuan taipan is PNG's most venomous snake. Its venom is overwhelmingly neurotoxic and hemotoxic, and its bite seven times more lethal than that of the Indian cobra. The man was paralyzed and close to death. What little antivenin was available was administered, but it was expected that if the man did survive, he would remain in a serious condition for several weeks. The man was prayed over and, to the astonishment of all, recovered fully within twenty-four hours.

Then David remembered another occasion when he and his wife Allison, a registered nurse, were hosting David's parents during a visit to PNG. David was called urgently to the hospital. A woman had presented after giving birth to a stillborn child. She was bleeding heavily. Assuming there were retained products of conception, David examined her internally. "To my horror," he said, "I found my hand reached forever. I was internally palpating her spleen. She had ruptured her uterus."

He called for assistance but there was only family to help. The patient's relatives were summoned to provide blood for transfusion. David administered the anesthetic while his father, a Sydney surgeon who had never before performed a hysterectomy, operated with Allison assisting.

The patient survived. This was remarkable enough, but even more amazing was the fact that David had insisted his father obtain temporary medical registration for PNG before visiting. Curiously, his father had been invited to observe a surgical friend perform a partial hysterectomy one week before coming to PNG!

Buoyed on by what David had said, I spoke with Chris, an eminent pediatric cardiologist. He related how one evening he had been called to the bedside of a dying child, a little girl. As he stood by the bedside, God placed in his heart and mind a sense of urgency to pray in his own spirit for that child. As he did so, she grew in strength. By morning she was remarkably improved, and survived. He was so impressed by the turn of events that he felt convicted to share this experience with the parents.

He also told of young Ben, who was admitted for surgery to a narrowing of the aortic valve. Postoperatively, Ben had a stormy course. He was given digoxin, a drug used to treat heart failure, but continued to deteriorate. His heart developed a lethal heart rhythm called ventricular tachycardia (VT) proceeding to ventricular fibrillation (VF), where the heart contractions are entirely uncoordinated and blood ceases to flow around the body. He was countershocked but the effect did not last long. The doctor said that Ben was actually countershocked more than a hundred times over the period of an hour! His heart became weaker and eventually, despite all efforts, stopped.

The doctors went out to the parents to tell them that their little boy had died. But Chris was called back into the room. Ben's heart had begun to beat again, spontaneously. Three more times he developed VF and three more times he was countershocked.

Ben began to improve, and finally remained in normal sinus rhythm. A CT scan demonstrated a small brain hemorrhage in the region of the third ventricle. But he had no clinical evidence of brain damage.

The doctor followed Ben's progress for a number of years. He remained completely well. What he did not know at the time of surgery was that the boy's parents were committed Christians. They had numerous friends throughout New South Wales and South Australia who had been praying for Ben.

Chris also told of a baby boy born with a condition in which the heart fails to develop properly and the major vessels, the pulmonary artery and aorta, are reversed in position. The baby was severely ill and developed a grade ¾ periventricular brain hemorrhage. The hematologist and neurologist gave little hope of survival. He was ventilated and kept alive with the use of inotropes, drugs used to help the heart beat more strongly.

The baby continued to deteriorate. It was clear that he was dying and the decision was made to take him off the ventilator and return him to his mother for his final hours. All drugs were ceased. But he did not die. Rather, he began to feed. His mother took him home where he began to recover. Within six months he was strong enough to undergo corrective surgery for his transposition. He made a full recovery with no apparent brain damage.

Chris told me that the child had actually been discharged from hospital on the same day that he had been on a ventilator and was expected to die. The doctor followed him for years and he remained well. He was not aware of prayers for the child or of any faith which the mother may have had. But as a Christian doctor he was beginning to recognize the healing hand of God on his patient who otherwise would have perished.

Perhaps because doctors may tend to be skeptical, God seems to favor them with experiences that are faith-building and that cut across their conventional ideas of medical management and healing. The Bible says that faith is "the substance of things hoped for, the evidence of things not seen" (Hebrews 11:1). It also speaks of a "gift of faith," not to be confused with faithfulness, which is a fruit of the Spirit. I believe God occasionally gives us such an experience as a gift on which to build our faith.

I spoke with Graeme, a Sydney obstetrician. He had been a Christian since childhood but had some difficulty in accepting that God might intervene today in the healing process. He had been out jogging one Sunday morning when he was summoned urgently to his teaching hospital to perform an emergency Ceasarean section.

He said, "Ern, it all seemed to be fine, until about halfway through when everything went terribly wrong." The patient it seemed had placenta accreta, a condition occurring in 1 in 2,500 pregnancies where the placental tissue invades the muscle layers of the uterus making it difficult, sometimes impossible, to remove. She developed DIC, a condition where essential clotting agents are consumed by the body and bleeding is unable to be controlled, and began to hemorrhage torrentially. Graeme and the surgical team worked frantically to stop the bleeding. Finally a hysterectomy was performed, but bleeding persisted. It began to dawn on him that he just might lose this young woman. In desperation he quietly prayed and, immediately, the bleeding came under control!

I have recently spoken with Graeme again years after the event which had clearly made a permanent impact on his life.

"The situation was dire," he said, "I had closed the patient after surgery, but I knew all was not well. I called my wife at home and asked her to pray while I struggled to restore the patient's blood volume. She went to the evening service at St. Bede's, our church, and the whole congregation prayed. The patient recovered. You know, I still see the patient from time to time and I have made her aware of the miracle of her healing. I also see her baby, now as a patient."

Rob, a senior eye specialist, trained in Sydney but now practicing in Hong Kong, told of a personal experience in Jackie Pullinger's church in Hong Kong where he was an elder at the time.[55] At the conclusion of a service, he and his wife were asked to pray for a visiting Englishman said to be very ill. He related how his heart sank when he saw the man. He was wasted and jaundiced and apparently in the terminal stages of non-Hodgkin's lymphoma. Rob related how they dutifully prayed for the man, but with little hope. From that day the man began to improve. The last they heard he was in complete remission.

A Sydney surgeon called me one day to relate the following experience. He was called to see a young woman who was suffering from severe abdominal pain. He scheduled emergency surgery and opened the abdomen to find a ruptured appendix. There was also an abscess present and he drained a litre of purulent fluid. The post-operative course was stormy. The young lady remained unwell with a high swinging fever. He referred the patient to me for ultrasound of the abdomen, which revealed a large abscess. The surgeon decided to operate again to drain the abscess that day, but to his frustration was unable to schedule a time in the operating room.

On ward rounds the next morning, he was astonished to find that the patient's fever had resolved and that her condition had improved considerably. Progress ultrasound showed a small amount of clear fluid adjacent to the spleen, but no abscess. On questioning the patient, it seemed that she had settled a long-standing argument with her parents that night, and that she had asked the Lord to heal her. The fluid disappeared completely in subsequent ultrasound studies.

Finally I spoke also with Andrew from a large family practice where there are several other Christian doctors. They encourage one another and meet weekly with other members of staff for prayer.

Andrew believes that God wants all to be physically well and that sickness is allowed only by God's permissive will. A framed verse in his surgery states: "In all things give thanks."

Andrew is completely open about his faith with his patients. He believes that sharing his faith plays a part in their healing, and he prays with them when the opportunity arises, if they are agreeable. He does not differentiate his own healing ability from that of God. "All healing is of God," he says, "but when I pray for patients and they are open to the will of God, healing is enhanced."

Andrew has experienced healing in his own life. Some years ago he suffered from a severe whiplash injury. When an overseas speaker, reputedly with a healing ministry, visited Sydney, Andrew volunteered his services as a medical observer and examiner. He did not seek prayer for himself, but found that his neck pain completely resolved after attending one of the meetings. He observed that seeking the healer, rather than healing itself, allowed God to intervene.

Andrew also told of a young woman who came forward to testify to healing that she had received during the meeting. She was about eighteen years of age and had been profoundly deaf since birth. She wore two powerful hearing aids, which were of little assistance. Her speech was that of a woman who had never properly heard a normal human voice to allow her to develop her own speech patterns. Friends and family had brought her along that night believing God for a miracle.

She was prayed for and immediately began to hear. Andrew took her to a quiet place in the auditorium where he could assess her. He says that he was able to stand over ten feet behind her and whisper, and she was able to hear every word! That night she spoke openly of the love of God and of His healing power. Her family and friends were overwhelmed by her healing and were also able to testify to her healing. Andrew saw the young lady many weeks later and was able to confirm the enduring nature of her healing.

He also examined a man who claimed to have been healed of Parkinson's disease. He was severely impaired by tremor and muscle rigidity. "I asked him to stretch out his hands," he said. "There was a moderate tremor. I told him, 'Go home and keep praying, God hasn't finished with you yet. Trust Him to finish the work.' You see, some miracles are not instantaneous."

The man returned the next night. "And he was completely healed," said Andrew. "His gait, facial expression, and speech were normal and he had no tremor."

When I asked Andrew why we don't see such events more frequently he said it was a matter of faith. "Sometimes we and the patients only have sufficient faith for the symptoms such as a bad back, rather than for the bigger issue, the cancer causing the back pain."

These experiences were landmark events in the lives of those doctors. They did not conform to the expected or anticipated course of clinical medicine. Yet they cannot be ignored. Each was witnessed and scrutinized by clinical eyes and examined in the context of medical training and years of experience.

Though isolated events in themselves, they had far-reaching impact into the lives of each of the doctors—a number of whose stories are told in the chapters to follow.

Doctors are trained to be objective and analytical in their approach to medicine. They learn to test hypotheses and ideas for validity before implementing them, and to embrace programs that are proven to be of sound value. If this were not so, medicine would be in disarray. Doctors would have no benchmarks to observe or standards to uphold. They would be unable to communicate with other doctors in a meaningful way. Medical teaching in the universities and colleges would be chaotic.

Doctors' professional competence is based upon accredited training, which must be on-going, on proven ability validated by peer review and on experience. It is on the basis of these criteria that they may practice with confidence. To remain registered to practice, they must formally demonstrate that they have achieved these parameters by gaining continuing medical education (CME) points under the scrutiny of their learned college. They must also maintain payment of their professional indemnity insurance, and in my situation pay annually for a licence to dispense and administer radiopharmaceuticals.

Is it any wonder that doctors protect and guard the pillars of their professional experience zealously? Any new information must be carefully scrutinized, tested, and validated before it is accepted. And in the interest of good medicine that is exactly as it should be.

Our profession becomes our identity and we tend to feel that our identity is sacrosanct. We can dismiss issues and events that we do not understand and cannot accept, as long as they are peripheral to us. But once they encroach upon our very identity, they must be addressed. At that stage our security and self-confidence are threatened. We become uneasy and insecure. The core values of our professional beliefs are challenged.

Such is often the case when Christian doctors are faced with the possibility that God may intervene in the healing process.

It is not uncommon for God to challenge professional belief. Simon Peter did not know Jesus well at all. He had met him through John the Baptist, Jesus' cousin, and had no doubt been impressed by the way in which he had healed his mother-in-law: "But Simon's wife's mother was sick with a high fever, and they made request of Him concerning her. So He stood over her and rebuked the fever, and it left her. And immediately she arose and served them" (Luke 4:38,39).

Simon Peter was a professional fisherman, and with several others ran two fishing boats. In the fifth chapter of Luke, we read that he had been fishing all night with no success and was washing his nets with the others when Jesus approached.

Jesus was surrounded by people wishing to hear Him, and asked Peter if he might speak to the crowds from his boat a little way out from the shore. After he had finished speaking, Jesus told Peter to "launch out into the deep and let down your nets for a catch" (Luke 5:4). Peter was reluctant. He was tired. He had been fishing all night (the best time to fish) with no success, and he and his men had already washed their nets. What would a carpenter know about fishing anyway?

But he was obedient. Luke tells us that the catch was remarkable to the point that the nets began to break and the boat began to sink. These professional fishermen were "astonished" at the size of the catch.

Peter had experienced an event which had been in total contradiction to his professional experience and expectation. He and his friends were simply overwhelmed. He had no alternative but to recognize Jesus as Lord and Master, and fell to his knees. The event was to change not only the nature of his professional life, but his entire future.

As I listened to the experiences recounted by the doctors, it became clear that these were life-changing events with implications reaching far beyond the immediate for both doctors and patients alike. Just as with Peter, they impacted upon the very substance of the doctors' professionalism and the nature of their life journey from that point on.

It is one thing to witness a doctor's response to God's intervention in the health and welfare of a patient. But it is simply breathtaking to observe the impact of God's intervention in a doctor's life when mortality itself is challenged.

The man of God must have insight into things spiritual. He must be able to see the mountains filled with the horses and chariots of fire; he must be able to interpret that which is written by the finger of God upon the walls of conscience; he must be able to translate the signs of the times into terms of their spiritual meaning; he must be able to draw aside now and then, the curtain of things material and let mortals glimpse the spiritual glories which crown the mercy seat of God. The man of God must declare the pattern that was shown him on the mount; he must utter the vision granted to him on the isle of revelation...None of these things can he do without spiritual insight.[56,57]

20

The Higher Mountains

Render to scientific medicine the discipline of science and to God and His Word the discipline of faith.

John Saxton

———————————

"**H**eavy the head that wears the crown," said my father when I accepted the Westmead Hospital job. He was right. He was also right when he told me to "surround yourself with people that you trust and respect."

One such friend who became a lifelong confidant was Dr. John Saxton. I had known him as a senior radiologist at Royal Prince Alfred Hospital during my internship. He later became a senior partner in a much-respected radiology practice in Parramatta, and remained in that capacity when I moved into private practice. He was my business competitor, but a wonderful Christian friend. In quiet moments we would call one another to share experiences and encourage each other.

John celebrated life in its fullness. A frustrated farmer, he loved horses and cattle. He also had a passion for fine cars, and whenever I saw a brilliant red Mercedes I knew it would likely be John. But his consuming interest was for family and, in particular, his wife, Janet.

John retired ten years ago with the expectancy of a quiet life on his semi-rural property, but those years had proven to be the most challenging of all.

It was a cold wintry afternoon as I negotiated the long and winding driveway to John's home in the Hills district, north-west of Sydney. He was waiting for me. With silver hair slicked back, red sweater and brilliant blue eyes, his appearance was striking. We made our way up the stairs and into the living room where a log fire beckoned. Janet gave me a warm welcome and disappeared to prepare afternoon tea.

John stoked the fire as I settled back into the lounge. "As a young guy," he said, "I spent time in the Royal Australian Navy before going on to study medicine." He had thrived on college and university life, throwing himself into drama, music, the visual arts and sport, and had been stimulated by the cut and thrust of intellectual discussion.

Janet was seventeen when they met, and about to commence the first year of an arts degree. "She was beautiful," he said, "and we spoke the same language." But in Janet he also found "honesty, openness, and a fearless vulnerability" that he found irresistible.

On a visit to her home in country New South Wales, John was to discover that her family members were practicing Christians. "They would meet around the breakfast table to read the Bible and pray before riding out to check the lambing ewes." He sensed in that home an assurance of God's ability to meet practical need, and observed a quiet intimacy with a living God.

But he was unable to share their faith. Was it valid? Was it relevant to contemporary life and to medicine? He was a scientist, and placed value on valid hypothesis and rational thought processes.

At Sydney University, a public meeting was arranged for students to hear a prominent Christian speaker, the Reverend Dr. Howard Guinness. Dr. Guinness was a medical doctor. In 1930 he encouraged students to begin the Sydney University Evangelical Union (EU), the first of its kind in Australia. He also initiated Crusader groups in schools that same year.

John challenged him: "You have no scientific basis for what you are saying."

"You say you are a scientist," said the speaker. "Have you examined the evidence?"

"What evidence?"

"The thousand pages of documented evidence of eyewitnesses—the Bible."

John admitted that he had not.

"Then until you are 'fair dinkum,' don't play games with me," was the response.

The speaker continued, "As a scientist, you would surely understand the value of practical experiments. Christians believe when they pray to God He answers. Are you prepared to try that?"

John returned to his room disturbed and challenged. Long into the night he examined and re-examined the issues raised by the speaker, finally reading through the entire Gospel of John. Eventually he took the challenge put by Dr. Guinness. He had been anticipating for some time a certain phone call which would have implications for the future direction of his life. His challenge to God was this: that if he received the call by 9 a.m. that morning, it would be a sign to him that God was personally interested in his life. The call arrived on schedule. True to his word, John repented and gave his life unreservedly to God. But, as he said, it would take him years to fully understand the significance of what he had done.[58]

He began to attend a local church, but found it stifling. "Christians," he said, "were castrated and cloned." Their smiles were artificial and unconvincing. He enjoyed "real" people and didn't find them in church.

After graduation, John became a resident at the Royal Prince Alfred Hospital. But he was unwell, and tests proved that he was suffering from brucellosis, a bacterial condition causing fever, headache, weakness, and muscle pain, generally contracted by contact with livestock. The rigors of a cardiology term left him exhausted. A friend suggested that he apply for a radiology residency, because it would not be as physically or emotionally demanding and would give him a chance to recover his strength.

He well remembers his first barium study. "It's easy," said the senior radiologist. "Just stand here in front of the fluorescent screen while the patient drinks the contrast, and describe anything that doesn't look smooth."

As it happened, the first patient was a nurse known to John. To his dismay, the study revealed a large tumor. She died within the year. But her faith and trust in God demonstrated to John in a practical way the Christian virtues that he had not found in church life. "Her life and death," he said, "exhibited reality, not churchianity."

John despised hypocrisy. He would not tolerate doctors who were not 100 percent dedicated. He sought out honest men of integrity for his own business partners. Together they developed a highly respected imaging practice in western Sydney.

As the specialty of radiology developed in the 70s, it became more sophisticated and computer dependent. Computed Tomography (CT) began to play a major role in imaging, as did real-time ultrasound, and MRI was on the horizon. The partners decided that they would need a new building, purpose-built, to house their practice and the new technology.

None were experienced with building programs or practice development, and with the demands of a heavy clinical load they found the new challenge daunting. Reluctantly, John took on the task. "The Lord gave me skills I simply didn't have," he said.

But the new building placed serious constraints on the practice. One partner called him at 2 a.m. one morning, unable to sleep.

"How do you handle the worry?" he asked.

"Come on over and I'll show you," was the answer.

As the partner walked through the door John greeted him, then got down on his knees and said, "This is what I do." The partner joined him and together they asked God for help. "I literally needed a million dollars by the next morning," John said. "That was the raw truth of the matter." The current bankers could offer no further assistance.

John had heard that the governor of the Reserve Bank of Australia was a good man, and a Christian. "In desperation, and naively," he admits,

"I put in a call to that man the next morning. He agreed to see me. Of course he could not help me directly, but he gave me the boldness to approach the chairman of the AMP Society." (Australian Mutual Provident was one of Australia's oldest insurance companies.) An immediate appointment was made for John and the practice accountant to meet with the board the next morning.

"I have no secured assets but my integrity," John told them. "I do have a $1,000 life policy that my father took out for me as a child. I need a million dollars. I am asking you to back me with a million dollars." The board agreed to help and the undertaking was sealed with a handshake. The money was to be made available that same day. John, and the accountant, were overwhelmed by the turn of events. The accountant, not known to be a Christian man, barely made it down the steps of the AMP building at Circular Quay in Sydney, where he sat while John fetched him a coffee. "From that experience," John said, "I realized that I worshipped a mighty God, and I began to expect Him to do the impossible."

Soon after, a woman came to the practice for a barium enema. It demonstrated an extensive carcinoma of the large bowel. She told the partners present on the day that she would not accept surgery, but expected God to heal her. They commiserated. She would surely die. Some months later she returned for a progress study. No tumor was found! John was astounded. There must have been a mix-up with the films. Perhaps they had been mislabeled. But this was not the case. The woman had been genuinely healed. John does not recommend the patient's course of action but, from that day, he began to expect to see the hand of God move in his medical practice.

"God began to extend my ability as a radiologist. As I looked at a difficult CT sequence or ultrasound study it would come clear to me," he said. John would make a diagnosis but God would say to him, "Look again."

"God would alert me to go back and revise a report," he said. "I developed the habit of taking my sandwich down to the park for lunch. I would ask God for strength and wisdom for the afternoon reading session."

But then, early in 1998 John became unwell. He became progressively short of breath to the point that he was having difficulty climbing the stairs at home. Advice was sought from a leading Sydney lung specialist. The news was devastating. He had fibrosing alveolitis, a condition in which there is progressive fibrosis of the small air pockets of the lungs making them stiff and preventing the necessary exchange of oxygen and carbon dioxide. There was no cure. The specialist estimated that he had just twelve months to live.

The day after receiving this news, John and Janet met with Christian friends for a long-standing dinner engagement. Their friends encouraged them and gave them copies of Canon Jim Glennon's books, *Your Healing is Within You*[59] and *How Can I Find Healing?*[60] For the first time, John and Jan became aware of the wonder and all-encompassing power of the Holy Spirit. They began to search the Scriptures for verses relevant to healing. They had faith for salvation, but did God *really* heal today?

At about the same time, John noticed a small lump in the palm of his right hand. It seemed innocent enough, but when it was removed, it was found to be an extremely aggressive tumor, a synovial sarcoma. Furthermore, the excision had been incomplete. It was expected that the tumor would spread rapidly, and the surgeons recommended forequarter amputation of the right upper limb. This is a radical amputation involving the entire arm and shoulder.

But John's lung disease precluded such surgery. This posed a major problem, as the tumor was not thought to be sensitive to radiotherapy. They decided to "hit it anyway," and to their amazement it responded. In the months that followed, there was no recurrence.

"As a doctor I had a problem with this," said John. "I had been trained to accept nothing that did not stand up to rigorous scientific scrutiny. My medical career was based on this. The specialist had given me twelve months to live, now partially gone. Where did faith in God fit in?" He was in a real dilemma. And then Jesus' words came to him: "Render therefore to Caesar the things that are Caesar's, and to God the things that are God's" (Matthew 22:21).

"I had my answer," he said. "Render to scientific medicine the discipline of science and to God and His Word the discipline of faith."

John realized that he had been using his mind and experience as a yardstick, rather than the Word of God. He repented of this and began to look to the instructions and promises of God's Word. He bought himself a walking stick and called it "Faith."

But he was frightened. He had a "gut fear," as he put it. Searching the Scriptures he found these words: "For God has not given us a spirit of fear, but of power and of love and of a sound mind" (2 Timothy 1:7). He immediately adopted this verse as his own. Within fifteen minutes, fear and the symptoms associated with it were dispelled, never to return.

But the fibrosing alveolitis progressed. John and Janet continued to search the Scriptures and found the passage: "Is anyone among you sick? Let him call for the elders of the church, and let them pray over him, anointing him with oil in the name of the Lord. And the prayer of faith will save the sick, and the Lord will raise him up. And if he has committed sins, he will be forgiven" (James 5:14,15).

In Mark's Gospel they were shown the prayer of faith:

> So Jesus answered and said to them, "Have faith in God. For assuredly, I say to you, whoever says to this mountain, 'Be removed and be cast into the sea,' and does not doubt in his heart, but believes that those things he says will be done, he will have whatever he says. Therefore I say to you, whatever things you ask when you pray, believe that you receive them, and you will have them"(Mark 11:22-24).

At the healing service at St. Andrew's Cathedral in Sydney, they met Canon Jim Glennon and Canon Jim Holbeck who taught them to "affirm the *answer* not the *problem*." They learned to depend on God more, to thank Him expectantly, and to allow their faith to grow as prayers were progressively answered. They were anointed with oil in accordance with the Scriptures and had prayer and laying on of hands.

John was invited to a retreat for cancer patients at Golden Grove in Newtown, an outreach for the ministry activities of the Healing Ministry at St. Andrew's Cathedral. He was reluctant to go. "All they'll talk about is their cancer," he said. But he was wrong; they spoke of God's promises and answers. It was here that John received the fullness of the Holy Spirit. He recalls a rush of warmth passing through his body that made him gasp. It was here, he said, that he met Jesus again in a new role, as the Great Physician.

John *knew* that he had experienced a healing encounter with God. He and Janet decided to spend some days away in solitude. They headed south from Sydney to Shoalhaven Heads. In the overnight accommodation John was severely breathless. Even walking up the few steps to his apartment was a major task. But his faith was strong.

The next day they traveled on to Coolangatta Mountain, a large hill rather than a mountain, but John was testing the healing that he knew he had received. He began to climb it one step at a time. "As I climbed higher and higher," he said, "I knew that God was doing something wonderful."

The following day they traveled further south to Tilba Tilba at the foot of Mt Dromedary, the 3,000-foot double peak sighted and named by Captain James Cook as he sailed up the eastern seaboard of Australia in April 1770. They began to climb and as they did so, John realized that the impossible was happening. Finally, as they were approaching the summit, a cloud descended and they were enveloped in a cool mist.

"We stood there," he said, "transfixed by the awesome sight of the massive tree trunks ascending into cloud. It was God's cathedral and we claimed it as his theophony. We stood there praising and worshipping Him."

Six years later, at the time of my interview, John at age seventy-seven continued to lead an active life. His breathlessness had returned somewhat, but he was able to cut wood with his chainsaw for his open fire and to care for his family. Both he and his family were regular attenders at the Cathedral healing service where they played an active role encouraging and praying for others.

At the age of seventy-eight, John finally passed into the presence of his loving heavenly Father on May 27, 2005. He died peacefully in the presence of his loved ones, remaining conscious to the very end and praising God.

John's life demonstrates a journey, or climb if you like, from the planes of student skepticism to the peaks of mature insight into the mind of God. While faith in God and scientific rationalism may to the rationalist seem diametrically opposed, there is in fact no conflict for those who embrace a faith in God. Francis Collins is a Christian geneticist and director of the National Human Genome Research Institute. When asked by *Time* whether he believed science was compatible with Christian Faith he answered that the existence of God was either true or not true. However, calling it a scientific question implied that science could provide the answer. But God cannot be totally contained within nature, so His existence is beyond the ability of science to deduce.[61]

John's experience of faith and rationalism is similar to what Moses experienced with the rod he used to lead the people of Israel out of Egypt (Exodus 4:1-5). Moses carried the rod as his staff, his shepherd's crook, and his walking stick. But God told Moses to throw it to the ground. It was only then that he saw it take on the form of a snake. Then God told him to pick it up again. By faith he did so and straight away it turned back into a rod. But God had sanctified it for His use.

It was not until John was prepared to put his faith in God before his scientific credentials that God was able to bring about a major healing in his life. John learned, as did Moses, that sometimes we have to submit our most precious, familiar, and treasured possessions to Him before He can truly bless us. Sometimes He will restore them to us, sometimes not. In true style, however, God restored to John what had been surrendered, but in a new form acceptable to Himself but also to John: Render to scientific medicine the discipline of science and to God and His Word the discipline of faith.

In the deserts of the heart
Let the healing fountain start,
In the prison of his days
Teach the free man how to praise

W.H. Auden, "Another Time"
The Wylie Agency (UK) Ltd., 1940

— 21 —

Specialist Consultation

Man's extremity is God's opportunity.

Rees Howells[62]

I once attended a Trivial Pursuit night at the local school to discover to my delight that our team was formidable. It included a high school teacher, a senior doctor well-versed in classical music and literature and, our secret weapon, a Qantas pilot. We won convincingly. Part of the reason for our perhaps unmerited success was that the pilot seemed to know the correct answers even when the quizmaster did not.

"You must always have an answer," he said. "Passengers won't thank you if you don't." And so with medicine. Patients expect their doctor to have the solution to their problem.

But it is not sufficient to have an answer. It must be the correct one. If a doctor is uncertain how to proceed with a patient's management, he has the option of seeking advice from his peers or from a specialist with expertise in that particular area.

Likewise as Christians, when we are asked to pray for someone who is ill, we have the option of asking God how we should pray. Many would argue that the Scriptures are clear enough. After all, it says in the book of James, "Is anyone among you sick? Let him call for the elders of the church, and let them pray over him, anointing him with oil in the name of the Lord. And the prayer of faith will save the sick, and the Lord will raise him up. And if he has committed sins, he will be forgiven" (James 5:14,15).

I have no issue with this, except to say that there are many ways in which God may heal and it is helpful to seek God's mind on this issue. Not to do so may lead to presumption and to disappointment when prayers seem not to be answered.

A dear friend had experienced many years of undiagnosed pain. An attractive and vivacious professional woman, her life had been compromised by chronic nausea, pain after eating, and food intolerance, resulting in progressive weight loss. She had been hospitalized on several occasions without cause being found, and her condition was beginning to take a toll on her lifestyle and that of her family. Doctors had performed serial ultrasound and nuclear medicine studies, CT, numerous blood tests and endoscopy. All were unremarkable in their findings. There was the suggestion to remove her gall bladder on spec, as symptoms were of a "biliary" nature, but surgeons were reluctant.

Lynne and I found ourselves praying often into the early hours, desperate for a breakthrough, for the right diagnosis. We received a leading from God to seek advice from a professorial friend who suggested that the problem may be of a vascular nature, perhaps cyclical vomiting, a migrainous type of condition occurring in younger women and affecting the blood flow to the bowel. But when treated for this condition, her symptoms became considerably worse. My professorial friend remained convinced that the problem was vascular, so I arranged a Doppler ultrasound study in my rooms to examine blood flow in the abdominal arteries. My spirits soared as I observed indications of obstructed blood flow in the celiac axis, the main artery to the liver, spleen, and stomach. Surely here was the answer. This was median arcuate ligament syndrome, a rare condition where a ligament from the diaphragm compresses and narrows this artery.

The CT study performed weeks earlier was reviewed. It was normal. An MRI was arranged with some urgency. It was also reported as normal. No evidence of median arcuate ligament syndrome. Discouraged and angry, I challenged God. What was the story here? Why the false hope? I repeated the Doppler lying down, standing, on inspiration and expiration. The findings were indisputable. In my mind the diagnosis was confirmed. That weekend, symptoms became intolerable and, with some trepidation, I approached a senior Sydney vascular surgeon. The condition was affirmed yet again by Doppler in his lab on the Monday morning. Surgery was performed two days later. There was immediate and lasting relief from the symptoms which had plagued this woman's life for many years.

Contemporary health care is a team effort between professionals, patients and family, drawing upon all of the modern resources now available. The inclusion of God into that partnership introduces a level of wisdom and insight otherwise not available.

Some years ago, Lynne and I were acquainted with two women who had both been diagnosed with gynecological cancer. Sheila was an older lady, the mother of one of my advanced trainees, Paul. Lyndell was the young wife of an Anglican cleric. We prayed for both, asking for God's healing and seeking His wisdom in the matter. For the younger woman we received an inner conviction that she would be physically healed, as unlikely as that seemed. For the older lady we received an understanding that she would not survive physically, but that she would be assured of her salvation in Christ and experience a great sense of peace.

The older lady's illness progressed. She had the best of care, but unfortunately the tumor was inoperable. Her son, Paul, had been awarded a prestigious research fellowship to work at Massachusetts General Hospital in Boston to study nuclear cardiology. As the day of his departure approached, Sheila became progressively weak. Finally, the day before the family was to fly out, she was admitted for terminal care.

Paul and his wife were placed in a dreadful position. They decided to delay their trip. But Sheila was adamant. They must leave on schedule. Tickets had been purchased, the family was packed and ready to go, and the hospital in Boston was expecting them. Reluctantly they respected her wish.

By the next evening, Sheila's condition had deteriorated. I sat with her in the darkened hospital room. The ward was quiet; the night staff were busy reviewing schedules and checking medications. Most of the patients were asleep. Morphine had partially numbed Sheila's senses but she spoke rationally. I took her hand, "How are you, Sheila?"

"I'm in pain."

We prayed against the pain and it eased. I continued to question her, "How are you now?"

"I'm frightened."

We prayed against the fear and it passed. Sheila had been a practicing Catholic all of her life but to my understanding, like many churchgoers, she had never actually taken the step of submitting her life to the Lord Jesus Christ. I led her through a believer's prayer. She received a great sense of peace, and within a few hours passed away.

The younger lady, Lyndell, was twenty-three years of age. She and her husband, Richard, had just returned from an overseas trip, a wedding gift from his parents.[63]

Routine gynecological screening had revealed abnormal cell types and she was summoned to the local teaching hospital for further investigation. These tests confirmed the worst. She had a rare "clear cell carcinoma." The doctor's words were devastating: she would require radiotherapy followed by chemotherapy and finally, radical surgery. There was no chance of ever having children. Survival was not guaranteed.

This rare form of carcinoma was known to occur in women whose mothers have taken diethylstilbestrol (DES) during pregnancy.[64] Lyndell's mother had been treated with this medication. The chance of the tumor developing in patients at risk was 1 in 1,000. The condition was said to occur primarily in young women up to the age of 30, and only about 750 cases had been described worldwide.[65]

The young couple prayed and sought further medical advice. The professor at another teaching hospital recommended surgery alone. There would be no chance of ever having children. Lyndell and Richard, understandably distraught, continued to pray for guidance.

The professor consulted with other specialists in his field and confirmed that he wished to operate immediately.

The option of surgery alone gave some hope for later pregnancy, if only hysterectomy could be avoided. Lyndell and Richard were shaken by the turn of events. One management program involved radiotherapy, chemotherapy, and radical surgery; the other, surgery alone. Both approaches had been offered by men highly respected in their field. Lyndell prayed for guidance and searched the Scriptures. In the book of Jeremiah she was encouraged by the words: "Before I formed you in the womb I knew you; before you were born I sanctified you" (Jeremiah 1:5).

With the support of family and friends, and aware of a widening group of people who were praying for them, they decided to proceed with surgery alone.

Their church family was supportive and encouraging. The senior pastor was a tower of strength. Lyndell's mother remembers his words, "Whatever else you can't hold onto, hold onto this: that God is sovereign."

The day before surgery, Richard was to preach at the evening service. He spoke on suffering. At the conclusion of his address, he broke down and wept openly. Those in attendance said that he "stood ten feet tall."

Surgery proceeded as scheduled. Much to the family's relief, the professor decided not to perform a hysterectomy. But surgery was extensive, involving much of the reproductive system and adjacent normal anatomy because the tumor had invaded adjacent tissues. The professor and his team were able to reconstruct the birth canal from tissues which had been preserved. This was groundbreaking surgery and the details are described in the surgeon's published case report.

Lyndell went on to make a total recovery. The operation had been a first in Australia, and her story was covered on the Channel Ten television news and reported as a two-page spread in a Friday edition of the *Sun* newspaper. The *Sydney Morning Herald* published an article on the risks of maternal treatment with DES and the *Sixty Minutes* program on the Nine network also covered the issue.

Best of all, Lyndell went on to have a child by natural means. I met Simon last week for the first time, now a fine young man of 21. "A miracle baby," the professor had called him. As we sat discussing a book that he had been reading, it occurred to me that he would never have been born at all if a hysterectomy had been performed.

Since speaking with Lyndell, I have thought long and hard about the words of the church's senior pastor, "Whatever else you can't hold onto, hold onto this: that God is sovereign." This may sound like an easy option, even a cop-out. But the words are vital to the person in need, and profound almost beyond understanding. They are the rescue rope thrown to the drowning man, something to keep the head above water until the situation can be seen in perspective, until help can be mustered and rescue arranged.

In my specialty of imaging I meet many people who have just received bad news. They are often angry, impatient, and demand attention. They are frightened and confused. Such people, Christian or not, need a rescue rope to hold onto to stop them from drowning. Often it is sufficient for them to know that God is sovereign. He is there and He loves them.

I am confident that there is no simple predictable means by which God intervenes in our lives or the lives of our patients. In the Old Testament he announces, "I am Jehovah Rophe, the God that heals." However, this should not be interpreted in a simplistic manner. If we adopt this approach we will be left with many difficult and unresolved questions.

As an intern I had the privilege of working with Dr. John Sands, a senior consultant physician at Royal Prince Alfred Hospital. With double-breasted suit always buttoned, jet-black slicked-back hair and a soft but resonant, almost gravelly voice, he never failed to remind me of the actor George Raft. He had a giant intellect yet was humble and approachable. Unlike some, he could be contacted at any hour of the day or night without fear of reproach. I called him at 2 a.m. one morning to advise him that a patient had been admitted under his care after taking an overdose of potassium permanganate. Without hesitation he told me what to look for and how to proceed. As a novice, this made a lasting impression on me.

It soon became clear that as I developed a clear line of communication with Dr. Sands and sought his advice on the best way to manage his patients, so he was able to entrust them to my care. So it is with God, when we seek His mind on issues, asking in faith for the best way to proceed, He will often give us an inner witness of how to do this. To determine and to understand God's will in a matter, and then to pray it through, is the highest ideal that we can aspire to as Christians. Sometimes, however, it simply remains a matter of trust.

The principle of consulting with peers and with those more experienced is sound and well established in medical practice. Lyndell and Richard asked God for wisdom on how to proceed while seeking the best medical advice. The professor in turn sought advice from his peers. Finally the best path was chosen.

I stand amazed and truly in awe of God's grace and of His healing power, finding myself firmly plotted on a learning curve which seems to have no end. Though a senior physician now, I will always remain at best an intern of a God whose ways are unknowable and truly remarkable. All He asks is our trust and our availability.

Lyndell remains well and tumor-free and was told in 2007 that she would require no further follow-up. Lyndell's husband, Richard, died suddenly after an acute illness in February 2007. He was 59 years of age. Richard's death poses difficult questions for the believer. Here was a loving husband and father taken from his family at a relatively young age. He was a busy Anglican rector fulfilling a vital role in his parish with many dependent on him for guidance and leadership. He had experienced the miraculous healing and restoration of his wife and the birth of his child, and had seen the hand of God move in a sovereign way.

Why then did God take him? Could not his illness have been cured? Can death be a part of healing?

They shall awake as Jacob did, and say as Jacob said, Surely the Lord is in this place, and this is no other but the house of God, and the gate of heaven,

And into that gate they shall enter, and in that house they shall dwell, where there shall be no Cloud nor Sun, no darknesse nor dazling, but one equall light,

no noyse nor silence, but one equall musick, no fears nor hopes, but one equall possession, no foes nor friends, but an equall communion and Identity,

no ends nor beginnings; but one equall eternity.

John Donne (1572-1631)
Excerpt from his sermon XV

22

More than Conquerors

*T*he *Woodies* is an Australia-wide radio talk show for home improvement enthusiasts. Broadcast weekly on ABC radio 702, it is an absolute must for every do-it-yourself enthusiast. The interest lies not so much in the nature of the questions or even the answers, but in the witty and informative way that they are fielded by resident experts. One such expert was Les.

A regular segment was "Boofhead of the Week" where people painfully related Do-It-Yourself (DIY) disasters. One man was given the job of demolishing a beach house. "Why not," he thought, "tie a rope to the front porch, the other end to the rear end of my truck and pull the house down." He described how he had attached the rope, revved up the motor and dropped it into gear. The truck took off, wrenching the post from its housing, catapulting it out of the yard, back over the truck and across the road, where it hit the electrical wires taking out the power to the entire street. Les was merciless in his response.

Driving home from work one Friday, listening to the radio, I was surprised to hear the announcer fighting back tears. He had received a message from Les's son, "Dad has left the workshop, and he did it in style." Unbeknown to most, Les had been battling a malignancy for some time. It finally caught up with him and he had passed away that morning.

My own father died recently. He was ninety-one, near blind from macular degeneration, and had difficulty hearing, but was mentally alert. He was a fine man and maintained a strong Christian witness. In his last conscious moments he said to my sister, Rose, "I told one of the nurses about Jesus this morning. Do you think she heard me?"

Both of these men, Les and my father, died, and they died well!

Death is guaranteed. It may be delayed by "miracles" of modern medicine, but it is inevitable. To the non-believer, it is finality. To the Christian it has been described as "promotion to glory."

To the Christian, death is transition into the presence of God. To those left behind, it can be painful and harrowing. The mind says one thing, the heart another and, for a season at least, the two are irreconcilable.

To those without faith, death brings closure to a life which may have been wonderful, but is without hope for the future. To the Christian, it is a moment of triumph, the culmination of a life lived in an imperfect world, but entrusted to a perfect God.

I can't begin to imagine what heaven will be like. Singing hymns for eternity is not a proposition that I find attractive. But I know this, heaven will be far more wonderful than anything I can conceive of with my finite mind. As the apostle Paul said, "Eye has not seen, nor ear heard, nor have entered into the heart of man the things which God has prepared for those who love Him" (1 Corinthians 2:9).

Ian McCormack relates an experience that gave him some insight into what heaven might be like. He was night-diving in Mauritius when he was stung five times by lethal box jellyfish. "*C'est fini pour vous*, Ian!" his friends despaired as they witnessed the burns and lymphangitis rapidly developing on his right arm. The potent neurotoxin rapidly took its toll and, after fighting progressive paralysis, he lapsed into coma. Finally he was pronounced dead. But fifteen minutes after he had been taken to the hospital mortuary, to the horror and amazement of the attendant, he regained consciousness.

He describes, as have others, moving through a dark tunnel towards a source of intense light. At the end of the tunnel he saw a realm so wonderful that he could scarcely describe it, but comments, "I knew this was where I was always meant to be." He subsequently made a full recovery, but the event so changed his life that he has spent the subsequent twenty-one years passionately sharing his story and his faith. Skeptics have attributed the phenomenon of witnessing a "bright light" to cerebral ischemia, a situation where insufficient blood reaches the brain. They attribute the religious connotations to prior Christian belief and conviction. Ian, however, freely admits to having no Christian experience or commitment prior to his brush with death.

The Christian's attitude to approaching death will perhaps remain their most effective witness to family and friends. My father's impatience to be with the Lord was something he frequently spoke of, and this comforted and supported our own faith in the days following his death.

Final words often bear witness to people's lives when other memories have faded. The Oxford martyrs Hugh Ridley, Nicholas Latimer, and Thomas Cranmer were burned at the stake in October 1555. As the flames rose round them and before the bags of gunpowder tied to their necks had ignited, Latimer called to Ridley: "Be of good cheer, Master Ridley, and play the man, for we shall this day light such a candle in England as I trust by God's grace shall never be put out."[66] Five hundred years later, those words resound in our ears.

Few of us will have the opportunity to utter such words, but then few will suffer as these men did for their faith.

Dwight L. Moody died in 1899 at the age of sixty-two. His last words were: "I see earth receding; heaven is approaching. This is my triumph. This is my coronation day. It is glorious. God is calling and I must go. No pain...no valley...it is bliss."[67]

Nevertheless, the concept of death is daunting to many because it is unknown territory. However, it is appropriate and desirable that every man and woman approach death in a state of peace and acceptance in which they are able to relate to others their convictions, reflections, and aspirations.

Prominent radiation oncologist John Boyages is Professor of Radiation Oncology at Westmead Hospital and Director of the New South Wales Breast Cancer Institute. John told me, "There is nothing more tragic than when a patient is clearly terminal and refuses to acknowledge this. It denies the opportunity for healing of relationships, closure of issues, and celebration and thanksgiving for that person's life." He has seen this issue cause friction between couples at times when they are most in need of each other's honest and open support.

John came to faith later in life, through a man he met at a father-and-son church camp. He does not conceal his faith from patients and will often tell them that "prayer can really help" their situation. There is to be a new breast center built at Westmead Hospital, and it is his sincere desire that a prayer support group will be an integral part of that center to help patients cope with all aspects of their disease. He places great credence in the words of Philippians 4:6,7: "Be anxious for nothing, but in everything by prayer and supplication, with thanksgiving, let your requests be made known to God; and the peace of God, which surpasses all understanding, will guard your hearts and minds through Christ Jesus."

His palmtop is with him at all times. It contains a modern version of the Bible, in which he has marked certain verses with special significance for him, in particular, Proverbs 3:5,6: "Trust in the LORD with all your heart, and lean not on your own understanding; in all your ways acknowledge Him, and He shall direct your paths."

John has seen many patients die of cancer, young and old, Christian and non-Christian alike. He does not challenge the fact that God may intervene to change the course of a patient's illness, but emphasizes that ultimately we must accept the sovereign will of God. He believes that we must be sensitive to what God is saying in terms of a patient's illness. Maybe an illness is unto death, maybe not.

Contemporary society cushions us from the harsh realities of death and dying. Coffins are now caskets and dying is "passing." "Guarded prognosis," "cardiac event," and "aggressive lesion" are essentially euphemisms. This approach can help us to cope with confronting situations, but can be a problem if it encourages us to remain aloof from the dying process, and from the patient who more than ever needs nurturing, an attentive ear, and compassionate support.

Dr. Martyn Lloyd-Jones agreed that doctors need a healthy objectivity towards patients in crises. Without this, they would be heading for a breakdown. But he also warned that sometimes this could work to the disadvantage of doctor and patient alike. When speaking to a group of doctors, he said that one of the most remarkable things about the average medic was that they faced death more often than anybody else—but did they see it, and apply the fact to themselves, and their day-to-day life? He went on to add that doctors may answer that they are not interested in death, but in health and life. But there is nothing that affects life more than death.[68]

My good friend Dr. George Kostalas is gifted in his approach to the management of the dying patient. His positive manner and readiness to respond are a comfort to his patients. I recall my father's words to him, "Doctor, why won't God take away the pain?"

He replied, "Mr. Crocker, God's task is not to take away the suffering but to lead us through it."

But then George went beyond this. He provided palliative care so that physical suffering also abated, managing pain and distress, and improving quality of life through those uncharted and untested hours. His management of my father's final hours demonstrated in a very practical and specific way a moment-to-moment working relationship with his Silent Partner.

When either the doctor or the patient is a Christian, they introduce into that relationship a third entity. That person is God Himself. People often ask me if I can recommend a good Christian doctor. I tell them that I will recommend a good doctor. That doctor may or may not be a practicing Christian. The faith and trust of the patient alone will place him in God's care. In a situation where the doctor is a Christian and the patient not, the doctor himself brings God into the equation whether or not the patient is aware of that fact. There will be an added dimension of communication when both doctor and patient are Christians. However, God's power to intervene will not be limited if only one has faith.

The personal and family issues surrounding a patient's death may be very complex, requiring sensitivity, and discernment. Health care workers need be aware that there are ways in which they may have a positive input into those final moments of a person's life. These are best understood when they enter into a partnership with Father God and are prepared to draw upon His greater wisdom.

And how can this Silent Partner help? Certainly by bringing peace and acceptance, but also by giving insight and understanding of the issues that need to be dealt with, and by teaching us how to pray them through.

And how do we pray? Do we pray for healing? Do we pray for peace? Do we pray for salvation or for those left behind? However we pray, we must not be presumptuous, nor try to force God's hand to a solution which may not be in the best interest of the patient. What is important is to seek His will in the matter and to pray it through.

As we pray for people, we must remain sensitive and receptive to the manner in which God directs our prayers. A friend recently told me of James Dwyer, his nephew, who had been on a tour of duty in Afghanistan for four months. As a young South African, he had joined the British armed forces. His parents and grandparents were Christian, and three of his relatives had also served with the armed forces. As is often the case with young men, he struggled with the beliefs held dearly by his family members.

His grandfather, Professor Philpot, an eminent South African gynecologist and a Christian, vehemently opposed his enlistment. However, later he became his grandson's greatest supporter, writing to him regularly and encouraging him. James's return letters revealed that he was searching, honestly, for truth, and this in a theater of war where truth is often the first casualty.

His grandmother faithfully prayed for him, pleading with God for his salvation. But then, quite suddenly, as she continued to intercede, her prayer changed. The cry of her heart was this: that he would become a Christian "before the Lord took him." This change in her prayer focus was upsetting to some family members.

On December 27, 2007, on his father's birthday as it happened, his jeep hit an improvised explosive device (IED). Despite valiant efforts by his friends under the most difficult of circumstances, James died within half an hour.

Lieutenant Colonel Rory Bruce of Royal Marines posted of the moving sight of the coffin as it was taken into the RAF transport aircraft, into the empty cargo hold.[69] The last post sounded and there was a salute by two guns of 29 Commando.

James's last letter to his grandfather revealed that he had made his peace with God shortly before his death. He still questioned why there were so many Christian denominations, but he had made a sound commitment of his life to God. He was given a military funeral with full honors in Plymouth, an Anglican service. In South Africa today as I write, the Methodist church in his hometown will hold a memorial service to his life and memory. In the same town the Catholics will hold a requiem mass. He was 22 years of age.

Why this should happen to a fine young man is beyond our understanding, and perhaps too painful to be contemplated at this time. But a loving God knew the train of events and, by the intercession of his grandmother and the encouragement and ministry of his grandfather, brought about a miracle that was to change his destiny. God became James's Silent Partner at the eleventh hour, just in time to lead him home.

Both young and old alike die, often leaving us perplexed and questioning, *why should this be so?* Is God unreliable or inconsistent in His response to our prayers? Does He sometimes fail to anticipate situations? Is He incapable of intervening? Do people die because of lack of faith, or some impasse in their lives which has not been properly dealt with? Do people die because the faith of intercessors is not sufficient? All of these possibilities have been grappled with at some stage.

The fact is this, that we have a sovereign God who holds our lives in the palm of His hand (Psalm 31:15). Throughout my life I have been amazed by His attention to detail, even in minor issues. I have been able to call on Him for wisdom and strength in times of crisis and for help in matters which now seem embarrassingly trivial. He is interested in every aspect of our lives. It would be absurd to contemplate that He is not interested in life/death situations.

My friend Ken lay terminally ill in Royal Prince Alfred Hospital with prostate cancer. His PSA level,[70] which helps monitor the extent and activity of prostate cancer, had risen from 130 in May to in excess of 1,000 in early June. It was now 2,700. He had been admitted this time after a massive gastrointestinal bleed, losing over six quarts of blood.

Blood tests revealed the development of DIC,[71] a condition where essential clotting agents are consumed by the body, and bleeding is unable to be controlled. He became progressively pale and weak as blood loss continued. Finally, after consultation with Ken and his family members, the medical team withdrew active measures of support. Drips were removed and he was transferred to a private room. We gathered around his bed to pray for him and to support him. He was able to repeat after us the words of the 23rd Psalm and this appeared to bring him great comfort.

And then, the next day, the impossible happened. He began to improve, dramatically. Day by day he grew in strength.

I spoke to his resident by phone. "It's remarkable, it really is. It's just wonderful really," she said. "We call him Lazarus. Two days ago his hemoglobin was thirty-nine. We gave him two units of blood. He's awake and telling jokes. We've asked the physical therapists to start to mobilize him and we'll be sitting him out of bed today."

Ken's improvement continued to the point that he was discharged home. Lynne and I visited him that week and shared a meal with the family. He sat at the head of the table and was the perfect host, pouring drinks, and leading the conversation. After the meal we prayed and he retired around 9:30 p.m.

Then, three months later, after a sudden further hemorrhage, Ken passed quietly and peacefully into the presence of his Lord and Master. "I don't want to go," he said, "but I'm ready."

Since his return home, Ken had been able to confirm his Christian faith and had recommitted himself to the Lord. He had also been able to deal with issues in his life that had required attention for some time and was able to bring closure. God gave him that extra time and he knew it. He was aware of these words: "He restores to man His righteousness...He will redeem his soul from going down to the Pit, And his life shall see the light. Behold, God works all these things, twice, in fact, three times with a man, to bring back his soul from the Pit, that he may be enlightened with the light of life" (Job 33:26,28-30).

James and Andrew Melville were known as the "Little Men who would not Bend." They played a pivotal role in the establishment of the Church of Scotland in the sixteenth century, suffering persecution and imprisonment. As James Melville lay dying, he with others celebrated his life and his death. He asked that the candle burning behind him be brought forward that he might "sie to die" and then quoted words from the Psalms: "I will both lie down in peace, and sleep; for You alone, O LORD, make me dwell in safety" (Psalm 4:8).[72]

God is with us at all times. He planned our lives before we were born. He watches over us in the womb and through our early years. When we are old enough and are able to make an informed commitment to Him, He becomes our Savior and our Silent Partner. Through life He is our strength and guide, and in death He is able to lead us home.

Through uncharted days
The light moves on
Like a desert caravan negotiating
The transience of the sand
Like a ship in unsounded waters
Testing the winds

A white form on a narrow road
A solitary figure
Brings light into darkness
Looking forward, always forward
Unstoppable, unquenchable

A seamless garment
Trails in the dust of the day
Is it a shroud?
Is it a robe?
Does it hide or reveal my destiny?

I take hold
But my grip falters
Hand reaches over hand
Taking hold again and again
I will not let go
I will not let go
I will not let go

Until you bless me.

E.F. Crocker, 2006

23

This Hope We Have

My hope is built on nothing less, than Jesus' blood and righteousness...

Edward Mote, 1797-1874

"Whatever I do it must be honoring to God," said James, his words weighed and measured. He had planned to be a surgeon since student days and a neurosurgeon since internship. And now, after years of study, grueling rosters and a rigorous training schedule, he was well advanced in his neurosurgical training.

But something had happened, something he hadn't planned. He had developed a severe form of inflammatory arthritis. His hands were dusky and his fingers swollen. The rheumatologist had not ruled out a career for him in neurosurgery, but he was aware that progression of the condition would severely affect his dexterity.

Others might have been devastated by this recent turn of events, but not Jim. It was tough, but as a Christian he knew that his life and his future lay in God's hands. I marveled at his serenity as he continued, "Whatever I do, it should have an application to the mission field...just in case." He was intelligent and determined and, best of all, he was prepared to submit himself to God's will in the matter.

There was no immediate solution, but the answer would come. He was buoyed on by trust and hope, based on living faith. That hope would be his anchor until the situation was resolved.

As a departmental director of Westmead Hospital, I enjoyed a close working relationship with the chaplains. Many became personal friends, and would often drop in for coffee and a chat.

A businessman invited me to display copies of a Christian men's magazine in our patients' waiting room. It contained testimonies of businessmen, professionals, and academics whose lives had been changed by their faith in God.

One of the most interesting stories was that of Dr. Ben Carson, an eminent pediatric neurosurgeon at the Johns Hopkins University Hospital in Baltimore. Ben had begun life in a Detroit ghetto. His mother was one of twenty-three children. As a lone parent she struggled to raise her two young boys without financial support, while having to cope with recurring bouts of depression often requiring hospitalization. As a child, Ben was plagued by failing grades. As a teenager, he developed a violent temper, on one occasion almost killing one of his friends. His mother had a strong Christian faith. She affirmed and encouraged her boys constantly. Her faith and trust bred hope and encouragement within her sons. They began to realize the potential within themselves to do great things. Ben improved his grades dramatically and with God's help overcame his temper. He went on to top his school academically. He was offered a scholarship to West Point, but his great passion was to study medicine. Completing pre-med at Yale, he went on to specialize in neurosurgery at the University of Michigan and Johns Hopkins University Hospital, Baltimore.[73]

Ben continues to practice at Johns Hopkins, where he has been Director of the Division of Pediatric Neurosurgery since 1984. He is currently Professor of Neurosurgery, Oncology,[74] Plastic Surgery and Pediatrics. He is also co-director of the Johns Hopkins Craniofacial Center. His special interest is the separation of conjoined twins, fused at the head.

Ben's story was a true story that would surely bring hope to anyone in need. Wishing to remain politically correct, I asked the chaplains for permission to display the magazine. Some were in favor, some non-committal. One openly opposed my request. "Why, you might give patients false hope," he argued. I considered his words: "False hope." Surely to deny the validity of hope was to embrace hopelessness. Was hope in God misplaced and therefore false?

I thought of prominent Christians who had been in seemingly hopeless situations. The German theologian Dietrich Bonhoeffer was hanged on the personal order of Heinrich Himmler after being walked naked to the gallows, but maintained his hope and faith in God to the end. His life has been an inspiration to generations.[75] Bonhoeffer's hope transcended that of physical deliverance from Nazi persecutors. It was hope in the eternal deliverance of Almighty God. Surely it had not been misplaced.

I thought also of my friend, Dr. Li, in Central China, whose story is told in chapter 5. He had been stripped of medical responsibilities, humiliated in front of his family, and criticized publicly. But he maintained hope and faith in a God who would never let him down.

I considered what it meant to hope in God. In Hebrews Paul says, "This hope we have as an anchor of the soul, both sure and steadfast, and which enters the *Presence* behind the veil, where the forerunner has entered for us, even Jesus" (Hebrews 6:19,20).

Paul had been speaking of God's promise to Abraham that he would have a son even though he was an old man and his wife was well beyond childbearing age. William Barclay explains that in the ancient world the anchor was a symbol of hope.[76] The important thing about an anchor is that it holds the whole ship, not just part of it. Hope in God sustains the whole person, body, mind, and spirit.

An anchor can hold a ship in treacherous waters. The anchor chain passes through depths which are unseen and unknown, to hold the anchor which is secured by bedrock. To the Christian that rock is Christ himself.

Worldly hope is optimism or positive thinking—to be encouraged for sure, but dependent on factors that are temporal and uncertain. Christian hope is a free gift poured out in our hearts through the Holy Spirit who has been given to us" (Romans 5:5). The Amplified translation says that hope "never disappoints or deludes or shames us." *The Message* paraphrases Romans 5:3-5 this way:

There's more to come: We continue to shout our praise even when we're hemmed in with troubles, because we know how troubles can develop passionate patience in us, and how that patience in turn forges the tempered steel of virtue, keeping us alert for whatever God will do next. In alert expectancy such as this, we're never left feeling shortchanged. Quite the contrary—we can't round up enough containers to hold everything God generously pours into our lives through the Holy Spirit!

We understand from reading God's Word that we will never be left feeling shortchanged. There will be trials and tribulations, but these produce patience, and patience produces character. Character brings hope and hope does not disappoint.

Hope sustains us and gives us reason to go on. When we hope for healing, the initial plea of the heart is for physical healing and relief from suffering.

There are many causes of illness and suffering. Sometimes we are responsible by exposing ourselves to stress, smoking, excessive alcohol, drugs, or poor diet. Other times a disease process may simply declare itself with no obvious underlying cause or precipitating factor. In whatever situation, God is receptive to our prayers.

I believe our first recourse is to conventional medicine. If conventional means fail, then God alone is able to intervene. He may choose to heal us physically. He may call us home to be with Him. In either situation, He is sovereign and His decision is beyond questioning. Either way, hope must be linked with trust in a loving God who wants only the very best for us.[77]

In Proverbs we read, "Hope deferred makes the heart sick, But when the desire comes, *it is* a tree of life" (Proverbs 13:12). To deny hope to a patient is to compound an illness by adding to it a negative spiritual dimension which may adversely affect the disease process. I have seen patients who have given up hope and accelerated their demise. The absence of hope also gives false credence to the voluntary euthanasia movement which is rapidly gaining momentum in our society.

I am not saying that as Christian doctors we should withhold our considered opinions from patients regarding the seriousness of their illness.

It is our responsibility to be frank and honest. Patients expect and deserve this from us and most want to hear it "as it is." However, God's healing often starts where medical expertise fails, and we have no right to crush a patient's spirit by denying them hope.

Christian doctors are in a unique position to counsel and advise. They must be sensitive to their patient's hopes and expectations, considering these in the context of medical knowledge, yet remaining receptive to the many ways in which God may wish to intervene.

Occasionally, healing may be rapid and without incident. Other times it may occur over an extended period and require prolonged prayerful support. The physical healing process should not be seen in isolation. Often the Lord has a wider agenda of healing that deals with spiritual issues, family relationships and personal matters that need to be put right. It is important to be mindful of God's promise that "All things," yes, "All things work together for good to those who love God, to those who are called according to *His* purpose" (Romans 8:28), and sometimes this requires time.

There should also be an understanding that a patient may not recover physically. There is nothing more tragic than the patient who dies hoping for physical healing but unable to countenance that this may not occur. There are affairs to be settled, relationships which need attention and family members to be prepared. I have had close friends die, adamant that they would be physically healed. There were many things that I wished to say to them, but these were not acceptable as they would be interpreted as a lack of faith on my part.

Hope is valid for both doctor and patient alike. It applies to every aspect of life: personal, professional, and spiritual. It is not something to be left at the office when we return home at night, or to remain on our bedside table when we set off for work in the morning.

Enduring hope is one of God's great gifts to us. It is His will that we embrace it wisely. When problems come they are generally unexpected. The first casualty is often peace of mind, even before we have had the opportunity to assess the gravity of a situation or decide how it might be approached. For this reason we are told to put on as a helmet, "the hope of salvation" (1 Thessalonians 5:8). This helmet will clothe and protect our minds until the situation is understood and finally resolved. Hope is truly an anchor of the soul (Hebrews 6:19).

And so my young neurosurgical friend continues to wait upon God for guidance. He is actively seeking direction and knows that God will not fail him. Maybe he will continue in neurosurgery, maybe not.[78] One thing is sure, when we place our complete hope and our trust in God, He will guide and lead us according to his own perfect plan. And when the right decision is made it will be confirmed by a peace of mind and spirit that only comes to those who abide in Him.

> This I recall to my mind, therefore I have hope. Through the LORD'S mercies we are not consumed, because His compassions fail not. They are new every morning; *Great is Your faithfulness.*
>
> *(Lam. 3:21-23, italics mine)*

Sports people, media personalities, even ex-presidents and prime ministers use their influence to sway public opinion. Yet members of the medical profession are forbidden to use their position of influence to impose their personal opinions and beliefs on their patients. And this is exactly as it should be. When patients approach a doctor, they do so from a position of dependency and trust. It would be unethical for a doctor to knowingly and wilfully take advantage of this.

Nevertheless, doctors must remain true to themselves. Their approach to issues that encroach upon the sanctity of life, such as abortion, human cloning, and euthanasia, must be in harmony with their spiritual convictions. They may have chosen a career path in medicine in response to their faith, and it is reasonable to expect that they will practice in that context. Ideally, the doctor's approach to patient problems is determined by knowledge, experience, compassion, and by clear, objective insight. Each of these is tempered by the doctor's moral values and spiritual awareness. This is not something to be legislated against or suppressed.

In Australia we respect the rights of the individual, and freedom of religion is sacrosanct. Doctors should not only be able to worship freely, but also to live and practice according to their convictions, as long as these are not in conflict with the law of the land.

However, just as the doctor's rights are respected, so too must the rights of the patient be respected. It is therefore not unreasonable that a patient be aware of the doctor's spiritual convictions in so far as they may impact his decision-making and patient management.

A doctor's compassion for those in need is focused by faith and finds expression in practical means, arising from a relationship with the Living God.

24

Being There

While the earth remains, seedtime and harvest, cold and heat, winter and summer, and day and night shall not cease.

Genesis 8:22

"Please come to the patient waiting area immediately." The voice over the paging system was compelling and I knew that I must act immediately.

The patient was sitting with his wife, who was clutching a small child. The little girl, clinging to her mother's knee, was sobbing.

I had not met him before. He was a big man—353 lbs. according to his chart—and with the appearance of a Pacific Islander. He was young, early thirties, but despite his youthful and robust appearance was clearly unwell. Turning to his notes I read that he suffered from dilated cardiomyopathy, a condition where the heart muscle weakens and contracts poorly. It had weakened to the point where he had developed left ventricular failure. His lower limbs were swollen and he was breathless. He had been waiting for transportation back to hospital after a procedure, but had become light-headed and nauseous. His heart was racing and his systolic blood pressure was low.

I moved him onto a bed and gave him oxygen to breathe. An ECG showed no acute changes and he soon began to feel better. His wife sat closely by, holding his hand. Both were fearful and clearly intimidated by the austere clinical environment. She began to cry. My heart went out to them and I wondered what I might do to comfort and assure them.

Placing a hand on his shoulder I quietly prayed in my spirit, asking God to strengthen him and to take away their fear. Transport soon arrived and they were gone, but they were comforted, and they were assured. Somebody cared, somebody understood.

A doctor is often rewarded with the opportunity of being in the right place at the right time. It is wonderful to bring comfort and support to patients in need. It is even better to be able to bring them good news. Patients talk about "good news" and "bad news" all the time. "Is it good news, doctor? I hope it's good news. I can't deal with any more bad news."

One of the richest rewards in medicine is to be able to reassure a patient and allay their fears. The expression on the patient's face is its own reward. But it's better still if we are in that place of privilege where we can sensitively share our own faith and hope, and speak into their own situation of need.

My friend, Dr. Tony Dale, relates tending to an elderly gentleman who had suffered a cardiac arrest and been resuscitated. Tony attended the patient on the morning of his discharge to confirm that all was in order and to say his goodbyes. As he walked away from the bed and out of the ward, the Lord spoke to him and said: "That man thinks you are wonderful. All of the people here think you are wonderful. But none of them know why!"

Immediately, Tony was reminded of a verse from Isaiah: "How beautiful upon the mountains are the feet of him who brings good news" (Isaiah 52:7). "I knew," he later told me, "that God was challenging me to be much more open about the source of life within me, and to share with my patients, staff, and colleagues about Jesus." He was also acutely aware of a second verse in Isaiah 42:8 where God says, "I am the LORD, that is My name; and My glory I will not give to another, nor My praise to carved images." God will not share His glory with another.

Patients will often recognize in Christian doctors a dimension of love and care not always extended in health care. Sometimes the patient knows that the doctor is a Christian, sometimes not. The love and compassion the patient senses flows from the very heart of God.

People miss wonderful opportunities not just with strangers but also with close friends and relatives, because they are uncomfortable with illness and perhaps a little embarrassed. Sometimes just being there is enough. A word in season can be a powerful blessing. And it is more important to listen than to talk. Physical contact too is extremely important. A firm grip of the hand and a quiet word of assurance can make a world of difference.

Sam is one of the new breed of medical students who has entered medical training as a postgrad. He was born in South Korea where his father was assistant pastor to the renowned church leader, Paul Yongi Cho. "When I was a kid and sick in bed," he said, "my mum or dad's hand on my head as I went to sleep meant so much more to me than any of the medicines they might have. I really believe that it's so important to support patients and offer them strength and comfort."

As Christians we have within us the Holy Spirit, that same Holy Spirit who raised Jesus from the dead. One characteristic of the Holy Spirit is described by the Greek word "Paracletos," which means to come alongside to strengthen and comfort. By sharing our Christian love with patients, we bring them into contact with God's Holy Spirit who will comfort, nurture, strengthen, and encourage.

It is important to lean heavily on God for wisdom and for the right word to say. This is rarely given in advance, but generally comes just as it's needed. I stood discussing a patient's test result with him one afternoon only to hear that he had experienced a dreadful personal tragedy that very day. My mind raced ahead looking for some way to help him. But there seemed no way. I quietly asked God for wisdom. Almost immediately the conversation turned, providing an opportunity to bring a helpful word. That quiet word in the busy waiting room brought healing to us both.

"Being there" is all about appropriating God's purpose and timing. The opportunities of which I speak are not random events. They may be pivotal in the lives of those to whom we speak, and occur at times of critical need. This is often recognized only in retrospect. My eye doctor friend, Rob, whose story is told in chapter 7, says that he has given up trying to convince anybody of anything. And he's probably right. "It's the Holy Spirit who convicts, in *His* time," he says. Our responsibility is to be receptive, available, obedient, and ready.

Peter and Rachel are Christian GPs who do not overtly promote their practice as Christian, but have Scripture verses on display in their surgeries. They see themselves as treating the whole person, attending to the patients' physical needs, but also to their personal, social, and, where appropriate, spiritual needs. *Holistic* is a term they happily apply to their method of practice. They pursue excellence in practice, and see the provision of "quality medicine" as an integral part of their Christian witness.

Both pray for their patients privately, and also with the patient when they feel it appropriate to do so. Peter sees himself as "planting seeds" that will one day bear a harvest.

Rachel says, "All healing is of God. He will often give me specific insight as I require it. Sometimes when I need wisdom for an individual patient I pray for it and it comes. He gives me a bigger vision of what to do."

Peter is often involved in palliative care, and he marvels how God will give him the strength to deal with difficult situations. One patient, a relatively young woman with widespread malignancy, was not seeking physical healing but believed that her life and death would be a witness to many. Her faith and trust in God, Peter says, was a powerful witness to the entire medical practice.

Rachel tells of two sisters who would not allow their father to discuss his faith with them. Within a twelve-month period one of the sisters developed cancer and their father also became terminally ill. As he lay dying, one of the daughters read the Scriptures to him. He was just sufficiently conscious to hear the words. The daughter was challenged by the words she read and has since become a Christian. It is likely that the father had prayed for his daughters all of their lives, hoping and trusting to see them saved. But God was faithful, and the seeds sown over the years finally generated new life, in God's perfect timing.

I recently reviewed the studies of a man with metastatic cancer which had spread throughout his body. There had clearly been an improvement in his situation after chemotherapy.

"Something's working for you," I said.

"I believe that God is helping me," he replied. Then he told me a remarkable story. Fifty-eight years before, his mother in Italy had given him a crucifix. He was not a religious man, but he had kept that crucifix in his bottom drawer all those years. When he developed cancer he took out that crucifix and began to pray.

In Australia we know that seeds may lie in the ground for years until an event such as a bushfire causes them to germinate. So with the seeds that we plant in people's lives. They may lie dormant for decades until some crisis causes them to germinate, as with this man.

The days of our lives are as seasons. In Ecclesiastes we read:

> To everything there is a season,
> A time for every purpose under heaven:
> A time to be born,
> And a time to die;
> A time to plant,
> And a time to pluck what is planted;
> A time to kill,
> And a time to heal;
> A time to break down,
> And a time to build up;
> A time to weep,
> And a time to laugh;
> A time to mourn,
> And a time to dance...

Ecclesiastes 3:1-4

As Christians, God uses us to speak into the lives of people according to their needs, according to their season. Sometimes we plant the seed. Other times we tend to seeds planted by others. Sometimes, just sometimes, we

201

participate in the harvest. But one thing is sure: "While the earth remains, seedtime and harvest, cold and heat, winter and summer, and day and night shall not cease" (Genesis 8:22).

Lie Shian, just Lie to her friends, has been a solo practitioner in western Sydney for most of her working life. Petite, attractive, and in her early fifties, she is feisty, animated, and her voice rings with confidence and hope. She refers to God as her "invisible boss" who encourages her, strengthens her and gives her wisdom to press on, even in the most difficult situations. As she speaks, her face radiates God's love. But it has not always been that way.

Lie was born in China. Her family migrated to a small village in Western Borneo after the communist takeover, a region now notorious for independence violence. Family members were not Christian, and most of the villagers engaged in animism (the belief that spirits inhabit natural objects) and ancestral worship. But Lie's grandfather converted to Catholicism shortly before his death and, as a result, the whole family converted. Family members would gather in the evening to recite the rosary, under the strict supervision of Grandmother. During one of those family gatherings, Lie experienced a spiritual encounter that has remained with her all of her life. "Christ came to me," she said, "and held my hand. He had such a look of love on His face. Even now I see Him holding my hand in the home." She was eight years old at the time.

At fifteen years of age, Lie traveled to Sydney to join her brothers and sisters to complete her education, and after graduating from high school, was accepted into the medical course at the University of New South Wales. She embraced all of the student distractions of university life. "God was still there," she said, "but I just saw Him as the one to help me when I was in need." She continued to recite the rosary and dutifully attended confession and mass. "But I had no personal relationship with God."

Two years out of medical school, she commenced general practice in the western suburbs of Sydney. She met David, a young attorney, fell in love, and soon they were married. "All of my goals were achieved," said

Lie. "I had success, respect, financial security, and a happy marriage. But my life was focused on *my* goals and *my* glory. There was something missing and I felt empty inside. My self-centeredness brought me great pain.

"But the mercy and grace of God had not left me."

At twenty-eight, looking for meaning and fulfillment, she began to attend a local church where she experienced the love of Jesus in a personal way. She went on to accept Him as her Savior. "My life changed completely," she said. "I saw His hand on every part of my life. I remembered my experience as a child when He came to me and took my hand. I had hurt Him but He forgave me. He rescued me, and gave me a new heart."

Lie's new relationship with God has revolutionized the way in which she practices medicine. "I was released," she said. "I am no longer pressured to look good or perform, in front of patients." There is often pressure from patients to support personal needs. This might involve agreeing to termination of an unwanted pregnancy, submitting a favorable medical report, or providing an unjustified certificate. "Sometimes I say to God: 'What do I say and what should I do?' He always provides the answer. I have counseled so many young women against termination. They come back later with their baby and thank me for my advice."

Lie was recently consulted by an older man seeking euthanasia for a terminal illness. She counseled him against this. Visiting him at home she encouraged him and read passages from the Bible, in particular the 23rd Psalm: "Yea, though I walk through the valley of the shadow of death, I will fear no evil; for You are with me" (v. 4). She also read from Revelation about heaven and what he should expect. The man eventually died of his illness, but before doing so, accepted Christ as his Savior. He died well, at peace, without fear and with great expectation.

She thanks God also for wisdom and strength to deal with patients who may be seeking drugs of addiction, and has learned to write prescriptions in such a way that they cannot be tampered with.

With their permission, Lie will often pray with patients. One patient had severe limb pain due to nerve root compression, which had not responded to surgery. The patient was a computer programmer. Sitting for hours at a computer console produced agonizing pain. After prayer he was completely relieved of his pain.

A close friend developed small cell carcinoma of the lung, and was treated by removal of part of the lung. But the tumor recurred in the other lung, close to the cardiac border. The area was treated with radiotherapy. Lie and her friends gathered together and prayed for this man. The tumor completely disappeared and, five years later, has not recurred. Subsequent X-rays showed no evidence of tumors or of post radiotherapy fibrosis. The man has subsequently become a Christian and has entered a theological training college.

Lie makes no secret of her faith. Emblazoned across her waiting room on a banner last Christmas were the words: "Jesus is the reason for the season." She is occasionally challenged regarding her beliefs, but is greatly respected in her community for her caring attitude, her quality of practice, her passion, and her faith. I have had the opportunity of speaking with many of her patients. Without exception they have expressed love and affection for her.

Recently, Lie was baptized in her local church. She had been baptized as a Catholic in her Indonesian village at age ten, but felt the need to reaffirm her faith in a public manner. On the day of her baptism she wrote these words:

> "I want to know Christ and the power of His resurrection and the fellowship of His suffering, becoming like Him in His death" (Philippians 3:10). I want to be baptized as a true believer. In my spiritual walk over the years, my old self often raises its ugly head. My struggle and my sinful desire have not been easy. My baptism shall be a mark of grace to remind me daily that "It is no longer I who live but Christ who lives in me."

Three times Geoff was suspended from Granville Boy's High, and fifteen times he was caned. *Aput se pugne*, the school motto, translates: "He prepares for the challenge." But the boys had another interpretation: "Ready for the fight."

"Some guys carried knives and you had to defend yourself," he said. "You could never show your soft side."

It was the late '70s in the wake of Vietnam. Young people questioned everything, trusted nobody—authority figures and politicians in particular. Skinheads and gangs ruled in the western suburbs of Sydney. Geoff was a Christian, and helped to lead the Interschool Christian Fellowship. He constantly had to defend himself and to give an account of what he believed.

With help he managed to transfer to another school where he applied himself diligently. At the final exams, to his delight, he qualified to study medicine at the University of New South Wales.

As a medical student he doubted his abilities. An older friend advised him to take his mind off himself by reaching out to others. "If you can help one person a day you've done well. Ask yourself each morning: 'Who can I help today?'" Geoff found that as he extended himself to others, so he regained confidence and self-assurance.

During the clinical years, Geoff incurred the wrath of one of his professors, a man well known for his ready temper. Finally, things deteriorated to the point that Geoff appealed to the dean. The issue was resolved in his favor, and Geoff was grateful to God for His help. "I knew He got me into medicine and I knew that He wouldn't let me down," he said.

Geoff completed general practitioner training, gaining extra qualifications in obstetrics and pediatrics, and joined a group practice in Sydney. A young mother brought a sick child to the surgery suffering from what appeared to be a mild viral illness. Geoff treated him symptomatically and arranged some tests, but that night the child collapsed and died. It was later established that he had a pre-existing problem. But Geoff felt "gutted." He began to doubt the reality of his Christian belief. Why would a loving God allow this to happen?

"What if it's all a hoax?" he asked. "What if it's all a façade? What if Phillip Adams is right after all?" (Adams is a well-known Australian atheist.) Geoff believed in a historical Jesus. But was Jesus alive today and was He relevant? Searching for confirmation, he finally resolved to ask God for a sign.[79]

Soon after, a friend invited him over one Saturday afternoon "to pray for a young man who needs help." The young fellow was described as demon possessed. Here was something of which Geoff had no experience whatever.

The young man had been heavily involved in the occult and his mother claimed to be a witch. "He seemed normal enough and was well presented." As they began to pray, the man's voice changed. It became guttural and unrecognizable. He began to blaspheme, utter obscenities, and behave in an indecent manner. "He passed wind for forty-five minutes," said Geoff. "I didn't know that was physiologically possible!" With growing spiritual awareness, Geoff perceived the man's voice as demonic. "Finally," he said, "I was aware of a 'cold presence' leaving the man. His voice returned to normal and he regained composure." The cycle was repeated several times until finally the man appeared to be free of whatever powers had controlled him, and was at peace. Geoff returned home, shaken.

The events of that day remain clearly etched on his mind. "I'd been looking for a sign, a reality," he said, "some proof that I could lock into. God showed me that all right. He said to me, 'You want a sign, I'll show you the other guy.'" Geoff never again doubted the reality of spiritual powers or the existence of a personal God.

Geoff describes God as his Enabler and Empowerer. "Sometimes I will be astounded by a diagnosis that I am able to make and I ask myself: 'Where did that come from?'"

He has observed healing beyond his comprehension. A patient with an inoperable brain tumor was prayed for by her church and family. Her symptoms resolved and a progress CT scan showed no sign of the tumor. "Such situations are extremely rare in my experience," he says, "but when they do occur they are a powerful witness to God's presence."

Geoff lives in a semi-rural area of Sydney. He is a warden of his local Anglican church and also runs the men's group. "Men and their sheds— that's what we call it," he said. "Each month we visit a guy's home. He gives us a guided tour of his shed and tells us what he does there. After that we have a time of devotion, and then supper. It's a really good night.

There was one guy, he had five beautifully restored vintage cars in his shed. You'd never know it to talk with him."

Geoff's life is spent helping and encouraging others, both in clinical practice and in the wider community. That's the nature of the man. Perhaps it is because of this that God has entrusted to him and his wife a child who is incapacitated, but making wonderful progress.

"As I get older I recognize more and more that God uses ordinary people to do extraordinary things," he said. "It all depends on whether we are willing to make ourselves available when He calls us. I am constantly aware of how vulnerable we are in this life, and you can't take it with you. You'll never see a hearse with a tow bar."

25

A Country Practice

God planned it. We didn't do it. We didn't even try. He just did it.

Rob, general practitioner

It was still dark as I dragged the heavy farm gate and closed it behind me. Snow was falling and a biting south-westerly reminded me that spring was several weeks away. The drive east to Cooma would take an hour, maybe longer, and would be treacherous. I strained to see the road ahead through the icy windshield, the headlights navigating a passage through falling snow.

I was to meet several partners from one of the Cooma practices over breakfast. In my pocket was a list of questions, but I knew that I must put aside any preconceived ideas of where the discussion might lead.

Winding through the sleeping town of Berridale, I recalled my first meeting with Brian, one of the doctors, twelve months earlier.

"Oh, Brian, he's a champion fellow," said one of the locals. It was clear that the doctor was well respected by the members of this farming and business community. Young and vital, he had a permanent smile and a tousle of blond hair. He wore an open-neck, checkered shirt and a red thermal jacket. Though quietly spoken, he was a man's man, keen to share his faith and his passion for rural medicine.

Brian had grown up on Sydney's North Shore where his father was a doctor and his grandfather a clergyman. He had been captain of The

King's School, one of Sydney's most prestigious schools, and had also captained their first eleven at cricket.

Graduating from Sydney University and completing residency, he studied anesthetics in the UK, returning to Australia to take up a training position at Gosford Hospital, north of Sydney. After short periods in general practice, one in a mining town in the Northern Territory where he was doctor to an Aboriginal community, he returned to country New South Wales to practice in the town of Inverell.

Brian's wife, Effie, also a doctor, with specialty training in obstetrics, had grown up in the Greek Orthodox tradition, but without a personal faith. Brian was nominally Anglican. While living in Inverell, they decided to have their first child baptized. The minister at the Uniting Church introduced them to a program called "Christianity Explained" and it was through this that they both became Christians.

Soon after, Brian was invited to join a group practice in Cooma, a town of 8,000 people at the foot of the New South Wales snowfields. He was to discover that other doctors in the practice were also Christians.

Brian explained that he and his partners made no secret of their faith, but did not openly promote their practice as Christian. "We're strongly orientated to family needs," he said. "We provide hope and love where it's needed. As doctors we carry some influence in the community. It opens doors for us to help people.

"The partners," he told me, "meet weekly for prayer and to discuss practice issues." This also gives them opportunity to pray about their patients. "We've looked for ways to help our community beyond medical means. We run parenting classes, and are planning a course on sexual health issues for adolescents.

"I am reassured by God's presence and I am comfortable in my belief," he added. "This allows me to help others in difficult times...even though the going can be very tough. I can look back and trace God's hand moving in situations." Brian takes comfort in Philippians 4:6,7: "Be anxious for nothing, but in everything by prayer and supplication, with thanksgiving, let your requests be made known to God; and the peace of God, which surpasses all understanding, will guard your hearts and minds through Christ Jesus."

A few days before we met, Brian had worked until midnight at the base hospital only to be called again at 4 a.m. to continue until 7 p.m. that night. One evening he was called in to resuscitate a newborn baby. At the same time an elderly man, critically ill, was brought into emergency.

"I really had to depend on God for strength and wisdom. But I find my strength in weakness, and I can honestly say, 'when I am weak then I am strong'" (2 Corinthians 12:10).

I had pondered Brian's comments a great deal since that first meeting. The sky cleared as I approached Cooma. The temperature was just a few degrees above freezing and the wind howled down the broad main street. A few souls braving the elements scurried to their destinations in parkas and thermals, faces turned from the gusting wind.

We had arranged to meet in a small café next to the surgery. It was bustling with people in mountain gear quaffing coffee and making short work of large helpings of eggs and bacon. The shopkeeper directed me to a back room, where Brian and David were warming themselves before an open fire. We greeted one other warmly, ordered hot drinks and settled into comfy chairs around the fire.

I had spoken with David before about his experiences in Papua New Guinea (PNG) with the patient bitten by a taipan snake and another with a ruptured uterus (chapter 19), and was glad to renew his acquaintance. "After moving back to Australia," he said, "I learned to fly a light plane, and it was at that stage that one of my friends suggested that I consider joining a Christian medical practice. We decided that our Christian faith should be an integral part of our professional and personal lives."

David and his partners experience all of the advantages and disadvantages of working in a rural community. Together with a second practice, they are responsible for the wellbeing of the 8,000 residents of the town and surrounding farmlands, and of many visitors to the snowfields each year. Although they practice obstetrics, anesthetics, and some general surgery, there is no specialist surgeon in Cooma, and medical imaging is limited. There is now no private radiology in Cooma, and until recently the hospital had no CT facility. Ultrasound is available, but there are no specialist imaging doctors to provide on-site reports. They are also required to participate in the seven-day, twenty-four-hour on-call roster at the base hospital.

David values the collegiality and mateship of his partners, and the immediate availability of their wide-ranging skills. "But I still need to walk in God's strength as I did in PNG," he said. "Here I am surrounded by confidence and competence. Here it's easy to depend on others more and God less. This has been one of the biggest challenges to me, especially as I move more and more into procedural work. Sometimes with a difficult appendix I just have to ask God for help. Difficult deliveries can be a real problem, especially shoulder dystocia,[80] where there is a risk of breaking the baby's arm. In those situations you just need God's help."

We ordered a second round of coffee as Christian arrived. He was the most recent doctor to join the practice, a big man, bespectacled, with a wonderfully honest and open face. "I'm still settling in," he said. "It will take me a while."

Christian was from a Lutheran background. His family had migrated from Germany when he was a year old. He had been baptized as a small child and confirmed at age fifteen, but then left the church. "But at twenty, I came back to the church. This is when the Gospel first hit me. It was then that I realized what it was all about. I had come back to something real, to family," he said.

At Flinders University he completed medical training, and then went on to study theology in the Lutheran seminary at Adelaide. The partners refer to him as their practice theologian.

"The work is busy and very demanding," he said, "especially the on-call. You just can't predict what will come up next. I don't always have the continuity of patient care that I would like. People with injuries from the snowfields just want to be fixed up and go home. Often my wife and

I pray for them after they have left, that God will continue to look after them."

Rob was the last to join us. He was on-call for the base hospital and was anticipating a busy day. In red wool jacket and rural attire, he looked very much part of the practice. He shook my hand firmly. From his confident manner and open smile, it was clear that he was a man with purpose and direction.

Rob joined the practice in 1992. He grew up a nominal Presbyterian in Sydney, and became a Christian through Dawn, his wife-to-be, when they met in the UK in 1988. "You can't marry me unless you are a Christian," she said. Rob became a Christian and his life has never been the same since. But it has been full of challenges. "Eleven years ago I developed melanoma. They gave me two years to live. And now, eleven years later, there is no sign of disease. That again changed my life.

"We had no vision for what we were to do here," he said, "but God knew. He *told* us what to do. I had always thought it was better to be a Christian doctor working in a non-Christian practice. But God had a different idea. When Brian and David and I needed another doctor we advertised on the web for two years with no result. Finally we decided to advertise for a Christian doctor, and within forty-eight hours we had one—Christian! God planned it. We didn't do it. We didn't even try. He just did it."

There are now seven doctors working in the practice. These include the full-time partners, a casual, and Brian and Rob's wives on a part-time basis.

All of the doctors attend the local Baptist church. "Many churches consist of groups of people holding hands looking in," Rob said. "We want to be a group of people holding hands looking out."

The church operates a parenting program called "Growing Kids God's Way." The practice also supports a program called Childwise. It is "Growing Kids God's Way" in a non-Christian format, and as such it can operate through the community college. The doctors applied unsuccessfully for federal funding and have underwritten the program financially themselves. It has now been extended to include pre-teen and teen components.

Brian excused himself. There were patients to see. But Rob settled back. There was more to say, and he hadn't yet received his first call out. "I'm aware of the growing pressures on the doctors of this practice," he said. "We have to get priorities and relationship with God right. God first, family second, practice third. There is no point if your practice is running well and your boy is out in the back shed shooting himself."

The partners are aware of the demands upon them personally and on their families and practice. "A country GP is used to being able to handle all of the situations that arise. But our practice has developed into something different, and will require different people with different areas of expertise working together to help share the load, if we are to participate in the wider plan that God has for us," said Rob.

Some years ago at a medical conference in Sapporo, in the northernmost Japanese island of Hokkaido, I found myself looking for a quiet spot to prepare my notes. Entering the great hall of the conference center, I found it to be completely empty. As I sat in the half darkness, a young woman in casual clothes walked on stage, violin in hand. She was soon joined by others with various instruments. Each began to tune up and then practice. The combined sound of the musical instruments, together with the chatter, was an assault to the ears.

And then a young man walked to center stage dressed in faded blue jeans and a black T-shirt. A *stagehand*, I decided. But within seconds there was absolute silence and then, with one stroke of his hand, the auditorium was filled with the most glorious music. This was the Sapporo Symphony orchestra, and the man in blue jeans, the conductor. Each member had come together with a specific skill and a mutual love for music. Under the hand of the conductor, uncoordinated noise was transformed into the most beautiful music.

The doctors of this country practice have specific skills and strengths. Some are anesthetists, others have obstetric or surgical expertise and another, an interest in palliative care. One has a pilot's licence and mission field experience. One has a love for teaching and one, formal theological training. Another has worked in an Aboriginal community. But

God brought them together, finely tuned their skills, and set them to work to accomplish something truly wonderful. As Rob said, "God planned it. We didn't do it. We didn't even try. He just did it."

— 26 —

Watch One, Do One, Teach One

And in Your book they all were written, the days fashioned for me, when as yet there were none of them.

Psalm 139:16

The lines of his Bible were underscored and highlighted with yellow ink, but he pointed enthusiastically to words which had come to mean so much to him: "The days of our lives are seventy years; and if by reason of strength they are eighty years, yet their boast is only labor and sorrow" (Psalm 90:10).

I listened in astonishment. Most people in their early 70s would find these words daunting. But Doug's interpretation was somewhat different. "I am seventy-one," he said, with a broad smile, "and this verse tells me that maybe I have ten years, and there is so much to do in that time."

Doug had been a general practitioner all of his working life and has recently retired, although he will never retire in the true sense. He greeted me with a bear hug and his trademark grin. A big man, partly balding and with a goatee beard, he is the kind of person that immediately puts you at ease. We sat on his balcony overlooking bushland, the chime of bellbirds loud in our ears.

Doug has a number of chronic illnesses, most of them potentially serious. But unlike others I have met, he is not debilitated by these. Rather, he focuses on them as a means of maintaining his wellbeing.

Doug was born in Wollongong, an industrial town south of Sydney, into a non-Christian family. His sister had been disabled by birth injury and his parents, bitter and disillusioned, could not entertain the concept of a loving God. At seven years of age, Doug experienced an overwhelming awareness that one day he would become a doctor. "Dr. Doug," his mother mused, wondering what the future might hold for this small boy.

As a young man, he began medical studies at Sydney University. Campus life offered more to a boy like Doug than academia alone, and he embraced it all to the point that by the end of year one he had managed to fail every subject. "I can't afford to keep you," said his father. "Pass next year or you are out." A wiser man, Doug repeated year one, this time passing every subject, with some credits. It seems likely that his newfound success was partly attributable to Shirley, also a medical student who was to become his life partner.

Doug joined the Evangelical Union, and under the ministry of its president, Dudley Foord, developed a strong Christian faith. His parents protested, but there was little they could do. Doug and Shirley were also strongly influenced by the ophthalmic surgeon Dr. John Hercus who was renowned for testing patient's eyesight by their ability to read verses from his Bible. They were also influenced by Dr. Paul White, the "Jungle Doctor," who spent much time with them and other Christian medical students, counseling, and encouraging.

After final year they were married, and accepted residency positions at The Royal Newcastle Hospital, with the intention of training for country practice. Residency completed, they were invited to practice at Delegate, a small town an hour's drive from Cooma in the southern snow country of New South Wales, population 600. There were no other doctors in town, and facilities were extremely limited. Anesthesia, when necessary, was still given by drip ether. They accepted the posting on condition that the town purchase a modern anesthetic machine.

Doug and Shirley very quickly learned to practice what they called "survival medicine." There was no specialty support, no satisfactory means of transporting critically ill patients, and no transfusion service. But they built a mutual trust with the townsfolk and local farmers, tending to their needs 24/7. "I believed then, as I do now," said Doug, "that people just need a doctor who will be on their side."

Doug performed simple surgery while Shirley gave the anesthetic. "I remember an impossible appendix," he said. "I just could not find it. I had to send up one of my 'Please help!' prayers."

Major trauma from working farms and resulting from motor vehicle accidents on country roads posed enormous problems. "I just couldn't get the patients out. They would die in transit." His answer: to build an airstrip large enough for a small plane to land. For the first time, patients could be airlifted to regional centers to receive specialist emergency attention.

There was also an urgent need for a blood transfusion service. Doug set up a transfusion register, which included 100 townsfolk. At last, blood could be cross-matched for transfusion on demand.

In 1961, sensing the time was right, Doug and Shirley moved on to Wee Waa. This larger town in northern New South Wales had a forty-bed hospital. Again they would be the only doctors. The scenario was the same: no modern anesthesia, poor transport, and no transfusion service. Doug enlisted the help of the local Rotary Club to build an airstrip. A transfusion registry was established, and of course a modern anesthetic machine procured.

The town's climate was severe. For more than six months of the year, the temperature rose above 95 degrees (35 degrees C). But this meant it was ideally suited for cotton. When Doug and Shirley arrived, twenty-eight acres were under cotton. When they left in 1975, 50,000 acres were under cultivation. And with cotton came American immigrants. The town population grew dramatically.

In the early 70s, the charismatic movement swept Australia. Doug and Shirley discovered a new dimension to their faith. Twenty-three people in their small Anglican church experienced what they referred to as "the baptism in the Holy Spirit." The richness and the intimacy of the fellowship, with God and with each other, lives with them still.

Doug had always wanted to teach, and the isolation of rural practice provided little opportunity. In 1975 he learned of a Department of General Practice to be established at Liverpool Hospital on the western outskirts of Sydney. Here was an opportunity to train other young doctors. After prayer and long consideration, Doug and Shirley were so convinced that this was what Doug was meant to do that they sold up and moved to Sydney. It was a huge step of faith—but in retrospect, somewhat presumptuous.

Doug was to discover that without a postgraduate degree he could not be admitted to the faculty at Liverpool Hospital. There followed a time of searching and deep questioning of God's purpose. They had left their home, their friends, their practice, and there was a growing family to support.

Doug took on locum assignments, searching for new direction, and finally established a family practice at North Rocks in north-west Sydney. The practice was built on Christian principles. As it grew and partners were taken in, it was accredited for GP training, and Doug was able to fulfill his dream of training young doctors for general practice.

Doug has a wonderful approach to life. Where many people identify a problem, he sees an opportunity. In our contemporary lifestyle we expect everything to be available, on credit, automated, fully serviced, and procurable by means of a quick phone call or a few seconds punching keys at a computer terminal. If it is "too hard" we are often not interested. If one provider can't satisfy today, we turn to one who can. Our approach uses the system. Doug's approach sets the agenda for a new and better system, one that would not exist without prayerful consideration and perseverance.

Doug walked me back to the car. As I opened the door and felt the rush of heat from inside the cabin, I heard my cell phone. It was my mother. My dad was very ill. I knew that I would need to take him to hospital that afternoon. As I later sat in the emergency department watching my father receive an IV infusion, I thought of Doug's reaction to life's difficulties. "Maybe I have ten years," he said, "and there is so much to do."

Render unto Science

All I know is that it's people who are important, God and people—not the "sexy" side of medicine.

Sam, medical student

J ohn Carew Eccles strode the halls of John Curtin School of Medicine like a general, hands flourishing, white coat flapping in his wake. A small band of associates struggled to maintain the pace as he theorized and expressed his views on everything from postsynaptic inhibition to his passion for folk dancing.

As a medical student I had been privileged to work with Sir John at the Australian National University during my Bachelor of Medical Science year. Perhaps it was because I was a student that he confided in me many of his philosophical views of life, including his belief in God. He challenged my own views, occasionally passing me handwritten manuscripts from friends abroad requesting, "Comments by morning please."

He was a polymath and one of the finest medical minds that Australia has known. Born in Melbourne in 1903, he won a Rhodes scholarship to Oxford in 1925 where he worked with Sherrington, the father of modern neurology. His work on the mechanism of neuronal transmission earned him a Nobel Prize in medicine and physiology in 1963, and that same year he was made Australian of the Year.

During the 1963 Nobel Prize celebrations, he gave a banquet speech on behalf of the laureates, concluding with these words: "I am passionately devoted to the study of life, and particularly to the higher forms of life. For me the one great question that has dominated my life is: What am I? What is the meaning of this marvellous gift of life?...May God bless you.[81]

He was a driven man, and ran his labs accordingly. Teams from abroad worked twelve-hour shifts in the many-shielded rooms of his department, some commencing at 6 a.m., others at 6 p.m. Over a sixty-six year period from 1928, he contributed 567 papers to the literature, one published posthumously in 1998.

In 1966, facing compulsory retirement from the Australian National University, he left Australia to take up a prestigious research position in Chicago, later moving to the State University of New York. I never met the man again, but watched his progress with interest. In 1983 he published a series of papers on the meaning of life. These included: "The human mystery: a lifelong search for truth,"[82] and "The self-conscious mind and the meaning and mystery of personal existence."[83]

Sir John retired to Switzerland where he died in 1997. To my understanding he died as he had lived, in a personal quest for God and for the meaning of life.

He was one of the most remarkable men I have known. Having known him, I knew that I could not complete this book without talking to Christians involved in pure (laboratory) research. Such people do not have the immediate feedback or rewards of those in clinical medicine. Theirs is an often lonely walk towards an unseen goal, with little encouragement or reward. Failure is a recurring companion, but often the substrate from which many of their ideas evolve. What drives these people, and in what manner do they relate to God?

I arranged to speak with Dr. Nick West, a young molecular biologist on the way up. Nick is engaged in tuberculosis research at Sydney's Centenary Institute.

"Did you know that there are 2 million deaths from tuberculosis each year," he said, "and 8 million new cases? One third of the people in the world are infected with tuberculosis." He went on to tell me of the increasing problem of co-infection with HIV, especially in African countries, and of the huge problem of multi-drug resistance. There is a new term, "extensively drug resistant," now written XDR-TB.

Whereas much of Nick's work has been directed towards the development of new vaccines, he is now focused on the gene structure of the Mycobacterium. "It's amazing," he said. "How can simple bacteria attack and destroy so many tissues and adapt to tolerate every onslaught the body and modern drugs can throw against it?"

Nick was recently awarded a prestigious New Investigators Grant by the National Health and Medical Research Council, to study the genetic profile of TB and to see how this could be modified to make it vulnerable to therapy.

He explained that he was examining gene sequences in the bacterium. "We need to recognize the important ones, knock them out, and then see what the bacterium can't do," he said. "If we can find the essential gene products that the bacterium needs to survive and cause disease, we can devise drugs to block those pathways."

I asked him if there was a particular verse of Scripture that had special meaning for him. "Yes..." he said, hesitating, "I don't want to seem bigheaded, but these words from the Psalms are important to me: "The steps of a good man are ordered by the LORD, And He delights in his way" (Psalm 37:23). In these words he finds promise of purpose and direction. The end point of his work is often not clear and he must trust God for direction and the means to proceed.

Nick is very much aware that discipline and order are vital to him as a Christian and as a researcher. He must accept the disappointments with the successes, knowing that God is in control and that he alone has the foresight and the vision. His PhD project as a young science graduate did not appeal at all. It involved a study of the bacterium which causes a whooping cough-like disease in animals (also known as kennel cough). After praying the matter through and committing himself to the work, he was surprised to find that the research equipped him with the experience he required for the next stage of his career.

He qualified to participate as a key member in a four-country EU-funded research program in Oxford working with principal researchers from Oxford, Paris, Rome, and Brussels. This experience enabled him to return to Sydney to a prominent research laboratory, and has impacted on the success of his current research grant.

Leanne is Nick's wife. She has a degree in biotechnology and is responsible for the design and implementation of new clinical trials for a pharmaceutical company. Her work relates to drugs which make cancer cells sensitive to chemotherapy agents. "Sometimes I battle with the results," she said, "and I ask God to help me understand what it all means. He gives me that knowledge and sometimes I have to ask myself: Where did that come from?"

The scientific training they share allows them to advise and support one another in an informed manner. But their mutual faith in God, the third partner in their marriage, allows them to share in a deeper way the challenges and the blessings of their journey, and to pray for one another when times are tough.

I interviewed Professor Warwick Britton at his home on a wet winter's evening in July 2007.

After negotiating Sherpa, the family dog, and meeting family members, I settled into discussion with Warwick and his wife, Annette—a dialogue which would continue past midnight.

My questions were put aside and, as Warwick spoke, I wrote, and prayed that God would show me how his hand had been extended through the life of this extraordinary man. He did.

Sydney's Royal Prince Alfred Hospital in the 70s was a production line for prospective physicians. A well-oiled machine fueled by tradition and zealous institutional pride cranked out candidates at an alarming rate. There were twenty-four in my year alone, with few failing to pass the mark.

It was onto that stage that young Dr. Britton, university medal in hand, made his entrance into the medical residency program. His aspirations, fired by an undergraduate degree in pathology and a short stint at a mission hospital in Thailand, were towards scientific research and missionary work, an unlikely combination. Mission work was not viewed as appropriate by the powers that be for someone of his academic potential.

Residency completed, and after a short dalliance with pediatrics, Warwick entered into a coveted gastroenterology training position and was on track to becoming the clinical superintendent. But the lure of the Third World was far too strong and, in 1978 Warwick, with Annette, also a doctor, and their 2-week-old son set off for training at All Nations Christian College near London. From here they traveled to India, and finally on to a 100-bed hospital in a remote area of Nepal.

Warwick took charge of adult medicine and pediatrics, and Annette oversaw obstetrics and the leprosy patients. With the help of a surgeon and medical assistants, they triaged and treated 600 hospital outpatients per day, often three at a time. All of their resources were stretched and they were sorely tested. "Nepal is one of the poorest nations on earth, and 85 percent of our income to run the hospital came from the patients," said Warwick. "We only had thirty-nine drugs, but with those we could treat 95 percent of illnesses."

Even so, God surprised them by His grace. One day a man came to the clinic. The whites of his eyes were yellow and it was clear that he was deeply jaundiced. "I suspected he had liver cancer and that there was little I could do for him." His family planned to take him down to the 'sacred river,' Kali Gandaki, which flowed down from the high plains, so that according to Hindu ritual he could sit with his feet in the water to die. They believed that his spirit would flow into the waters and downstream into the Ganges. As a parting gesture, Warwick gave the man a large dose of the drug metronidazole. It would have no effect on cancer, but it might help if the man was suffering from amebic dysentery and its complications.

The man sat with his feet in the water for three days waiting to die.

Three months later a group of men came to the clinic and sat in a corner until others had gone. "Do you know who this man is?" asked one. He pointed to the man who had been jaundiced, now perfectly well. After sitting with his feet in the river for three days, the man had been taken home by his family. There he had made a full recovery. "And you said he was going to die," chided the spokesman, to the amusement of his friends. Warwick suspects that the man indeed may have had a large amebic abscess in his liver which responded to the medicine.

But after three years in Nepal, the desire to participate in research remained strong. Warwick made the decision to return to Sydney to begin a PhD program which would take several years. This would be difficult as he was already 32.

In Nepal he had developed a fascination for leprosy. "It was a great enigma," he said. Until 1960, nobody had been able to grow it in the laboratory. This was largely because the bacterium is so slow-growing. It takes fourteen days to double, compared to twelve hours for tuberculosis, and only twenty-two minutes for E.coli.

"Dapsone had been an effective medicine against leprosy in the 70s," Warwick continued. "But we were now noticing an increasing resistance to drug therapy. Treatment using multiple drugs in combination had been introduced and seemed to be working. But I thought: leprosy is a disease of the body's immune system. The whole disease process is an immune reaction against the organism."

Warwick wrote to the World Health Organization (WHO). If he could obtain the leprosy bacterium then he could make antibodies against it. "When I look back, it was a bit out of line for a PhD student to write to WHO offering his laboratory's facilities," he added, "but I did."

The response was short and to the point: "You provide the research protocol and we'll give you the bacteria."

"You are on your own," said his supervisor.

"We knew very little about the organism," Warwick explained. "The idea was to break it up into little bits that we could understand."

Ten milligrams of pure leprosy bacilli were received from the WHO. These were injected into mice, and eventually thirty-six antibodies were identified. "We shared these with laboratories around the world," he said. "A laboratory in Boston using one of my antibodies found the gene that stimulated T cells." These cells play a large role in immunity. The results were published in the prestigious journal *Nature*.[84]

Warwick remained torn between research and Third World medicine. In 1986, having completed his PhD studies, he was invited to return to

Nepal to run a research laboratory at the Anandaban (Forest of Joy) Leprosy Hospital about nine miles from Kathmandu. His thesis was submitted the night before the young family flew out to Kathmandu.

For eight months, local politics prevented Warwick from entering the hospital. During this time, he taught medical students in Kathmandu. When permission was finally given to enter the hospital, he worked six days out of seven. He shared time between teaching in Kathmandu and hospital work, traveling up to 31 miles per day by motorcycle. Some of the roads were treacherous and he suffered two serious falls. "You can't go into automatic when you ride there," he said.

With the help of Paul Roche, an Australian scientific officer, Warwick set up a small laboratory at the hospital to study leprosy. Since that time, fifty scientific papers have come from that lab.

In 1989, recognizing the growing educational needs for their family, Warwick and Annette decided to return to Australia. Remarkably, an invitation was received from Professor Tony Basten offering a senior lecturer position in Immunology at Sydney University. Warwick at that time did not regard himself as a clinical immunologist, but accepted the post and quickly geared up to the role.

With others he extended the work of his PhD thesis and built on results from the studies at Anandaban. Eventually he was able to develop a leprosy vaccine. This work took eighteen years to fully complete.

In the years that followed, Warwick's work expanded. "In the 90s, TB took off," Warwick said. In the eighteenth century it had claimed one in seven adult lives in Europe, but by the 1970s it had largely been controlled. In the 90s, fueled by the spread of HIV/AIDS, it became rampant again. In 1993 the WHO proclaimed it a world enemy. "At that time, most of the leprosy people switched their attention to TB research."

Warwick is currently working on developing improved vaccines for leprosy and TB. His research seeks to understand the body's immune response to leprosy and TB by examining the cells and the small protein molecules which carry signals between the cells to change them. There has already been good success in this area.

He is also trying to find out why some people are more prone to these diseases than others.

"Susceptibility to tuberculosis is 30 percent genetic and 70 percent due to environmental factors," Warwick continued. "Some people's DNA makes them more prone, whereas on the environmental side, conditions such as malnutrition, diabetes, and HIV/AIDS make people more susceptible."

Since 1990, sixteen PhD theses have been completed in the Centenary Institute under Warwick's supervision. He has recently been awarded a $4 million Wellcome[85] grant to work in collaboration with others to determine all of the genes in mice that control tuberculosis.

It was nearing midnight. I glanced at my pages of scribbled notes festooned with line diagrams and arrows drawn by Warwick, and marveled at the story I had heard. But there was more, something more, that God wanted to tell me about this man. I pressed in. "Does God lead you on a daily basis?" I asked.

"God is with me in a general sense," he said. "I pray and read my Bible, but I use the skills that He has given me. To be a researcher you must have perseverance, an eye for detail and, inquisitiveness most importantly, dogged inquisitiveness. In high-end science, most things don't work and you have to be inquisitive as to why. You can't do things in a slipshod manner. You must be sure of your methods and know that faulty technique is not the problem."

From Warwick I learned that one of the keys to success is being able to handle failure well. The first lesson from failure was to learn to examine your methods and techniques to see if they were faulty. The second was to determine why something had failed and to learn from that. The third was to pursue the possible benefits that may arise from an understanding of why something failed.

It was the very elements of this man's nature that had enabled him to discern and pursue God's will for his life and to realize such a level of success. A God-given interest in science and Third World medicine developed into a passion. From that passion grew a vision, and from the vision, a strategy. The strategy, however, was God's. It was clearly apparent in retrospect, but from Warwick's perspective it was a walk of faith, one day at a time.

"God calls us in ways that we would not predict," he said. "I could just as easily have gone to theological college. But he gave me an overall direction that I would never have chosen, especially through leprosy. We must understand," he went on, grinning broadly, "that God's will for our life is God's will for our life."

At this stage he became quite animated. "The best job we ever had was in that little 100-bed hospital in Nepal. We knew we were needed there and we knew we were in God's will. But God brought us back to Royal Prince Alfred Hospital in Sydney, where I knew if I rolled over tomorrow someone would step up to take my place. We asked ourselves: 'Why have we ended up here?' But as Christians, God taught us to trust Him."

Again and again, Warwick found himself in situations where, as he said, "I had the commitment, but others had the skills." In Nepal he required language skills, expertise in tropical medicine and a deeper understanding of physiology. Back in Sydney, newly learned skills allowed him to complete an outstandingly successful PhD project, eventually leading to the development of a vaccine for leprosy.

Warwick finds strength in community, both in his spiritual walk and as a professional. He understands that corporately as Christians we are the "body of Christ," each one contributing according to their own special attributes and strengths. In his work, Warwick claims that the best results are achieved in a community of researchers looking for ways to communicate and work together.

I had one more question. It was the first that I had planned to ask but somehow it now seemed almost irrelevant:

"How do you deal with the controversy between faith and rationalism?"

"I don't see it as a problem," he said. "When you have faith, you don't have to leave your brain at the door. Ultimately you come to a place where you need faith, faith in God. I would say to Richard Dawkins[86] that you can argue against faith in God but eventually you will need forgiveness."

He then went on to tell me an amazing story about two young boys who had walked for fourteen days to reach the small hospital in Nepal where they knew they would find people to teach them of God's love and forgiveness. All the boys had to encourage them to go on were Bible texts written on strips of paper and a hunger for knowledge and forgiveness.

Every life begins as a new page, a fresh canvas, a new Word document. If we look carefully at that page and hold it to the light we will see there is always a watermark that reads: "God's plan for your life." As the plan is revealed it generates excitement, but often some uncertainty. It is not a plan that we might rationally choose for ourselves and may not sit comfortably with family or friends. It is a plan that is destined to take us beyond our comfort zone. It is the only plan that if followed will bring peace and fulfillment.

"God's will for our life is God's will for our life," Warwick said, "and that's the truth of it."

> And it shall be that every living thing that moves, wherever the rivers go, will live. There will be a very great multitude of fish, because these waters go there; for they will be healed, and everything will live wherever the river goes.
>
> Along the bank of the river, on this side and that, will grow all kinds of trees used for food; their leaves will not wither, and their fruit will not fail. They will bear fruit every month, because their water flows from the sanctuary. Their fruit will be for food, and their leaves for medicine.
>
> *Ezekiel 47:9,12*

Epilogue: Programmed to Live

In 1867, primarily due to his wife's asthma, Dwight L. Moody went to England. As he sat with his wife and friends in a public park in Dublin, Evangelist Henry Varley remarked, "The world has yet to see what God will do with a man who is fully consecrated to him." That saying spoke to Moody's heart, and he determined to be just that man![87]

I n the preface to this book I described the hand of the master weaver moving across the loom to produce an intricate life tapestry far beyond our creative means and ability. The weave is as complex and varied as the lives of which it is composed.

There is, I believe, a golden thread which appears from time to time in the weave. It is often best seen from afar, but will occasionally shine brightly in the light of a normal day. It is the element of the fabric that ensures integrity and permanence. Without that thread the cloth would be erratic and unstable. It would fray and fragment. When seen it is unmistakeable. It is the hand of God himself.

The lives of witnesses recorded in this book are as varied as might be found in any profession, in any society, at any time in history. Though complex, they embrace all of the normal everyday experiences, the successes, failures, hopes and aspirations and, at times desperation, common to us all.

The experiences of God vary widely. Some have witnessed the miraculous, others have not. Some have been snatched from near certain death. Others have led more sheltered lives. But the nature and the character of God is unchanged by experience and each has clearly discerned the true character of God in their life.

Having read this book, you may ask: "Just what is a normal Christian life? What can I expect in my daily walk with God?" This question recurred to me each time I conducted an interview, or reviewed the manuscript. Each life was extraordinary. Each was unique. But each shared one common element of faith: trust in a Living God.

Watchman Nee in his book, *The Normal Christian Life*[88] maintained that the normal Christian life was something quite different from the life of the average Christian, and could be summarized: "I live no longer, but Christ lives His life in me." The normal Christian life is anything but normal.

Most of us live within the comfort zone of daily routine. Security is important to us, so too are success and lack of conflict, also the assurance that we have not missed our potential. The game plan for our lives is based on our concept of what constitutes success and happiness. What we fail to understand is that God has so much more in store for us than we could ever imagine. The potential for our life is so much greater when we allow Him to live in us and through us, than when we live by our own resources.

Each life represented in this book displays direction, design and a sense of destiny. Each also demonstrates a pattern of progressive spiritual growth and development. Each has been touched at some point by Almighty God and, from that encounter, has ensued a vision and a means to achieve that vision. Continuing trust has been required, as sometimes the vision has been revealed one day at a time, sometimes over many years, sometimes over a lifetime.

I began with the intention of exploring the way in which God impacts on the lives of Christian doctors and their families. The brief was a simple one, to faithfully record events and experiences of doctors both in their private lives and in their practice of medicine.

What I completely failed to anticipate was the torrential cascading effect of God's grace into the lives of patients, staff, families, friends, and acquaintances. The grace of God is not contained within individuals but overflows into the lives of many. What in the life of one might begin as a small stream flows into the fertile plains of the spirits of others, bringing healing and new life. As it flows into new territories it gathers volume and momentum, exposing, cleansing, shaping, and regenerating. It may be contained for a season, but will eventually overflow its banks and move on. It is unquenchable.[89]

So I observed that where God brought healing into the life of John, my radiologist friend, so God used him to bring healing to the lives of others through the St. Andrew's Healing Ministry. Through John, God also influenced others to be actively engaged in this ministry. I saw also that where God brought healing into the life of Professor Don Tredway, an eminent teacher and physician in his own right, so those abilities were sanctified to reach out into the lives of many others internationally.

I observed that where God brought Christian doctors together into group practice, he first of all brought healing, regeneration, and encouragement to them as individuals and to their families. Through those doctors, God brought healing, restoration, and guidance to their community. They began to reach out to people with marital problems, and drug and alcohol addiction, and sponsored a course for young people on sexual health.

As I listened, I heard how God had touched the life of a grandfather in a small village in Western Borneo. The grace of God has continued to flow through three successive generations of his family, crossing cultural barriers, and geographic boundaries. The impact of his walk with God is now poured out upon the people of western Sydney through the love of his granddaughter, a busy general practitioner.

Donald Dale, born of medical missionary parents in south-western China, had no memory of those early years. After becoming a Christian, he developed a burning desire to serve God in China and did so for many years, bringing healing and salvation to many.

And God's plan for our lives may be revealed even before our walk with God begins. His Word says, "Before you were born I sanctified you"

(Jeremiah 1:5). At seven years of age, Doug had an overwhelming calling to become a doctor. "Doctor Doug," his mother mused. The work he commenced in remote country towns continues, and the Christian family practice he established in Sydney's northern suburbs continues to thrive in the hands of others.

It became clear that when men and women are prepared to submit their lives to God, they enter into a path that is both preordained and assured. Though steps may falter and direction seems unclear at times, God has the vision and the oversight. Trust in and obedience to Him will confirm, sometimes only in retrospect, that the course taken was the correct one. God does not take us down blind alleys but will sometimes take us into situations where experience is gained for the journey ahead.

As I spoke to doctors, the same words recurred over and over again: "He shall direct your paths; He shall direct your paths." Those paths led through the US, Britain, China, Nepal, Yemen, India, Taiwan, New Guinea, Indonesia, South Africa, Borneo, Afghanistan, universities, country New South Wales, and government departments. And always, God was there, preparing the way.

And as the direction of the path is defined—so too is the destination. The journey will not end one day before God's appointed time. As a doctor I have watched young Christians die, and I have seen people taken in their prime. Always the question is: Why? Why would a loving God allow this to happen? I have seen other Christians live to advanced age. There is no simple answer, but my belief is this: that God has a specific purpose for our lives. That purpose may be achieved over many years, or in just a few. Our times are indeed in His hands (Psalm 31:15), and the days of our lives were written in his book, "When as yet there were none of them" (Psalm 139:16).

I marveled as Professor Bob Batey related how God had miraculously saved him from near-certain death on two occasions, and I have known others in similar situations. My own confidence is this: that I will live every day that is required to achieve the tasks that God has given me.

I observed that partnership with God is a two-way relationship. Whereas people may recognize God as their Silent Partner, the One who is always there to empower, encourage, and provide, they soon find that being God's partner lifts them into another realm, another dimension of living. As they submit their way to God and become available to Him, so they find themselves on His agenda, involved in fulfilling His will.

So my professorial friend, Warwick Britton, after making himself available, found himself ministering to lepers in the high country of Nepal. So the young Ken Clezy, a small boy growing up on a farm in Western Victoria with the "call of the gospel" on his life, found himself saving the lives of Christian missionaries struck down by the bullets of a Muslim extremist in the Middle East.

Though our search for God may begin as a personal quest for meaning and eternity, it has the potential to impact and change lives. Though an encounter with the living God may constitute a new beginning, it is so much more than that. It is the unleashing of a source of godly power, wisdom, and grace that will flow through us to the lives of others, as long as we are receptive and obedient to Him. This is our heritage, this is our inheritance, and this is our purpose.

And the new life that we live in Christ is a better path by far than any other that we may choose to travel. The way at times may be challenging and formidable, but God always provides the means to deal with new and unexpected tasks. And when the time is right, He will provide other hands to help carry the load so that others may "run with the vision."

How easy for me to live with You, O Lord!
How easy for me to believe in You!
When my mind parts in bewilderment
or falters,
when the most intelligent people see no further
than this day's end
and do not know what must be done tomorrow,
You grant me the serene certitude
that You exist and that You will take care
that not all the paths of good be closed.
Atop the ridge of earthly fame,
I look back in wonder at the path
which I alone could never have found,
a wondrous path through despair to this point
from which I, too, could transmit to mankind
a reflection of Your rays.
And as much as I must reflect
You will give me.
But as much as I cannot take up
You will already have assigned to others.

Aleksandr Solzhenitsyn
Words inspired by Psalm 73:25,26[90]

Therefore we also, since we are surrounded by so great a cloud of witnesses, let us lay aside every weight, and the sin which so easily ensnares us, and let us run with endurance the race that is set before us, looking unto Jesus, the author and finisher of our faith, who for the joy that was set before Him endured the cross, despising the shame, and has sat down at the right hand of the throne of God.

Hebrews 12:1,2

The Bottom Line

With each interview I waited patiently and expectantly, knowing that eventually each person would speak the words that I needed to hear, words that would reveal the very essence of that person's journey. Sometimes these words were lessons drawn from life experience and a progressive trust in God. Sometimes they reflected sheer wisdom that only God could reveal, and indeed I regarded these as words of knowledge given in critical times by the Spirit of God. Often these words were life-changing to the person involved, and many of them have had a major impact on my own life. As I listened, a light would switch on in my spirit as these words were uttered. I share some of them now for your own blessing.

- "God planned it. We didn't do it. We didn't even try. He just did it." *Rob, general practitioner, chapter 25*
- "We have to get priorities and relationship with God right. God first, family second, practice third. There is no point if your practice is running well and your boy is out in the back shed shooting himself." *Rob, general practitioner*
- "Whatever else you can't hold on to, hold onto this: that God is sovereign." *Lyndell's pastor, chapter 21*
- "God said to me, "Stop looking at yourself and try Me out." God gives me the capacity to get up and get on with the day." *Professor Bob Batey, gastroenterologist, chapter 10*

- "If you feel constrained and you feel you are talking with God, then you've got to do it." *Dr. Russell Clark, physician, chapter 8*

- "I realized that I worshipped a mighty God, and I began to expect Him to do the impossible." *Dr. John Saxton, radiologist, chapter 20*

- "Render to scientific medicine the discipline of science, and to God and His Word the discipline of faith." *Dr. John Saxton*

- "We stood there, transfixed by the awesome sight of the massive tree trunks ascending into cloud. It was God's cathedral and we claimed it as His theophany. We stood there praising and worshipping him." *Dr. John Saxton*

- "You never know what's next from day to day, so you have to be ready to 'go with the flow' no matter what happens. God never changes; He is the only constant. Without that knowledge I'd go nuts." *Jenny, nurse, chapter 7*

- "'The days of our lives are seventy years; and if by reason of strength they are eighty years, yet their boast is only labor and sorrow (Psalm 90:10).' I am seventy-one, and this verse tells me that maybe I have ten years, and there is so much to do in that time." *Doug, retired general practitioner, chapter 26*

- "I believed then, as I do now, that people just need a doctor who will be on their side." *Dr. Doug*

- "My life changed. I saw His hand on every part of my life. I remembered my experience as a child when He came to me and took my hand. I had hurt Him but He forgave me. He rescued me, and gave me a new heart...In my spiritual walk over the years, my old self often raises its ugly head. My struggle and my sinful desire have not been easy. My baptism shall be a mark of grace to remind me daily that 'it is no longer I who live, but Christ who lives in me.'" *Dr. Lie Shian, general practitioner, chapter 24*

- "I'm a depressive and it doesn't take much to push me over. But I've found that 'when I am weak, then I'm strong.' It's not my backbone, but God's backbone...that time of depression didn't make sense. I asked myself: where's God in this? But [He] took me out. He was very good to do that. It actually took my problems to prize me out of my comfort zone." *Michael, surgeon, chapter 14*

- "All I know is that it's people that are important, God and people—not the 'sexy' side of medicine." *Sam, medical student, chapter 27*

- "I know what it's like to say goodbye to God and go down to the path of the dead...The Hebrew man sells himself into slavery for six years and the seventh year he is freed. I went six years and six days...I learned how to seek God's face rather than His hand. I learned to seek God for Himself rather than His healing. I had to ask myself: Will I be led by Him? Will I trust Him?" *Linda, general practitioner, chapter 13*

- "It was like death and resurrection. I entered hospital on the Thursday to receive a death sentence that evening. Friday was all about dying. On the Saturday I slept for the first time in many weeks. But Sunday they moved me out of the ICU into the general ward. I was greatly improved. That was resurrection!" *Rosemary, heart patient, chapter 15*

- "Shut up, woman. If I can't explain it, it doesn't exist!" And later: "The more I praised God, the more my strength returned." *Don Tredway, professor, chapter 4*

- "When you have three close friends gunned down while you're having breakfast—that shocks you like nothing else can." And later: "When so many people in the Arab world think Christians are ogres of Caucasian origin who drop bombs on you if you are Muslim, it seemed important to do what we could to show that wasn't so." And again: "If you don't walk the walk you may as well forget about talking the talk. All I can do is display grace and peace. They'll say, 'Clezy, he either fits the mold or he doesn't.' They download the Scriptures from the Net, so they know what to expect." *Dr. Ken Clezy, general surgeon, chapter 12*

- "Maybe an illness is unto death, maybe not. There is nothing more tragic than when a patient is clearly terminal and refuses to acknowledge this, denying opportunity for healing of relationships, closure of issues, and the celebration and thanksgiving for that person's life." *Professor John Boyages, oncologist, chapter 22*

- "I knew He got me into medicine and I knew that He would not let me down." *Geoff, general practitioner, chapter 24*

238

- "I am a Christian, and I am not afraid." *Elderly professor in central China, chapter 5*

- "I wanted to be a neonatologist but God had other ideas and led me into general practice. He trained me, so I do it. He gives me a bigger vision of what to do." *Rachel, general practitioner, chapter 24*

- "It was like when the Israelites were led in the desert by a pillar of fire by night and a pillar of cloud by day. Well, my pillar was on the move." *Anna, Australian Embassy doctor, Jakarta, chapter 11*

- "I could not have made it through that day in my own strength. I was scared. I was five months pregnant and completely out of my depth. I had been running and jumping fences and I just wanted to go home...But I was the embassy doctor that day, relieving the regular doctor who was away on leave, and I just had to do it." *Anna*

- "I have given up trying to convince anyone of anything. It is up to the Holy Spirit to open hearts and minds, to allow people to see the Scriptures as they are." *Rob, ophthalmic surgeon, chapter 24*

- Q: "If you think you are nothing, how can you offer yourself to God?" *Kel Richards, Anglican Television*
  A: "You are offering God a total wreck and asking Him to make something decent out of it. It's amazing what He can do." *Dr. Donald Dale, missionary doctor, chapter 6*

- "When you have faith, you don't have to leave your brain at the door. Ultimately you come to a place where you need faith, faith in God." *Warwick Britton, professor of Medicine, chapter 27*

- "God's will for your life is God's will for your life." *Professor Warwick Britton*

- "I've lived thirty-five years. I have everything that I have ever wanted including a wonderful family. Do I keep going and live another thirty-five or am I supposed to die now?" *Bob, primary care doctor, chapter 15*

- "God showed me that He is the Great Physician and I'm just the assistant. He's the boss." *Brad, family doctor, chapter 16*

- "God said to me, 'All truth comes from Me and all people can do is to distort that truth or discover it.'" *Paul, psychiatrist, chapter 17*

- "You can see tears in their eyes. They've been looking in the wrong mirrors all their lives." (Speaking of the women inmates of a South Carolina prison.) *Paul, psychiatrist*

- "We had a group of native leaders come to our community. For three days they prayed for the bloodshed and the broken treaties and covenants in our region. They released a blessing and a prayer over the prison and over our program. Within one month the cost of medication that I was prescribing dropped by two-thirds." *Bob, primary care doctor, chapter 15*

- "We got into Bluefields Nicaragua just after Hurricane Mitch. We had two bags of medicine, a little money and not a clue where to go. The local mayor said, 'You've got money and medicine. We'll give you a boat and send you up the river. You pay for the gas.'" *Bob, primary care doctor*

Biographical Profile

D r. Ern Crocker graduated from the Medical Faculty of the University of New South Wales with honors in 1969. He was awarded the University Prize for Surgery, the HP and BL Melville Prize for Surgery, and the Gilbert Ashby Memorial Prize for General Proficiency. He had previously obtained a bachelors degree in Medical Science with honors. His thesis had related to the role of the alpha and beta adrenergic systems in the cardiovascular responses to hyperventilation during arterial hypoxia.

He completed his internship and residency at Royal Prince Alfred Hospital in Sydney and commenced advanced training in nuclear medicine. During this time he also trained in diagnostic ultrasound at the Commonwealth Acoustic Laboratories, later the Ultrasonics Institute, and became the first nuclear medicine physician to practice ultrasound in Australia.

In 1975 he completed his nuclear medicine training as a research fellow at the University of Pennsylvania, before returning to Sydney to be admitted as a fellow of the Royal Australasian College of Physicians. He was made founding Director of Nuclear Medicine and Ultrasound at Westmead Hospital and continued in that position for a ten-year period, establishing it as one of the major diagnostic nuclear medicine departments in Australia.

During his years at Westmead, he sat on many committees, including the Council of the Australian and New Zealand Association of

Physicians in Nuclear Medicine, the ASUM Board of the Diploma of Medical Ultrasonography, the Federal Government Nuclear Medicine Fees Committee, the Nuclear Medicine Advisory Committee of the New South Wales Government, and the Public Works Advisory Committees for Nuclear Medicine and Ultrasound. He was also secretary of the Royal Australasian College of Physicians Nuclear Medicine Training Advisory Committee.

Dr. Crocker has contributed seventy-five scientific papers to the literature in his specialties of nuclear medicine and ultrasound.

He has had a particular interest in Christian outreach to China, and has visited China many times to participate in medical seminar programs. With his wife, Lynne, he was the Australian representative for the Jian Hua Foundation and was a board member of Australian China Endeavour.

In 1986 he was involved in the establishment of a private nuclear medicine and ultrasound practice in western Sydney. He continues to operate in that practice.

Dr. Crocker's other interest is photography. He has been published in Australian and international journals and has been widely represented in exhibitions.

He lives in the Hills district of Sydney with Lynne, who is an artist. They have a daughter, Sascha, and two sons, Brook and Sam. Brook's wife, Lucinda, is also a medical practitioner and they have two beautiful children, Rory and Louella.

Contact Ern Crocker

Dr. Ernest Crocker is an author, speaker and physician living in Sydney, Australia. He is an honors graduate and final year medalist of the University of New South Wales who completed his postgraduate training in Nuclear Medicine at the University of Pennsylvania.

Dr. Crocker has a particular interest in the intervention of God in the healing process and in the lives of doctors and their patients. This grew from a remarkable experience that he had as a young doctor operating an emergency after-hours medical service and continues to this present day.

His experience as a physician over thirty years has placed him in an ideal position to use medicine as a model to investigate the ways in which God intervenes in the lives of men and women today, changing them from the mundane to the extraordinary.

He maintains that God has a specific and strategic plan for each of us personally and professionally. This plan is revealed when as Christians we find our identity in Father God and allow His Holy Spirit to encourage and empower us. He becomes our *silent partner*.

Nine Minutes Past Midnight is a book about doctors and patients who took God at His word and were astonished at what followed.

Website: www.ernestcrocker.com
Book website: www.nineminutespastmidnight.com
Twitter: @ErnestCrocker
Key You Tube links: http://www.youtube.com/watch?v=rbhKZnh)50A
www.youtube.com/watch?v=dyKX98qi53

End Notes

Introduction

[1] Barclay, William, 1955. *And He Had Compassion On Them*. Edinburgh: The Church of Scotland Youth Committee.

Chapter 1: Now is the Time

[2] Author's Note: Cardiopulmonary resuscitation: in this case, mouth to mouth resuscitation alternating with chest compression.

Chapter 2: Where Can a Young Man Put His Trust?

[3] Author's Note: *Pegged trousers* were the trendy trousers of the 60s with very narrow drainpipe legs a-la-Beatles and *winkle pickers* were the very pointed toe shoes of the day.

[4] Author's Note: Feeding of the five thousand is recorded in Mark 6:30–44:

Then the apostles gathered to Jesus and told Him all things, both what they had done and what they had taught. And He said to them, "Come aside by yourselves to a deserted place and rest a while." For there were many coming and going, and they did not even have time to eat. So they departed to a deserted place in the boat by themselves.

But the multitudes saw them departing, and many knew Him and ran there on foot from all the cities. They arrived before them and came together to Him. And Jesus, when He came out, saw a great multitude and was moved with compassion for them, because they were like sheep not having a shepherd. So He began to teach them many things. When the day was now far spent, His disciples came to Him and said, "This is a deserted place, and already the hour is late. Send them away, that they may go into the surrounding country and villages and buy themselves bread; for they have nothing to eat."

But He answered and said to them, "You give them something to eat."

And they said to Him, "Shall we go and buy two hundred denarii worth of bread and give them *something* to eat?"

But He said to them, "How many loaves do you have? Go and see."

And when they found out they said, "Five, and two fish."

Then He commanded them to make them all sit down in groups on the green grass. So they sat down in ranks, in hundreds and in fifties. And when He had taken the five loaves and the two fish, He looked up to heaven, blessed and broke the loaves, and gave them to His disciples to set before them; and the two fish He divided among *them* all. So they all ate and were filled. And they took up twelve baskets full of fragments and of the fish. Now those who had eaten the loaves were about five thousand men.

[5] Author's Note: John the Baptist prophesied of Jesus saying, "I indeed baptized you with water, but He will baptize you with the Holy Spirit"(Mark 1:8).

[6] Crocker E.F., A.V. McLaughlin, J.G. Morris, R. Benn, J.G. McLeod and J. Allsop. 1974. "Technetium brain scanning in the diagnosis and management of cerebral abscess." *American Journal of Medicine*, 56:192.

Chapter 3: The Silent Partner

[7] Cooke, Graham. 2005. (Personal communication from an address), "Abiding in God's Rest." Sydney: Dayspring Church Conference.

Chapter 5: Open Door to China

[8] Author's Note: PET scanning uses positron emitting radionuclides such as F18 to image organ systems. It is especially useful in the early diagnosis and staging of malignancy. The technique was developed in the mid-1970s, but has only recently been generally accepted in Australia. PET scanners now incorporate CT scanners and the imaging technique is called PET/CT.

[9] Author's Note: The director of the Chinese State Administration for Religious Affairs (SARA), Yie Xiaowen, has recently said that the number of Christians in China has now reached 130 million. *The Christian Post* quoted President Bob Fu of the China Aid Association as saying that the unprecedented growth of the Chinese Church had happened under relentless persecution, and that they were praying that China would soon realize true religious freedom.

Michelle Vu. January 8 2007. "Police Raid Chinese Bible Study at Communist School" The Christian Post (online): <http://www.christianpost.com/news/police-raid-chinese-bible-study-at-communist-school-24854>.

Chapter 6: Donald

[10] Dale, Penny. 2006. *Ten Sacks of Rice: Our Way to China*. Austin, Texas: Karis Publishing, second edition.

Chapter 7: China Syndrome

[11] Author's Note: History of the Walled City noted from: Kowloon Walled City Park Leisure and Cultural Services Department: 24 November, 2011.
<http://www.lcsd.ggov.hk/parks/kwcp/en/index.php>

[12] Author's Note: On 1 October 2006, a 45-foot South African Leopard sailing catamaran set sail from Hong Kong to circumnavigate the world, led by Jenny and a crew of two. Her course took her to Singapore, through pirate-infested waters off Vietnam, to Phuket, Chagos and to Mozambique (after surviving a major storm). Next to Durban, around the Cape to St. Helena in the South Atlantic, to Fortaleza Brazil, and then on to Panama via Trinidad after managing to avoid Level 5 hurricanes Felix and Dean. At 3:30 AM local time, March 8, 2008, she arrived back in Hong Kong completing circumnavigation, with Henry the dog, Coco a cat from the Seychelles, and crew (herself and husband Rob).

Chapter 8: From Mundane to Extraordinary

[13] Author's Note: She had anemia and thrombocytopenia, a reduced level of platelets in the blood.

14 Author's Note: Thrombotic Thrombocytopenic Purpura (TTP): hemolytic uremic syndrome mainly affecting young women and characterized by abnormally low levels of platelets in the blood, the formation of blood clots in the small vessels of many organs and neurological damage. Large aggregates of von Willebrand factor (which causes platelets to adhere to membranes) accumulate.

15 Author's Note: This is a metal surgical retractor used by a surgical assistant to retract tissues so that the surgeon is able to access the surgical site. They are an American invention.

Chapter 9: New Horizons—Deeper Waters

16 Author's Note: A growler is a piece of ice about the same size as a small car.

Chapter 11: Fire by Night

17 USA Today, September 8, 2004.
18 smh.com.au, November 24, 2004.
19 *The Age* newspaper, September 9, 2004.
20 Moore, Matthew and Rompi, Karuni. *Sydney Morning Herald*, September 9, 2004.

Chapter 12: A More Excellent Sacrifice

21 Author's Note: Lynwood café was the home of school teacher Napoleon Richard Poidevan, whose son Leslie Oswald Poidevan (1876–1931) surgeon, cricketer and tennis player, was signed by W.G. Grace to the London County Cricket Club and later, in 1906, represented Australia in the Davis Cup.

22 Corcoran, Mark. *The Yemen Option*, Foreign Correspondent, Lead Story Series 13, Episode 24, ABC Television, March 2, 2004.

23 *BBC News*, World Edition, December 30, 2002.

24 *Wall Street Journal*, Eastern Edition, December 31, 2002.

25 Author's Note: Kamel was executed by firing squad in the southern Ibb province of Yemen February 27, 2006. His accomplice, Ali al-Jarallah, had been executed in November of the previous year. Elliott, Hannah. March 2, 2006. Associated Baptist Press.

[26] *The New York Times*, Late East Coast Edition, April 22, 2003.

[27] *The Lancet*, March 29, 2003.

[28] Olson, Ted (compiler). Weblog: January 19, 2003. "Yemeni Missionaries, Killer had Earlier Sought Their Help," *Christianity Today*. <www.christianitytoday.com/ct/2003/101/51.0.html>

[29] Boreham, F.W. 1922. "A Handful of Stars: Texts That Have Moved Great Minds," New York: Abingdon Press.

[30] Author's Note: Dr. Ken Clezy, AM OBE FRCS FRACS was awarded the Royal Australasian College of Surgery International Medal for extraordinary contributions to surgery in Third World countries by the college president on February 10, 2001 in Tasmania.

Chapter 13: A Very Present Help

[31] Author's Note: The cliff in Sydney called "The Gap" is a notorious site for suicides.

[32] Hartwig, B. and Nichols, A., 2000. *GP Health and Well-Being: The Issues Explored*. Brisbane North Division of General Practice.

[33] Caplan, R.P., 1994. "Stress Anxiety and Depression in Hospital Consultants, GP's and Senior Service Managers." *BMJ* 309:1262.

[34] Lawrence, J., 1997. "The Tragedy of Doctor Suicide." *Journal of the Queensland Branch of the Australian Medical Association*:12,13.

[35] May 29, 1997. "Doctors Mental Health Working Group Report and Recommendations."

[36] Author's Note: The Doctors' Mental Health Working Group was chaired by Professor Beverley Raphael, director, Center for Mental Health, and included representatives from government, doctor's associations, and numerous other interest groups representing hospitals, medical residents, and medical specialties. The board reported a substantially higher suicide rate in doctors than occurred in the general population and in relation to other professionals. They found that the increase in relative risk was even more marked for female doctors ranging from 2.5–5.7 times age matched standards.

[37] Gibson, N., and Gibson, P., 2000. *Excuse Me Your Rejection is Showing*. Sovereign World Ltd.

[38] Author's Note: A process whereby certain proteins are removed from the circulation.

Chapter 14: One Man's Walk

³⁹ Author's Note: 1 Kings 18: 25–40:

Now Elijah said to the prophets of Baal, "Choose one bull for yourselves and prepare it first, for you *are* many; and call on the name of your god, but put no fire *under it*."

So they took the bull which was given them, and they prepared *it*, and called on the name of Baal from morning even till noon, saying, "O Baal, hear us!" But *there was* no voice; no one answered. Then they leaped about the altar which they had made.

And so it was, at noon, that Elijah mocked them and said, "Cry aloud, for he *is* a god; either he is meditating, or he is busy, or he is on a journey, *or* perhaps he is sleeping and must be awakened." So they cried aloud, and cut themselves, as was their custom, with knives and lances, until the blood gushed out on them. And when midday was past, they prophesied until the *time* of the offering of the *evening* sacrifice. But *there was* no voice; no one answered, no one paid attention.

Then Elijah said to all the people, "Come near to me." So all the people came near to him. And he repaired the altar of the LORD *that was* broken down. And Elijah took twelve stones, according to the number of the tribes of the sons of Jacob, to whom the word of the LORD had come, saying, "Israel shall be your name." Then with the stones he built an altar in the name of the LORD; and he made a trench around the altar large enough to hold two seahs of seed. ³³And he put the wood in order, cut the bull in pieces, and laid it on the wood, and said, "Fill four waterpots with water, and pour it on the burnt sacrifice and on the wood." Then he said, "Do it a second time," and they did it a second time; and he said, "Do it a third time," and they did it a third time. So the water ran all around the altar; and he also filled the trench with water.

And it came to pass, at the time of the offering of the evening sacrifice, that Elijah the prophet came near and said, "LORD God of Abraham, Isaac, and Israel, let it be known this day that You are God in Israel and I am Your servant, and that I have done all these things at Your word. Hear me, O LORD, hear me, that this people may know that You are the LORD God, and that You have turned their hearts back to You again."

Then the fire of the LORD fell and consumed the burnt sacrifice, and the wood and the stones and the dust, and it licked up the water that *was* in the trench. Now when all the people saw *it*, they fell on their faces; and they said, "The LORD, He *is* God! The LORD, He *is* God!"

And Elijah said to them, "Seize the prophets of Baal! Do not let one of them escape!" So they seized them; and Elijah brought them down to the Brook Kishon and executed them there.

[40] Author's Note: A nuclear medicine procedure for assessing blood flow to the brain.

[41] Author's Note: South Africa won by five wickets. Australia scored 228 runs.

Chapter 15: No Retreats, No Reserves, No Regrets

[42] Words completed by W. Borden of Yale in his Bible shortly before his untimely death from meningitis in Cairo April, 1913, at age 25. Quoted from: Taylor, Mrs. Howard. *Borden of Yale '09*, Philadelphia: The Bingham Company (for the China Inland Mission, undated).

[43] Author's Note: David Wilkerson (1931–2011) American evangelist, best known for his book *The Cross and the Switchblade*. Founder of Teen Challenge, and founding pastor of the Times Square Church in New York.

[44] Author's Note: Charles Wendell Colson (1931-2012) was one of the original "Watergate Seven" and was known as "Nixon's hatchet man." At the time of his conversion to Christianity in 1973 his life radically and permanently changed. In 1976 he established *Prison Fellowship*, America's largest outreach to prisoners, ex-prisoners, and their families.

[45] Author's Note: A global movement of church and missions leaders from many denominations and agencies to finish Christ's Great Commission to take the gospel to all peoples and nations.

Chapter 16: Letting Go—Letting God

[46] Author's Note: A balloon-like swelling of the main artery from the heart with splitting of the wall allowing blood to pass between the layers of the blood vessel.

[47] Author's Note: A special computer subtraction X-Ray using dye to show blood flowing through blood vessels.

[48] (1 John 4:18.)

Chapter 17: Set the Prisoners Free

[49] Author's Note: Rheumatoid factor is an autoantibody directed against the body's own tissues. In high levels it in an indicator of active rheumatoid arthritis.

[50] Edman, V. Raymond, 1984. *They Found the Secret.* Grand Rapids, Michigan: Zondervan Publishing House.

Chapter 18: A New Heart for Rosemary

[51] Wyngaaden, J.A., and Smith Jr., L.H., 1985. *Cecil Textbook of Medicine*, 17th Edition. St. Louis:W.B. Saunders Company:338.

[52] Author's Note: In the United States the prevalence (the number of cases of a specific disease present in a given population at a certain time) has been reported as one case per 1,300–15,000 live births.

[53] Author's Note: Where there was persisting heart enlargement the survival at five years was approximately 15 percent.

Chapter 19: A Gift of Faith

[54] Miller, Reverend Graham (Personal communication). Hurstville: St Giles Presbyterian Church.

[55] Jackie Pullinger is an Englishwoman who established a ministry to heroin addicts and Triad gang members of the walled city in Hong Kong. Her story is told in her book, *Chasing The Dragon.* Ventura, CA: Regal Books, 1980. More about Jackie in chapter 7.

[56] Powhatan, James, 1940. *George W. Truett: A Biography.* Nashville: Broadman Press.

[57] George W. Truett (1867–1944) began his career as a teacher in a one-room school in Crooked Creek, Georgia, eventually becoming president of Baylor College, and later president of the Southern Baptist Convention. He became a friend of presidents. His biographers described the man's ministry in two words: "heart-power."

Chapter 20: The Higher Mountains

[58] Author's Note: The call had come from a young lady who was no longer interested in pursuing a friendship with John. Because of this, John and Janet were able to grow in their relationship and eventually marry.

[59] Glennon, J., 1978. *Your Healing is Within You.* NJ: Bridge-Logos.

[60] Glennon, J., 1987. *How Can I Find Healing?* NJ: Bridge-Logos.

[61] van Biema, David. "God vs. Science," *Time*: Sunday November 5, 2006.

Chapter 21: Specialist Consultation

[62] Grubb, N., 1986. *Rees Howells Intercessor.* Cambridge: Lutterworth Press.

[63] Lyndell has requested that correct names be used.

[64] Author's Note: This synthetic non-steroidal estrogen was first produced in 1938. It was used in several areas in the United States between 1945 and 1955 and infrequently in the early 70s as a means of treating threatened miscarriage.

[65] National Institute of Health *DES Research Update* 1999, July 19–20, 1999.

Chapter 22: More than Conquerors

[66] Foxe, John, 1999. *Foxe's Book of Martyrs.* NJ: Revell.

[67] Chapman, J.W.,1900. *The Life and Work of Dwight Lyman Moody.* Now available as online book at: <www.Biblebelievers.com/moody>

[68] Martyn Lloyd-Jones. Part of an address given at the annual breakfast of The Christian Medical Fellowship July 15,1953, during the Annual Meeting of the British Medical Association at Cardiff.

[69] See:www.royalnavy.mod.uk>. A New Year—A New Man in Afghanistan. Operations Diary. Lieut. Col. Rory Bruce, Royal Marines, January 2007.

[70] Author's Note: Prostate specific antigen is a protein produced by the prostate and normally found in small quantities in men's serum.

[71] Author's Note: Disseminated Intravascular Coagulation.

[72] See:<http://christianlibrary.org.au/cel/documents/psalms/chap10.htm>

Chapter 23: This Hope We Have

[73] Carson MD, Ben, 1990. *Gifted Hands*. New York: HarperCollins.

[74] Author's Note: The study and management of malignancy.

[75] Duane, W.H. Arnold, 1991. *Prayers of the Martyrs*, 1st edition. Grand Rapids, MI: Broadmoor Book.

[76] Barclay, William, 1957. *The Letter to The Hebrews*, 2nd Edition. Fife: St Andrew's Press, 57.

[77] Author's Note: God has a plan for those who put their trust in Him, as promised in these verses:

"For I know the thoughts that I think toward you, says the LORD, thoughts of peace and not of evil, to give you a future and a hope" (Jeremiah 29:11).

"Trust in the LORD with all your heart, and lean not on your own understanding In all your ways acknowledge Him, and He shall direct your paths" (Proverbs 3:5–6).

[78] Author's Note: My young neurosurgical friend, James, has subsequently been accepted into a radiology training program in a major Sydney teaching hospital. He has an interest in PET/CT fusion imaging and may well train in neuroradiology.

Chapter 24: Being There

[79] Author's Note: Phillip Adams is an Australian journalist, broadcaster, social commentator and film maker. He is a self-proclaimed atheist. One of his books is *Adams versus God*. Melbourne: Nelson, 1985.

Chapter 25: A Country Practice

[80] Author's Note: An obstructed delivery when the shoulder impacts on the maternal pelvis.

Chapter 27: Render unto Science

[81] Copyright © The Nobel Foundation 1963. "Sir John Eccles—Banquet Speech." Nobelprize.org. January 27, 2011.
<http://nobelprize.org/nobel_prizes/medicine/laureates/1963/eccles-speech.html>.

[82] Eccles, J.C., 1983. "The Human Mystery: a Lifelong Search for Truth." *Civitas*: 38, 301–305.

[83] Eccles, J.C., 1983. "The Mystery of Personal Existence." *Scholar and Educator*,7, 5-18.

[84] Mustafa A.S., H.K. Nerland, Gil, A., Britton, W.J. et al, 1986. "Human T Cell Clones Recognize a Major M.leprae Protein Antigen Expressed in E.coli." *Nature*, 319:63–66.

[85] Author's Note: A large pharmaceutical company established in London in 1880.

[86] Dawkins, Richard, 2006. *The God Delusion*. London: Bantam Press.

Epilogue: Programmed to Live

[87] Dorsett, Lyle, 2003. *A Passion for Souls: The Life of D. L. Moody*. Chicago, IL: Moody Publishers.

[88] Nee, Watchman, 2002. *The Normal Christian Life*. Eastbourne: Kingsway Communications Ltd.

[89] Author's Note: I have also observed how the Spirit of God may flow in a retrograde fashion through generations from child to parent to grandparent.

[90] Solzhenitsyn, Aleksandr, 1974. *Solzhenitsyn: A Pictorial Record*. New York: Farrar Strauss and Giroux.